WEST-B Basic Skills
Teacher Certification Exam

By: Sharon Wynne, M.S.
Southern Connecticut State University

"And, while there's no reason yet to panic, I think it's only prudent that we make preparations to panic."

XAMonline, INC.
Boston

XAMonline, Inc.
21 Orient Ave.
Melrose, MA 02176
Toll Free 1-800-509-4128
Email: inof@xamonline.com
Web www.xamonline.com
Fax: 1-781-662-9268

Library of Congress Cataloging-in-Publication Data

Wynne, Sharon A.
  WEST-B Basic Skills Teacher Certification / Sharon A. Wynne.
  ISBN: 978-1-58197-638-0
    1. WEST-B Basic Skills   2. Study Guides.   3. WEST
    4. Teachers' Certification & Licensure.   5. Careers

Disclaimer:
The opinions expressed in this publication are the sole works of XAMonline and were created independently from the National Education Association, Educational Testing Service, or any State Department of Education, National Evaluation Systems or other testing affiliates.

Between the time of publication and printing, state specific standards as well as testing formats and website information may change that is not included in part or in whole within this product. Sample test questions are developed by XAMonline and reflect similar content as on real tests; however, they are not former tests. XAMonline assembles content that aligns with state standards but makes no claims nor guarantees teacher candidates a passing score. Numerical scores are determined by testing companies such as NES or ETS and then are compared with individual state standards. A passing score varies from state to state.

Printed in the United States of America   œ-1

WEST-B: Basic Skills
ISBN: 978-1-58197-638-0

TABLE OF CONTENTS

SUBAREA III.   MATHEMATICS

Great Study and Testing Tips!

What to study in order to prepare for the subject assessments is the focus of this study guide but equally important is *how* you study.

You can increase your chances of truly mastering the information by taking some simple, but effective, steps.

Study Tips:

1. <u>Some foods aid the learning process</u>. Foods such as milk, nuts, seeds, rice, and oats help your study efforts by releasing natural memory enhancers called CCKs (*cholecystokinin*) composed of *tryptophan*, *choline*, and *phenylalanine*. All of these chemicals enhance the neurotransmitters associated with memory. Before studying, try a light, protein-rich meal of eggs, turkey, or fish. All of these foods release the memory-enhancing chemicals. The better the connections, the more you comprehend.

Likewise, before you take a test, stick to a light snack of energy boosting and relaxing foods. A glass of milk, a piece of fruit, or some peanuts all release various memory-boosting chemicals and help you to relax and focus on the subject at hand.

2. <u>Learn to take great notes</u>. A by-product of our modern culture is that we have grown accustomed to getting our information in short doses (i.e., TV news, sound bites, or *USA Today*-style newspaper articles.)

Consequently, we have subconsciously trained ourselves to assimilate information better in <u>neat little packages</u>. Notes scrawled all over the paper fragment the flow of the information. Strive for clarity. Newspapers use a standard format to achieve clarity. Similarly, your notes can be much clearer through use of proper formatting. A very effective format is called the *"Cornell Method."*

> Take a sheet of loose-leaf, lined notebook paper and draw a line all the way down the paper about 1"–2" from the left-hand edge.

> Draw another line across the width of the paper about 1"–2" up from the bottom. Repeat this process on the reverse side of the page.

Look at the highly effective result. You have ample room for notes, a left-hand margin for special-emphasis items or for inserting supplementary data from the textbook, a large area at the bottom for a brief summary, and a little rectangular space for just about anything you want.

3. <u>Get the concept, then the details</u>. Too often, we focus on the details and do not gather an understanding of the concept. However, if you simply memorize only dates, places, or names, you may well miss the whole point of the subject.

A key way to understand things is to put them in your own words. If you are working from a textbook, automatically summarize each paragraph in your mind. If you are outlining text, do not simply copy the author's words.

Rephrase them in your own words. You remember your own thoughts and words much better than someone else's thoughts and words and subconsciously tend to associate the important details to the core concepts.

4. Ask "Why?" Pull apart written material paragraph by paragraph, and do not forget the captions under the illustrations.

> Example: If the heading is "Stream Erosion," flip it around to read, "Why do streams erode?" Then, answer the question.

If you train your mind to think in a series of questions and answers, not only will you learn more, but the training will also help to lessen the test anxiety because you are used to answering questions.

5. Read for reinforcement and future needs. Even if you only have ten minutes, put your notes or a book in your hand. Your mind is similar to a computer; you have to input data in order to have it processed. *By reading, you are creating the neural connections for future retrieval.* The more times you read something, the more you reinforce the learning of ideas.

Even if you do not fully understand something on the first pass, *your mind stores much of the material for later recall.*

6. Relax to learn, so go into exile. Our bodies respond to an inner clock called biorhythms. Burning the midnight oil works well for some people, but not for everyone.

If possible, set aside a particular place to study that is free of distractions. Shut off the television, cell phone, and pager and exile your friends and family during your study period.

If silence really bothers you, try background music. Light classical music at a low volume, over other types of music, has been shown to aid in concentration. Music that evokes pleasant emotions without lyrics is highly suggested. Try just about anything by Mozart. It relaxes you.

7. Use arrows, not highlighters. At best, it is difficult to read a page filled with yellow, pink, blue, and green streaks. Try staring at a neon sign for a while, and you will soon see that the horde of colors obscures the message.

A quick note, a brief dash of color, an underline, or an arrow pointing to a particular passage is much clearer than a horde of highlighted words.

8. <u>**Budget your study time.**</u> Although you should not ignore any of the material, *allocate your available study time in the same ratio that topics may appear on the test.*

Testing Tips:

1. <u>Get smart; play dumb</u>. **Do not read anything into the question.** Do not assume that the test writer is looking for something else than what is asked. Stick to the question as written and do not read extra things into it.

2. <u>Read the question and all the choices *twice* before answering the question</u>. You may miss something by failing to carefully read—and then re-read—both the question and the answers.

If you really do not have a clue as to the right answer, leave it blank on the first time through. Go on to the other questions because they may provide a clue as to how to answer the skipped questions.

If later on, you still cannot answer the skipped ones—*guess.* The only penalty for guessing is that you *might* get it wrong. Only one thing is certain: if you do not answer a question, it will be counted as wrong.

3. <u>Turn the question into a statement</u>. Look at the way the questions are worded. The syntax of the question usually provides a clue. Does it seem more familiar as a statement rather than as a question? Does it sound strange?

By turning a question into a statement, you may be able to spot if an answer sounds right, and it may trigger memories of material you have read.

4. <u>Look for hidden clues.</u> It is actually very difficult to compose multiple-foil (choice) questions without giving away part of the answer in the options presented.

In most multiple-choice questions, you can often readily eliminate one or two of the potential answers. This leaves you with only two real possibilities, and automatically your odds go to 50–50 for very little work.

5. <u>Trust your instincts.</u> For every fact that you have read, you subconsciously retain something of that knowledge. On questions about which you are not certain, go with your basic instincts. *Your first impression on how to answer a question is usually correct.*

6. <u>Mark your answers directly on the test booklet</u>. Do not bother trying to fill in the optical scan sheet on the first pass through the test.

Be careful not to mismark your answers when you transcribe them to the scan sheet.

7. <u>Watch the clock</u>! You have a set amount of time to answer the questions. Do not get bogged down trying to answer a single question at the expense of ten questions you can more readily answer.

THIS PAGE BLANK

COMPETENCY 1.0   GRAMMATICAL RELATIONSHIPS

Skill 1.1   Identify errors in use of adjectives and adverbs.

Adjectives are words that modify or describe nouns or pronouns. Adjectives usually precede the words they modify but not always; for example, an adjective may occur after a linking verb.

Adverbs are words that modify verbs, adjectives, or other adverbs. They cannot modify nouns. Adverbs answer such questions as how, why, when, where, how much, or how often something is done. Many adverbs are formed by adding -ly.

Error: The birthday cake tasted sweetly.

Problem: *Tasted* is a linking verb; the modifier that follows should be an adjective, not an adverb.

Correction: The birthday cake tasted sweet.

Error: You have done good with this project.

Problem: *Good* is an adjective and cannot be used to modify a verb phrase such as *have done*.

Correction: You have done well with this project.

Error: The coach was positive happy about the team's chance of winning.

Problem: The adjective *positive* cannot be used to modify another adjective, *happy*. An adverb is needed instead.

Correction: The coach was positively happy about the team's chance of winning.

Error: The fireman acted quick and brave to save the child from the burning building.

Problem: *Quick and brave* are adjectives and cannot be used to describe a verb. Adverbs are needed instead.

Correction: The fireman acted quickly and bravely to save the child from the burning building.

PRACTICE EXERCISE: ADJECTIVES AND ADVERBS
Choose the option that corrects an error in the underlined portion(s).
If no error exists, choose "No change is necessary."

1) Moving <u>quick</u> throughout the house, the burglar <u>removed</u> several priceless antiques before <u>carelessly</u> dropping his wallet.

   A) quickly
   B) remove
   C) careless
   D) No change is necessary.

2) The car <u>crashed loudly</u> into the retaining wall before spinning <u>wildly</u> on the sidewalk.

   A) crashes
   B) loudly
   C) wild
   D) No change is necessary.

3) The airplane <u>landed safe</u> on the runway after <u>nearly</u> colliding with a helicopter.

   A) land
   B) safely
   C) near
   D) No change is necessary.

4) The <u>horribly bad</u> special effects in the movie disappointed us <u>great</u>.

   A) horrible
   B) badly
   C) greatly
   D) No change is necessary.

5) The man promised to obey <u>faithfully</u> the rules of the social club.

   A) faithful
   B) faithfulness
   C) faith
   D) No change is necessary.

ANSWER KEY: PRACTICE EXERCISE FOR ADJECTIVES AND ADVERBS

1) A   The adverb *quickly* is needed to modify *moving*. Option B is incorrect because it uses the wrong form of the verb. Option C is incorrect because the adverb *carelessly* is needed before the verb *dropping,* not the adjective *careless*.

2) D   The sentence is correct as it is written. Adverbs *loudly* and *wildly* are needed to modify *crashed* and *spinning.* Option A incorrectly uses the verb *crashes* instead of the participle *crashing*, which acts as an adjective.

3) B   The adverb *safely* is needed to modify the verb *landed*. Option A is incorrect because *land* is a noun. Option C is incorrect because *near* is an adjective, not an adverb.

4) C   The adverb *greatly* is needed to modify the verb *disappointed.* Option A is incorrect because *horrible* is an adjective, not an adverb. Option B is incorrect because the adverb *horribly* needs to modify the adjective *bad.*

5) D   The adverb *faithfully* is the correct modifier of the verb *promised.* Option A is an adjective used to modify nouns. Neither Option B nor Option C, which are both nouns, is a modifier.

Skill 1.2 Identify errors in use of nouns.

Plural nouns
A good dictionary should replace the learning of the multiplicity and complexity of spelling rules based on phonics, letter doubling, and exceptions to rules if they have not been mastered by adulthood. Learning the use of a dictionary and thesaurus will be a more rewarding use of time.

Most plurals of nouns that end in hard consonants or hard consonant sounds followed by a silent *e* are made by adding -*s*. Some words ending in vowels only add -*s*.

> fingers, numerals, banks, bugs, riots, homes, gates, radios, bananas

Nouns that end in soft consonant sounds—*s, j, x, z, ch,* and *sh*—add -*es*. Some nouns ending in *o* add -es.

> dresses, waxes, churches, brushes, tomatoes

Nouns ending in *y* preceded by a vowel, just add -*s*.

> boys, alleys

Nouns ending in *y* preceded by a consonant, change the *y* to *i* and add -*es*.

> babies, corollaries, frugalities, poppies

Some nouns' plurals are formed irregularly or remain the same.

> sheep, deer, children, leaves, oxen

Some nouns derived from foreign words, especially Latin, may make their plurals in two different ways—one of which may be to make them English. Sometimes, the meanings are the same; other times, the two plurals are used in slightly different contexts. It is always wise to consult the dictionary.

> appendices, appendixes   criterion, criteria
> indexes, indices   crisis, crises

Make the plurals of closed (solid) compound words in the usual way.

> timelines, hairpins
> cupfuls, handfuls

Make the plurals of open or hyphenated compounds by adding the change in inflection to the word that changes in number.

> fathers-in-law, courts-martial, masters of art, doctors of medicine

Make the plurals of letters, numbers, and abbreviations by adding -s.

> fives and tens, IBMs, 1990s, *p*s and *q*s (Note that letters are italicized.)

Possessive nouns
Make the possessives of singular nouns by adding an apostrophe followed by the letter *s* (*'s*).

> baby's bottle, father's job, elephant's eye, teacher's desk, sympathizer's protests, week's postponement

Make the possessive of singular nouns ending in *s* by adding either an apostrophe or an (*'s*) depending upon common usage or sound. When making the possessive causes difficulty, use a prepositional phrase instead. Even with the sibilant ending, with a few exceptions, it is advisable to use the (*'s*) construction.

> dress's color, species' characteristics or characteristics of the species, James' hat or James's hat, Delores's shirt

Make the possessive of plural nouns ending in *s* by adding the apostrophe after the *s*.

> horses' coats, jockeys' times, four days' time

Make possessives of plural nouns that do not end in *s* the same as singular nouns by adding *'s*.

> children's shoes, deer's antlers, cattle's horns

Make possessives of compound nouns by adding the inflection at the end of the word or phrase.

> the mayor of Los Angeles' campaign, the mailman's new truck, the mailmen's new trucks, my father-in-law's first wife, the keepsakes' values, several daughters-in-law's husbands

Note: Because a gerund functions as a noun, any noun preceding it and operating as a possessive adjective must reflect the necessary inflection. However, if the gerundive following the noun is a participle, no inflection is added.

The general was perturbed by the private's sleeping on duty. (The word *sleeping* is a gerund, the object of the preposition *by*.)

—but—

The general was perturbed to see the private sleeping on duty. (The word *sleeping* is a participle modifying private.)

Skill 1.3   Identify errors in use of pronouns.

Rules for clearly identifying pronoun reference

Make sure that the antecedent reference is clear and cannot refer to something else.

A "distant relative" is a relative pronoun or a relative clause that has been placed too far away from the antecedent to which it refers. It is a common error to place a verb between the relative pronoun and its antecedent.

Error:	Return the books to the library that are overdue.
Problem:	The relative clause *that are overdue* refers to the *books* and should be placed immediately after the antecedent.
Correction:	Return the books that are overdue to the library.

—or—

Return the overdue books to the library.

A pronoun should not refer to adjectives or possessive nouns.

Adjectives, nouns, or possessive pronouns should not be used as antecedents. This will create ambiguity in sentences.

Error:	In Todd's letter, he told his mom he'd broken the priceless vase.
Problem:	In this sentence, the pronoun *he* seems to refer to the noun phrase *Todd's letter* though it was probably meant to refer to the possessive noun *Todd's*.
Correction:	In his letter, Todd told his mom that he had broken the priceless vase.

A pronoun should not refer to an implied idea.
A pronoun must refer to a specific antecedent rather than an implied antecedent. When an antecedent is not stated specifically, the reader has to guess or assume the meaning of a sentence. Pronouns that do not have antecedents are called **expletives**. "It" and "there" are the most common expletives, though other pronouns can become expletives as well. In informal conversation, expletives allow for casual presentation of ideas without supporting evidence. However, in more formal writing, it is best to be more precise.

Error: She said that it is important to floss every day.

Problem: The pronoun *it* refers to an implied idea.

Correction: She said that flossing every day is important.

Error: Milt and Bette returned the books because they had missing pages.

Problem: The pronoun *they* does not refer to the antecedent.

Correction: The customers returned the book with missing pages.

Using Who, That, and Which:
While *who, whom,* and *whose* refer to human beings and can introduce either essential or nonessential clauses, **that** refers to things other than humans and is used to introduce essential clauses. **Which** refers to things other than humans and is used to introduce nonessential clauses.

Error: The doctor that performed the surgery said the man would be fully recovered.

Problem: Since the relative pronoun is referring to a human, *who* should be used.

Correction: The doctor who performed the surgery said the man would be fully recovered.

Error: That ice cream cone that you just ate looked delicious.

Problem: *That* has already been used, so you must use *which* to introduce the next clause, whether it is essential or nonessential.

Correction: That ice cream cone, which you just ate, looked delicious.

Identify proper case forms

Pronouns, unlike nouns, change case forms. Pronouns must be in the subjective, objective, or possessive form according to their function in the sentence.

Personal Pronouns

Subjective (Nominative)		Possessive		Objective	
	Singular	Plural	Singular	Plural	Singular	Plural
1st person	I	We	My	Our Ours	Me	Us
2nd person	You	You	Your Yours	Your Yours	You	You
3rd person	He She It	They	His Her/Hers Its	Their Theirs	Him Her It	Them

Relative Pronouns

Who	Subjective/Nominative
Whom	Objective
Whose	Possessive

Error: Tom and me have reserved seats for next week's baseball game.

Problem: The pronoun *me* is the subject of the verb *have reserved* and should be in the subjective form.

Correction: Tom and I have reserved seats for next week's baseball game.

Error: Mr. Green showed all of we students how to make paper hats.

Problem: The pronoun *we* is the object of the preposition *of*. It should be in the objective form, *us*.

Correction: Mr. Green showed all of us students how to make paper hats.

Error: Who's coat is this?

Problem: The interrogative possessive pronoun is *whose*; *who's* is the contraction for who is.

Correction: Whose coat is this?

PRACTICE EXERCISE: PRONOUN CASE
Choose the option that corrects an error in the underlined portion(s).
If no error exists, choose "No change is necessary."

· 1)   Even though Sheila and <u>he</u> had planned to be alone at the diner,
        <u>they</u> were joined by three friends of <u>their's</u> instead.

        A) him
        B) him and her
        C) theirs
        D) No change is necessary.

2)   Uncle Walter promised to give his car to <u>whomever</u> would guarantee
      to drive it safely.

        A) whom
        B) whoever
        C) them
        D) No change is necessary.

3)   Eddie and <u>him</u> gently laid <u>the body</u> on the ground next to <u>the sign</u>.

        A) he
        B) them
        C) it
        D) No change is necessary.

· 4)   Mary, <u>who</u> is competing in the chess tournament, is a better player
        than <u>me</u>.

        A) whose
        B) whom
        C) I
        D) No change is necessary.

5)   <u>We ourselves</u> have decided not to buy property in that development;
      however, our friends have already bought <u>themselves</u> some land.

        A) We, ourself,
        B) their selves
        C) their self
        D) No change is necessary.

ANSWER KEY: PRACTICE EXERCISE FOR PRONOUN CASE

1) C   The possessive pronoun *theirs* does not need an apostrophe. Option A is incorrect because the subjective pronoun *he* is needed in this sentence. Option B is incorrect because the subjective pronoun *they*, not the objective pronouns *him* and *her*, is needed.

2) B   The subjective case *whoever*—not the objective case *whomever* —is the subject of the relative clause *whoever would guarantee to drive it safely*. Option A is incorrect because *whom* is an objective pronoun. Option C is incorrect because *car* is singular and takes the pronoun *it*.

3) A   The subjective pronoun *he* is needed as the subject of the verb *laid*. Option B is incorrect because *them* is vague; the noun *body* is needed to clarify *it*. Option C is incorrect because *it* is vague, and the noun *sign* is necessary for clarification.

4) C   The subjective pronoun *I* is needed because the comparison is understood. Option A incorrectly uses the possessive *whose*. Option B is incorrect because the subjective pronoun *who*, and not the objective *whom*, is needed.

5) D   The reflexive pronoun *themselves* refers to the plural *friends*. Option A is incorrect because the plural *we* requires the reflexive *ourselves*. Option C is incorrect because the possessive pronoun *their* is never joined with either *self* or *selves*.

Skill 1.4   Identify errors in use of verbs.

Past tense and past participles
Both regular and irregular verbs must appear in their standard forms for each tense. Note: the -ed or -d ending is added to regular verbs in the past tense and for past participles.

Infinitive	Past Tense	Past Participle
Bake	Baked	Baked

Irregular Verb Forms

Infinitive	Past Tense	Past Participle
Be	Was/Were	Been
Become	Became	Become
Break	Broke	Broken
Bring	Brought	Brought
Choose	Chose	Chosen
Come	Came	Come
Do	Did	Done
Draw	Drew	Drawn
Eat	Ate	Eaten
Fall	Fell	Fallen
Forget	Forgot	Forgotten
Freeze	Froze	Frozen
Give	Gave	Given
Go	Went	Gone
Grow	Grew	Grown
Have/Has	Had	Had
Hide	Hid	Hidden
Know	Knew	Known
Lay	Laid	Laid
Lie	Lay	Lain
Ride	Rode	Ridden
Rise	Rose	Risen
Run	Ran	Run
See	Saw	Seen
Steal	Stole	Stolen
Take	Took	Taken
Tell	Told	Told
Throw	Threw	Thrown
Wear	Wore	Worn
Write	Wrote	Written

Error: She should have went to her doctor's appointment at the scheduled time.

Problem: The past participle of the verb *to go* is *gone*. *Went* expresses the simple past tense.

Correction: She should have gone to her doctor's appointment at the scheduled time.

Error: My train is suppose to arrive before two o'clock.

Problem: The verb following *train* is a present tense passive construction, which requires the present tense verb *to be* and the past participle.

Correction: My train is supposed to arrive before two o'clock.

Error: Linda should of known that the car wouldn't start after leaving it out in the cold all night.

Problem: *Should of* is a nonstandard expression. *Of* is not a verb.

Correction: Linda should have known that the car wouldn't start after leaving it out in the cold all night.

PRACTICE EXERCISE: STANDARD VERB FORMS
Choose the option that corrects an error in the underlined portion(s). If no error exists, choose "No change is necessary."

1) My professor <u>had knew</u> all along that we would pass his course.

    A. know
    B. had known
    C. knowing
    D. No change is necessary

2) Kevin was asked to erase the vulgar words he <u>had wrote.</u>

    A. writes
    B. has write
    C. had written
    D. No change is necessary

3) Melanie <u>had forget</u> to tell her parents that she left the cat in the closet.

    A. had forgotten
    B. forgot
    C. forget
    D. No change is necessary

4) Craig always <u>leave</u> the house a mess when his parents aren't there.

    A. left
    B. leaves
    C. leaving
    D. No change is necessary

5) The store manager accused Kathy of <u>having stole</u> more than five hundred dollars from the safe.

    A. has stolen
    B. having stolen
    C. stole
    D. No change is necessary

ANSWER KEY: PRACTICE EXERCISE FOR STANDARD VERB FORMS

1. B   Option B is correct because the past participle needs the helping verb *had*. Option A is incorrect because *it* is in the infinitive tense. Option C incorrectly uses the present participle.

2. C   Option C is correct because the past participle follows the helping verb *had*. Option A uses the verb in the present tense. Option B is an incorrect use of the verb.

3. A   Option A is correct because the past participle uses the helping verb *had*. Option B uses the wrong form of the verb. Option C uses the wrong form of the verb.

4. B   Option B correctly uses the past tense of the verb. Option A uses the verb in an incorrect way. Option C uses the verb without a helping verb such as *is*.

5. B   Option B is correct because it is the past participle. Options A and C use the verb incorrectly.

Verb Tenses

Verb tenses must refer to the same time consistently, unless a change in time is required.

Error: Despite the increased number of students in the school this year, overall attendance is higher last year at the sporting events.

Problem: The verb *is* represents an inconsistent shift to the present tense when the action refers to a past occurrence.

Correction: Despite the increased number of students in the school this year, overall attendance was higher last year at sporting events.

Error: My friend Lou, who just competed in the marathon, ran since he was twelve years old.

Problem: Because Lou continues to run, the present perfect tense is needed.

Correction: My friend Lou, who just competed in the marathon, has run since he was twelve years old.

Error: The mayor congratulated Wallace Mangham, who renovates the city hall last year.

Problem: Although the speaker is talking in the present, the action of renovating the city hall was in the past.

Correction: The mayor congratulated Wallace Mangham, who renovated the city hall last year.

PRACTICE EXERCISE: SHIFTS IN TENSE
Choose the option that corrects an error in the underlined portion(s).
If no error exists, choose "No change is necessary."

1)   After we <u>washed</u> the fruit that had <u>growing</u> in the garden, we knew
     there <u>was</u> a store that would buy the fruit.

     A) washing
     B) grown
     C) is
     D) No change is necessary.

2)   The tourists <u>used</u> to visit the Atlantic City boardwalk whenever they
     <u>vacationed</u> during the summer. Unfortunately, their numbers have
     <u>diminished</u> every year.

     A) use
     B) vacation
     C) diminish
     D) No change is necessary.

3)   When the temperature <u>drops</u> to below thirty-two degrees Fahrenheit,
     the water on the lake <u>freezes</u>, which <u>allowed</u> children to skate across it.

     A) dropped
     B) froze
     C) allows
     D) No change is necessary.

4)   The artists were <u>hired</u> to <u>create</u> a monument that would pay tribute to
     the men who were <u>killed</u> in World War Two.

     A) hiring
     B) created
     C) killing
     D) No change is necessary.

5)   Emergency medical personnel rushed to the scene of the shooting,
     where many injured people <u>waiting</u> for treatment.

     A) wait
     B) waited
     C) waits
     D) No change is necessary.

ANSWER KEY: PRACTICE EXERCISE FOR SHIFTS IN TENSE

1) B   The past participle *grown* is needed instead of *growing,* which is the progressive tense. Option A is incorrect because the past participle *washed* takes the *ed*. Option C incorrectly replaces the past participle *was* with the present tense *is*.

2) D   Option A is incorrect because *use* is the present tense. Option B incorrectly uses the present tense of the verb *vacation*. Option C incorrectly uses the present tense *diminish* instead of the past tense *diminished*.

3) C   The present tense *allows* is necessary in the context of the sentence. Option A is incorrect because *dropped* is a past participle. Option B is incorrect because *froze* is also a past participle.

4) D   Option A is incorrect because *hiring* is the present tense. Option B is incorrect because *created* is a past participle. In Option C, *killing* does not fit into the context of the sentence.

5) B   In Option B, *waited* corresponds with the past tense *rushed.* In Option A, *wait* is incorrect because it is present tense. In Option C, *waits* is incorrect because the noun *people* is plural and requires the singular form of the verb.

COMPETENCY 2.0   STRUCTURAL RELATIONSHIPS

Types of Clauses
Clauses are connected word groups that are composed of *at least* one subject and one verb. (A subject is the doer of an action or the element that is being joined. A verb conveys either the action or the link.)

Students are waiting for the start of the assembly.
(Subject)   (Verb)

At the end of the play, students wait for the curtain to come down.
(Subject) (Verb)

Clauses can be independent or dependent.

Independent clauses can stand alone or they can be joined to other clauses.

Independent clause	for and nor	
Independent clause,	but or yet so	Independent clause
Independent clause	;	Independent clause
Dependent clause	,	Independent clause
Independent clause		Dependent clause

Dependent clauses, by definition, contain at least one subject and one verb. However, they cannot stand alone as a complete sentence. They are structurally dependent on the main clause.

There are two types of dependent clauses: (1) those with a subordinating conjunction, and (2) those with a relative pronoun.

Unless a cure is discovered, many more people will die of the disease.
        Dependent clause   +   Independent clause

The White House has an official website, which contains press releases, news updates, and biographies of the president and vice president.
(Independent clause + relative pronoun + relative dependent clause)

Fundamentals of Sentence Structure

Simple: Consists of one independent clause.

Joyce wrote a letter.

Compound: Consists of two or more independent clauses. The two clauses are usually connected by a coordinating conjunction (and, but, or, nor, for, so, yet). Semicolons sometime connect compound sentences.

Joyce wrote a letter, and Dot drew a picture.

Complex: Consists of an independent clause plus one or more dependent clauses. The dependent clause may precede the independent clause or follow it.

While Joyce wrote a letter, Dot drew a picture.

Compound/Complex: Consists of one or more dependent clauses plus two or more independent clauses.

When Mother asked the girls to demonstrate their newfound skills, Joyce wrote a letter, and Dot drew a picture.

Note: Do **not** confuse compound sentence elements with compound sentences.

Simple sentence with compound subject:

Joyce and Dot wrote letters.

The girl in row three and the boy next to her were passing notes across the aisle.

Simple sentence with compound predicate:

Joyce wrote letters and drew pictures.

The captain of the high school debate team graduated with honors and studied broadcast journalism in college.

Simple sentence with compound object of preposition:

Coleen graded the students' essays for style and mechanical accuracy.

Skill 2.1   Identify errors in use of comparison.

When comparisons are made, the correct form of the adjective or adverb must be used. The **comparative** form is used for two items. The **superlative** form is used for more than two.

	Comparative	Superlative
slow	slower	slowest
young	younger	youngest
tall	taller	tallest

With some words, *more* and *most* are used to make comparisons instead of -er and -est.

	Comparative	Superlative
energetic	more energetic	most energetic
quick	more quickly	most quickly

Comparisons must be made between similar structures or items. In the sentence, "My house is similar in color to Steve's," one house is being compared to another house, as understood by the use of the possessive *Steve's*.

On the other hand, if the sentence reads, "My house is similar in color to Steve," the comparison would be faulty because it would be comparing the house to Steve, not to Steve's house.

Error: Last year's rides at the carnival were bigger than this year.

Problem: In the sentence as it is worded above, the rides at the carnival are being compared to this year, not to this year's rides.

Correction: Last year's rides at the carnival were bigger than this year's.

PRACTICE EXERCISE: LOGICAL COMPARISONS
Choose the sentence that logically and correctly expresses the comparison.

1) A. This year's standards are higher than last year.
   B. This year's standards are more high than last year.
   C. This year's standards are higher than last year's.

2) A. Tom's attitudes are very different from his father's.
   B. Toms attitudes are very different from his father.
   C. Tom's attitudes are very different from his father.

3) A. John is the stronger member of the gymnastics team.
   B. John is the strongest member of the gymnastics team.
   C. John is the most strong member of the gymnastics team.

4) A. Tracy's book report was longer than Tony's.
   B. Tracy's book report was more long than Tony's.
   C. Tracy's book report was longer than Tony.

· 5) A. Becoming a lawyer is as difficult as, if not more difficult than, becoming a doctor.

   B. Becoming a lawyer is as difficult, if not more difficult, than becoming a doctor.

   C. Becoming a lawyer is difficult, if not more difficult, than becoming a doctor.

· 6) A. Better than any movie of the modern era, *Schindler's List* portrays the destructiveness of hate.

   B. More better than any movie of the modern era, *Schindler's List* portrays the destructiveness of hate.

   C. Better than any other movie of the modern era, *Schindler's List* portrays the destructiveness of hate.

ANSWER KEY: PRACTICE EXERCISE FOR LOGICAL COMPARISONS

1) C   Option C is correct because the comparison is between this year's standards and last year's [standards is understood]. Option A compares the standards to last year. In Option B, the faulty comparative *more high* should be *higher*.

2) A   Option A is correct because Tom's attitudes are compared to his father's [attitudes is understood]. Option B deletes the necessary apostrophe to show possession (Tom's), and the comparison is faulty with *attitudes* compared to father. While Option C uses the correct possessive, it retains the faulty comparison shown in Option B.

3) B   In Option B, John is correctly the strongest member of a team that consists of more than two people. Option A uses the comparative *stronger* (comparison of two items) rather than the superlative *strongest* (comparison of more than two). Option C uses a faulty superlative, *most strong*.

4) A   Option A is correct because the comparison is between Tracy's book report and Tony's (book report). Option B uses the faulty comparative *more long* instead of *longer*. Option C wrongly compares Tracy's book report to Tony.

5) A   In Option A, the dual comparison is correctly stated: *as difficult as, if not more difficult than*. Remember to test the dual comparison by taking out the intervening comparison. Option B deletes the necessary *as* after the first *difficult*. Option C deletes the *as* before and after the first *difficult*.

6) C   Option C includes the necessary word *other* in the comparison *better than any other movie*. The comparison in Option A is not complete, and Option B uses a faulty comparative *more better*.

Skill 2.2   Identify errors in use of correlation.

A verb must correspond in the singular or plural form with the simple subject; interfering elements do not affect it. **Note:** A simple subject is never found in a prepositional phrase (a phrase beginning with a word such as *of, by, over, through, until*).

Present Tense Verb Form

	Singular	Plural
1st person (talking about oneself)	I do	We do
2nd person (talking to another)	You do	You do
3rd person (talking about someone or something)	He She does It	They do

Error: Sally, as well as her sister, plan to go into nursing.

Problem: The subject in the sentence is *Sally* alone, not the word *sister*. Therefore, the verb must be singular.

Correction: Sally, as well as her sister, plans to go into nursing.

Error: There has been many car accidents lately on that street.

Problem: The subject *accidents* in this sentence is plural; the verb must be plural also—even though it comes before the subject.

Correction: There have been many car accidents lately on that street.

Error: Everyone of us have a reason to attend the school musical.

Problem: The simple subject is the word *everyone*, not the *us* in the prepositional phrase. Therefore, the verb must be singular also.

Correction: Everyone of us has a reason to attend the school musical.

Error: Either the police captain or his officers is going to the convention.

Problem: In either/or and neither/nor constructions, the verb agrees with the subject closer to it.

Correction: Either the police captain or his officers are going to the convention.

PRACTICE EXERCISE: SUBJECT-VERB AGREEMENT

Choose the option that corrects an error in the underlined portion(s).
If no error exists, choose "No change is necessary."

1) Every year, the store <u>stays</u> open late when shoppers desperately <u>try</u> to purchase Christmas presents as they <u>prepare</u> for the holiday.

   A. stay
   B. tries
   C. prepared
   D. No change is necessary.

2) Paul McCartney, together with George Harrison and Ringo Starr, <u>sing</u> classic Beatles songs on a special greatest-hits CD.

   A. singing
   B. sings
   C. sung
   D. No change is necessary.

3) My friend's cocker spaniel, while <u>chasing</u> cats across the street, always <u>manages</u> to <u>knock</u> over the trash cans.

   A. chased
   B. manage
   C. knocks
   D. No change is necessary.

4) Some of the ice on the driveway <u>have melted</u>.

   A. having melted
   B. has melted
   C. has melt
   D. No change is necessary.

5) Neither the criminal forensics expert nor the DNA blood evidence <u>provide</u> enough support for that verdict.

   A. provides
   B. were providing
   C. are providing
   D. No change is necessary.

ANSWER KEY: PRACTICE EXERCISE FOR SUBJECT-VERB AGREEMENT

1) D   Option D is correct because *store* is third person singular and requires the third person singular verbs *stays*. Option B is incorrect because the plural noun *shoppers* requires a plural verb *try*. In Option C, there is no reason to shift to the past tense *prepared*.

2) B   Option B is correct because the subject, *Paul McCartney,* is singular and requires the singular verb *sings*. Option A is incorrect because the present participle *singing* does not stand alone as a verb. Option C is incorrect because the past participle *sung* cannot function as the verb in this sentence.

3) D   Option D is the correct answer because the subject *cocker spaniel* is singular and requires the singular verb *manages*. Options A, B, and C do not work structurally with the sentence.

4) B   The subject of the sentence is *some*, which requires a third person, singular verb: *has melted*. Option A incorrectly uses the present participle *having*, which does not act as a helping verb. Option C does not work structurally with the sentence.

5) A   In Option A, the singular subject *evidence* is closer to the verb and thus requires the singular in the neither/nor construction. Both Options B and C are plural forms with the helping verb and the present participle.

Identify agreements between pronoun and antecedent
A pronoun must correspond to its antecedent in number (singular or plural), person (first, second, or third person), and gender (male, female, or neutral). A pronoun must refer clearly to a single word, not to a complete idea.

A **pronoun shift** is a grammatical error in which the author starts a sentence, paragraph, or section of a paper using one particular type of pronoun and then suddenly shifts to another. This often confuses the reader.

Error: A teacher should treat all their students fairly.

Problem: Since *teacher* is singular, the pronoun referring to it must also be singular. Otherwise, the noun has to be made plural.

Correction: Teachers should treat all their students fairly.

Error: When an actor is rehearsing for a play, it often helps if you can memorize the lines in advance.

Problem: *Actor* is a third-person word; that is, the writer is talking about the subject. The pronoun *you* is in the second person, which means the writer is talking to the subject.

Correction: When actors are rehearsing for plays, it helps if they can memorize the lines in advance.

Error: The workers in the factory were upset when his or her paychecks didn't arrive on time.

Problem: *Workers* is a plural form, while *his or her* refers to one person.

Correction: The workers in the factory were upset when their paychecks didn't arrive on time.

Error: The charity auction was highly successful, which pleased everyone.

Problem: In this sentence, the pronoun *which* refers to the idea of the auction's success. In fact, *which* has no antecedent in the sentence; the word *success* is not stated.

Correction: Everyone was pleased at the success of the auction.

Error: Lana told Melanie that she would like aerobics.

Problem: The person that she refers to is unclear; it could be either Lana or Melanie.

Correction: Lana said that Melanie would like aerobics.

-OR-

Lana told Melanie that she, Melanie, would like aerobics.

Error: I dislike accounting even though my brother is one.

Problem: A person's occupation is not the same as a field, and the pronoun *one* is thus incorrect. Note that the word *accountant* is not used in the sentence, so *one* has no antecedent.

Correction: I dislike accounting even though my brother is an accountant.

PRACTICE EXERCISE: PRONOUN/ANTECEDENT AGREEMENT
Choose the option that corrects an error in the underlined portion(s).
If no error exists, choose "No change is necessary."

1) <u>You</u> can get to Martha's Vineyard by driving from Boston to Woods Hole. Once there, you can travel on a ship, but <u>you</u> may find traveling by <u>airplane</u> to be an exciting experience.

   A. They
   B. visitors
   C. it
   D. No change is necessary.

2) Both the city leader and the <u>journalist</u> are worried about the new interstate; <u>she fears</u> <u>the new roadway</u> will destroy precious farmland.

   A. journalist herself
   B. they fear
   C. it
   D. No change is necessary.

3) When <u>hunters</u> are looking for deer in <u>the woods</u>, <u>you</u> must remain quiet for long periods of time.

   A. you
   B. it
   C. they
   D. No change is necessary.

4) The strong economy is based on the importance of the citrus industry. <u>Producing</u> orange juice for most of the country.

   A. They produce
   B. Who produce
   C. Farmers there produce
   D. No change is necessary.

5) Dr. Kennedy told Paul Elliot, <u>his</u> assistant, that <u>he</u> would have to finish grading the tests before going home, no matter how long <u>it</u> took.

   A. their
   B. he, Paul
   C. they
   D. No change is necessary.

ANSWER KEY: PRACTICE EXERCISE FOR PRONOUN AGREEMENT

1) D   Pronouns must be consistent. As *you* is used throughout the sentence, the shift to *visitors* is incorrect. Option A, *They*, is vague and unclear. Option C, *it*, is also unclear.

2) B   The plural pronoun *they* is necessary to agree with the two nouns *leader* and *journalist*. There is no need for the reflexive pronoun *herself* in Option A. In Option C, *it* is vague.

3) C   The shift to *you* is unnecessary. The plural pronoun *they* is necessary to agree with the noun *hunters*. The word *it* in Option B is vague; the reader does not know to what the word *it* might refer. *It* has no antecedent.

4) C   The noun *farmers* is needed for clarification because *producing* alone creates a fragment. Option A is incorrect because *they produce* is vague. Option B is incorrect because *who* has no antecedent and creates a fragment.

5) B   The repetition of the name *Paul* is necessary to clarify who the pronoun *he* refers to. (*He* could be Dr. Kennedy.) Option A is incorrect because the singular pronoun *his* is needed, not the plural pronoun *their*. Option C is incorrect because the pronoun *it* refers to the grading of the tests, not the tests themselves.

Skill 2.3   Identify errors in use of negation.

Positive	Negative

To Be

Positive	Negative
I <u>am</u> afraid of the dark.	I <u>am not</u> afraid of the dark. (I'm not)
You are going to the store.	You <u>are not</u> going to the store (you're not/aren't)
They <u>were</u> pretty flowers.	They <u>were not</u> pretty flowers. (weren't)
I <u>was</u> enjoying my day off.	I <u>was not</u> enjoying my day off (wasn't)

Conditionals

Positive	Negative
Charlotte <u>will</u> arrive at 8.	Charlotte <u>will not</u> arrive at 8. (won't arrive)
Robert <u>can</u> run 26 miles.	Robert <u>cannot</u> run 26 miles (can't run)
I <u>could have</u> been great!	I <u>could not</u> have been great. (couldn't have)

Present simple

Positive	Negative
I <u>want</u> to go home.	I <u>do not</u> want to go home (don't)
Veronica <u>walks</u> too slowly.	Veronica <u>does not</u> walk too slowly. (doesn't)

Past Simple

Positive	Negative
I <u>skipped</u> rope daily.	I <u>did not</u> skip rope daily. (didn't)

Present Perfect

Positive	Negative
My mom <u>has</u> made my costume.	My mom <u>has not</u> made my costume. (hasn't)
The Thompsons <u>have</u> just bought a dog.	The Thompsons <u>have not</u> just bought a dog. (haven't)

Have Versus Have Got

Positive	Negative
I <u>have</u> 2 sisters.	I <u>don't</u> have two sisters.
I <u>have</u> got 2 sisters.	I <u>haven't</u> got two sisters.
Jeremy <u>has</u> school tomorrow.	Jeremy <u>doesn't</u> have school tomorrow.
Jeremy <u>has</u> got school tomorrow.	Jeremy <u>hasn't</u> got school tomorrow.

Common negative words include:

no, not, none, nothing, nowhere, neither, nobody, no one, hardly, scarcely, barely.

A **double negative** occurs when two forms of negation are used in the same sentence. In order to correct a double negative, one of the negative words should be removed.

Error: I haven't got nothing.

Correction: I haven't got anything.
     -OR-
     I have nothing.

Error: Don't nobody leave until 7 o'clock.

Correction: Do not leave until 7 o'clock.
     -OR-
     Nobody leave until 7 o'clock.

It is also incorrect to combine a negative with an adverb such as "barely," "scarcely," or "hardly."

Error: I can't barely stand it.

Correction: I can't stand it.
     -OR-
     I can barely stand it.

Skill 2.4 Identify errors in use of parallelism.

Faulty parallelism
Two or more elements stated in a single clause should be expressed with the same (or parallel) structure (e.g., all adjectives, all verb forms, or all nouns).

Error: She needed to be beautiful, successful, and have fame.

Problem: The phrase *to be* is followed by two different structures: *beautiful* and *successful* are adjectives, and *have fame* is a verb phrase.

Correction: She needed to be <u>beautiful</u>, <u>successful</u>, and <u>famous</u>.
       (adjective) (adjective)   (adjective)
       -OR-
She needed <u>beauty</u>, <u>success</u>, and <u>fame</u>.
      (noun)   (noun)   (noun)

Error: I plan either to sell my car during the spring or during the summer.

Problem: Paired conjunctions (also called correlative conjunctions, such as either-or, both-and, neither-nor, not only-but also) need to be followed with similar structures. In the sentence above, *either* is followed by *to sell my car during the spring*, while *or* is followed only by the phrase *during the summer*.

Correction: I plan to sell my car during either the spring or the summer.

Error: The President pledged to lower taxes and that he would cut spending to lower the national debt.

Problem: Since the phrase *to lower taxes* follows the verb *pledged*, a similar structure of *to* is needed with the phrase *cut spending*.

Correction: *The President pledged to lower taxes and to cut spending to lower the national debt.*
       -OR-
The President pledged that he would lower taxes and cut spending to lower the national debt.

PRACTICE EXERCISE: PARALLELISM

Choose the sentence that expresses the thought most clearly and effectively and that has no error in structure.

1. A. Andy found the family tree, researches the Irish descendents, and he was compiling a book for everyone to read.

   B. Andy found the family tree, researched the Irish descendents, and compiled a book for everyone to read.

   C. Andy finds the family tree, researched the Irish descendents, and compiled a book for everyone to read.

2. A. In the last ten years, computer technology has advanced so quickly that workers have had difficulty keeping up with the new equipment and the increased number of functions.

   B. Computer technology has advanced so quickly in the last ten years that workers have had difficulty to keep up with the new equipment and by increasing number of functions.

   C. In the last ten years, computer technology has advanced so quickly that workers have had difficulty keeping up with the new equipment, and the number of functions are increasing.

3. A. The History Museum contains exhibits honoring famous residents, a video presentation about the state's history, an art gallery featuring paintings and sculptures, and they even display a replica of the Statehouse.

   B. The State History Museum contains exhibits honoring famous residents, a video presentation about the state's history, an art gallery featuring paintings and sculptures, and even a replica of the Statehouse.

   C. The State History Museum contains exhibits honoring famous residents, a video presentation about the state's history, an art gallery featuring paintings and sculptures, and there is even a replica of the Statehouse.

4. A. Either the criminal justice students had too much practical experience and limited academic preparation or too much academic preparation and little practical experience.

    B. The criminal justice students either had too much practical experience and limited academic preparation or too much academic preparation and little practical experience.

    C. The criminal justice students either had too much practical experience and limited academic preparation or had too much academic preparation and limited practical experience.

5. A. Filmmaking is an arduous process in which the producer hires the cast and crew, chooses locations for filming, supervises the actual production, and guides the editing.

    B. Because it is an arduous process, filmmaking requires the producer to hire a cast and crew and choose locations, supervise the actual production, and guides the editing.

    C. Filmmaking is an arduous process in which the producer hires the cast and crew, chooses locations for filming, supervises the actual production, and guided the editing.

ANSWER KEY: PRACTICE EXERCISE FOR PARALLELISM

1. B   Option B uses parallelism by presenting a series of past tense verbs *found, researched*, and *compiled*. Option A interrupts the parallel structure of past tense verbs: *found, researches*, and *he was compiling*. Option C uses present tense verbs and then shifts to past tense: *finds, researched*, and *compiled*.

2. A   Option A uses parallel structure at the end of the sentence: *the new equipment and the increased number of functions*. Option B creates a faulty structure with *to keep up with the new equipment and by increasing number of functions*. Option C creates faulty parallelism with *the number of functions are increasing (and uses a plural verb for a singular noun)*.

3. B   Option B uses parallelism by presenting a series of noun phrases acting as objects of the verb *contains*. Option A interrupts that parallelism by inserting *they even display*, and Option C interrupts the parallelism with the addition of *there is*.

4. C   In the either-or parallel construction, look for a balance on both sides. Option C creates that balanced parallel structure: *either had ... or had*. Options A and B do not create the balance. In Option A, the structure is *Either the criminal justice students ... or too much*. In Option B, the structure is *either had ... or too much*.

5. A   Option A uses parallelism by presenting a series of verbs with objects: *hires the cast and crew, chooses locations for filming, supervises the actual production, and guides the editing*. The structure of Option B incorrectly suggests that filmmaking chooses locations, supervises the actual production, and guides the editing. Option C interrupts the series of present tense verbs by inserting the participle *guided* instead of the present tense *guides*.

Skill 2.5   Identify errors in use of coordination and subordination.

Coordination means that ideas of equal importance are joined. Coordinating conjunctions include the **FANBOYS—For, And, Nor, But, Or, Yet, So.** A comma precedes a coordinating conjunction that joins two independent clauses.

Subordination means that one idea of lesser importance is joined to another. Dependent clauses are created one of two ways—with subordinating conjunctions (e.g., although, when, until, since, because, if) or with relative pronouns (e.g., who, whom, which, that).

Error:	Because college students need to be diligent in their job search, the market is tight.
Problem:	The problem here is one of inappropriate or illogical subordination. The tight job market is not caused by the need for diligence among college students. Rather, the tight job market is a reason college students need to be diligent.
Correction:	Because the job market is tight, college students need to be diligent in their job search.
Error:	The college newspaper is published every weekday, yet it is a useful source of information to students.
Problem:	These two independent clauses are equally important, but the wrong coordinating conjunction is used. The word *yet* implies a contradictory piece of information.
Correction:	The college newspaper is published every weekday, and it is a useful source of information to students.
Error:	The college newspaper is run entirely and completely by students, and they are often journalism majors.
Problem:	This sentence is wordy and needs to subordinate the less important idea.
Correction:	The college newspaper is run entirely by students, who are often journalism majors.

PRACTICE EXERCISE: COORDINATION AND SUBORDINATION

For the underlined sentences below, choose the option that expresses the meaning with the most fluency and the clearest logic within the context. If the underlined sentence should not be changed, choose Option A.

1. Charity fundraisers have had to be creative in their efforts to support their organizations. <u>At the arts fair each spring, some groups sell popcorn and drinks due to the fact that they need to raise money, and other groups sell homemade goods at the craft fairs held each fall.</u>

    A. At the arts fair each spring, some groups sell popcorn and drinks due to the fact that they need to raise money, and other groups sell homemade goods at the craft fairs held each fall.

    B. To raise money, some groups sell popcorn and drinks at the spring arts fair while other groups sell homemade goods at the fall crafts fair.

    C. Because charities want to raise money at the arts fair held each spring, some groups sell popcorn and drinks, and in the fall other groups sell homemade goods at the craft fair.

    D. Due to the fact that charities want to raise money, at the spring arts fair, some groups sell popcorn and drinks, but other groups sell homemade goods at the crafts fair in the fall.

2. The winter dragged on with recurrent cold fronts dashing our hopes of warm weather. <u>Then one morning we awoke, and we saw the deep purple of the redbud blooms, and there were the pink, white, and lilac-colored azaleas, and also the snow-white dogwoods.</u>

    A. Then one morning we awoke, and we saw the deep purple of the redbud blooms, and there were the pink, white, and lilac-colored azaleas, and also the snow-white dogwoods.

    B. Then one morning we awoke seeing the deep purple of the redbud blooms, and then there were the pink, white, and lilac-colored azaleas and also the snow-white dogwoods.

    C. Then one morning we awoke to see the deep purple of the redbud blooms, the pink, white, and lilac-colored azaleas, and the snow-white dogwoods.

    D. The one morning we awoke to see the deep purple of the redbud blooms as well as the pink, white, and the lilac-colored azaleas. We also saw the snow-white dogwoods.

3.   In the last twenty years, laser technology has facilitated delicate heart operations. <u>Although once unimaginable, a laser beam that has given new life to many gravely-ill heart patients is a surgical technique that enables drilling tiny holes in the heart wall.</u>

A.   Although once unimaginable, a laser beam that has given new life to many gravely ill heart patients is a surgical technique that enables drilling tiny holes in the heart wall.

B.   It once seemed unimaginable, but laser beam surgery, in which holes are drilled in the heart wall, is a new surgical technique, although it has given hope to gravely ill heart patients.

C.   Bringing new hope to gravely ill heart patients, a once unimaginable surgical technique enables doctors to drill holes in the heart wall with a laser beam.

D.   Although once unimaginable and now a new hope to gravely ill heart patients, a new surgical technique uses a laser beam to drill holes in the heart wall.

4.   To the dismay of NASA scientists, the Hubble telescope at first sent back out-of-focus pictures. <u>However, an extraordinary mission in December 1993 was when a space shuttle team accomplished restoring Hubble's "eye," and now the Hubble can send back pictures that are sharp and clear.</u>

A.   However, an extraordinary mission in December 1993 was when a space shuttle team accomplished restoring Hubble's "eye," and now the Hubble can send back pictures that are sharp and clear.

B.   However, now sending back sharp, clear pictures, the Hubble "eye" was restored in December 1993 by the extraordinary mission of a space shuttle team.

C.   However, the Hubble "eye" was restored in December 1993 in an extraordinary mission accomplished by a space shuttle team sending back sharp and clear images.

D.   However, in an extraordinary mission in December 1993, a space shuttle team restored Hubble's "eye," so it now sends back sharp, clear images.

ANSWER KEY: PRACTICE FOR COORDINATION AND SUBORDINATION

1. By using the infinitive phrase at the beginning of the dependent clause at the end, **Option B** most concisely and clearly expresses the idea of groups raising money for charities by selling food and homemade goods. Option A adds the wordy phrase "due to the fact that" and introduces the two sentences with a long prepositional phrase that only relates to the first independent clause. Option C creates a wordy dependent clause and coordinates the two sentences with a "but," indicating an inappropriate contrast.

2. **Option C** most concisely coordinates the series of ideas expressed in the sentence. Option A coordinates three independent clauses that can be condensed. Option B overuses the words "and then" and includes the illogical idea "we awoke seeing." Option D creates two sentences that can be condensed to save words.

3. **Option C** places the modifying words and phrases near the words they modify, and the main clause is concisely and clearly phrased. In Option A, the long relative clause after the subject "laser beam" is confusing. Option B creates a main clause out of an idea that should be subordinated for concise phrasing, and it adds a wordy modifying phrase after the subject "laser beam surgery." Option D creates an awkward introductory modifying phrase.

4. **Option D** places the prepositional phrase "in an extraordinary mission in December 1993" at the beginning of the sentence to avoid confusion, and the coordinating conjunction "so" emphasizes the cause-and-effect relationship of the team's repair of the "eye" and the improved pictures. Option A uses an awkward construction "was when." Option B offers an illogical sequence with the result first and then the action of repair following. Option C misplaces the modifying phrase so that the team is "sending back sharp and clear images."

COMPETENCY 3.0   IDIOM, WORD CHOICE AND MECHANICS

Skill 3.1   Identify errors in use of idiomatic expressions.

Idiomatic expressions are groups of words whose meaning, when considered as a whole, is something entirely different from the meaning of each individual word. This is called **non-compositionality**. For example, the expression "hit the hay" has nothing to do with hitting hay at all; it means to go to bed. In addition, idioms display **non-substitutability**, which means that you cannot replace a word in an idiom and maintain its meaning. For example, one cannot say, "hit the straw" instead of "hit the hay," even though straw and hay could be considered synonyms. Lastly, idioms are **non-modifiable**; if an idiom is modified with syntactic transformations, it loses its idiomatic meaning. "Katie hit the bale of hay with her car" changes the meaning.

Idioms are not hard and fast grammatical rules; rather, idioms are verbal habits that have become ingrained in standard English language usage. Learning correct usage of idiomatic expressions is about learning to trust your ear. Idioms come in the form of expressions such as "rain check" or "a penny for your thoughts," as well as phrases such as "in contrast to" and "not only … but."

Some Idioms

abide by	discriminate against
agreed to	in charge of
as…as	in contrast to
among	insist upon
between	neither… nor
concerned with	not only…. but also
different from	rely upon

Error: I am having trouble deciding between the chocolate, vanilla, and strawberry milkshakes.

Problem: Here there are more than two items being distinguished. In this case, you must use *among*, as *between* should only be used when comparing two items.

Correction: I am having trouble deciding among the chocolate, vanilla, and strawberry milkshakes.

Error: Eugena has less game tokens than Charlie.

Problem: *Less* is used to answer the question, "How much?" whereas *fewer* is used to answer the question, "How many?"

Correction: Eugena has fewer game tokens than Charlie.

Error: Sheryl is considered as the top executive in her field.

Problem: This sentence sounds awkward. The proper expression would be *considered the* instead of *considered as.*

Correction: Sheryl is considered the top executive in her field.

Error: The geography final exam featured such topics like state capitals, the seven seas, and world climate.

Problem: The correct expression should be *such as* instead of *such ___ like.* *Like* should be used only when there is a direct comparison: Cara looks a lot like her sister.

Correction: The geography final exam featured such topics *as* state capitals, the seven seas, and world climate.

or   The geography final exam featured *topics such as* state capitals, the seven seas, and world climate.

PRACTICE EXERCISE: IDENTIFY ERRORS IN IDIOMATIC EXPRESSIONS

1) My parents took everyone out for my birthday and agreed to <u>foot the bill</u>.

   A) kick the receipt
   B) leave without paying
   C) pay

2) On the first day of school, the teacher had planned several "getting-to-know-you" activities to help <u>break the ice</u>.

   A) break up a block of ice
   B) put everyone at ease
   C) learn names

3) My boss gave me the <u>green light</u> to begin the project I'd proposed last week.

   A) permission to start
   B) a large sum of money
   C) a hug

ANSWERS

   1. C
   2. B
   3. A

Skill 3.2   Identify errors in word choice.

Choose the most effective word or phrase within the context suggested by the sentences.

1)   The defendant was accused of _____ money from his employer.

A) stealing
B) borrowing
C) robbing

2)   O.J. Simpson's angry disposition _____ his ex-wife Nicole.

A) mortified
B) intimidated
C) frightened

3)   Many tourists are attracted to the Paradise Island because of its _____ climate.

A) friendly
B) peaceful
C) balmy

4)   The woman was angry because the tomato juice left an _____ stain on her brand new carpet.

A) unsightly
B) ugly
C) unpleasant

5)   After disobeying orders, the army private was _____ by his superior officer.

A) degraded
B) attacked
C) reprimanded

6)   Sharon's critical evaluation of the student's book report left the student feeling _____, which caused him to want to quit school.

A) surprised
B) depressed
C) discouraged

7) The life-saving medication created by the scientist had a _____ impact on further developments in the treatment of cancer.

   A) beneficial
   B) fortunate
   C) miraculous

8) *The Phantom of the Opera* is one of Andrew Lloyd Webber's most successful musicals, largely because of its _____ themes.

   A) romantic
   B) melodramatic
   C) imaginary

9) The massive Fourth of July fireworks display _____ the partygoers with lots of colored lights and sound.

   A) disgusted
   B) captivated
   C) captured

10) Many of the residents of Grand Forks, North Dakota, were forced to _____ their homes because of the flood.

   A) escape
   B) evacuate
   C) exit

ANSWERS: 1 A, 2 C, 3 C, 4 A, 5 C, 6 C, 7 A, 8 A, 9 B, 10 B

PRACTICE EXERCISE: WORD CHOICE

Choose the sentence that expresses the thought most clearly and most effectively and that is structurally correct in grammar and syntax.

1)   A. The movie was three hours in length, featuring interesting characters, and moved at a fast pace.

        B. The movie was three hours long, featured interesting characters, and moved at a fast pace.

        C. Moving at a fast pace, the movie was three hours long and featured interesting characters.

2)   A. We were so offended by the waiter's demeanor that we left the restaurant without paying the check.

        B. The waiter's demeanor offended us so much that without paying the check, we left the restaurant.

        C. We left the restaurant without paying the check because we were offended by the waiter's demeanor.

3)   A. In today's society, information about our lives is provided to us by computers.

        B. We rely on computers in today's society to provide us information about our lives.

        C. In today's society, we rely on computers to provide us with information about our lives.

4)   A. Folding the sides of the tent carefully, Jack made sure to be quiet so none of the other campers would be woken up.

        B. So none of the other campers would be woken up, Jack made sure to be quiet by folding the sides of the tent carefully.

        C. Folding the sides of the tent carefully, so none of the other campers would wake up, Jack made sure to be quiet.

ANSWERS: 1 B, 2 A, 3 C, 4 A

Choose the most effective word or phrase within the context suggested by the sentence(s).

1) The six hundred employees of General Electric were _____ by the company due to budgetary cutbacks.

   A) released
   B) terminated
   C) downsized

2) The force of the tornado _____ the many residents of the town of Russell, Kansas.

   A) intimidated
   B) repulsed
   C) frightened

3) Even though his new car was easy to drive, Fred _____ to walk to work every day because he liked the exercise.

   A) needed
   B) preferred
   C) considered

4) June's parents were very upset over the school board's decision to suspend her from Adams High for a week. Before they filed a lawsuit against the board, they _____ with a lawyer to help them make a decision.

   A) consulted
   B) debated
   C) conversed

5) The race car driver's _____ in handling the automobile was a key factor in his victory.

   A) patience
   B) precision
   C) determination

6) After impressing the judges with her talent and charm, the beauty contestant _____ more popularity by singing an aria from "La Boheme."

   A) captured
   B) scored
   C) gained

7)   The stained-glass window was _____ when a large brick flew through it during the riot.

A) damaged
B) cracked
C) shattered

8)   The class didn't know what happened to the professor until it was_____ by the principal why he dropped out of school.

A) informed
B) discovered
C) explained

• 9)   The giant penthouse on the top of the building allows the billionaire Industrialist _____ the citizens on the street.

A) to view from above
B) the chance to see
C) to glance at

10)   Sally's parents _____ her to attend the dance after she promised to return by midnight.

A) prohibited
B) permitted
C) asked

ANSWERS: 1 C, 2 C, 3 B, 4 A, 5 B, 6 C, 7 C, 8 C, 9 C, 10 B

Wordiness
Passages contain irrelevant, repetitive, and/or wordy expressions. Select the underlined word or word group that is unnecessary to the context of the passage.

1)   Some children decide to participate <u>actively</u> in <u>extracurricular</u> activities, such as after-school sports and <u>various</u> clubs. Many teachers and administrators <u>willingly</u> volunteer to supervise the activities during their <u>spare</u> time.

    A) actively
    B) extracurricular
    C) various
    D) willingly
    E) spare

2)   Our high school reunion, was held at the <u>swanky</u> Boca Hilton, which is known for its elegance and <u>glamour</u>. We arrived in a <u>rented</u> stretch limo and prepared to dance and have a good time, <u>reminiscing</u> with our <u>dear</u> friends.

    A) swanky
    B) glamour
    C) rented
    D) reminiscing
    E) dear

• 3)   Once we reached <u>the top of</u> the mountain, a <u>powerful</u> storm came from <u>out of</u> nowhere, bringing rain and <u>large</u> hailstones from the dark <u>black</u> skies above.

    A) the top of
    B) powerful
    C) out of
    D) large
    E) black

•4) Policemen often undergo a rigorous, <u>harsh</u> training period to prepare them <u>adequately</u> for the <u>intense</u> dangers and stresses of the job. <u>Only</u> the most physically fit candidates are capable of handling the challenges of dealing with the <u>criminal</u> elements of our society.

A) harsh
B) adequately
C) intense
D) Only
E) criminal

•5) The <u>early morning</u> hurricane struck at dawn, knocking out power lines and <u>ripping the roofs</u> from buildings <u>all</u> throughout Broward County. <u>Massive</u> winds and rain wreaked havoc, and terrified residents ran <u>madly</u> for shelter and safety.

A) early morning
B) ripping the roofs from
C) all
D) Massive
E) madly

6) Alan's alcoholism affected the entire family <u>deeply</u>. When his father asked <u>him to</u> stop drinking, he <u>refused and</u> drove off in his sister's car, which he crashed into a utility pole. <u>Fortunately</u>, Alan miraculously survived and now is undergoing intensive treatment in a top-notch facility <u>that is well-regarded</u>.

A) deeply
B) him to
C) refused and
D) Fortunately
E) that is well-regarded

7) Soap operas are popular among <u>many</u> television viewers because of the ability to <u>blend</u> real issues such as drug abuse, infidelity, and AIDS <u>with melodramatic plots</u> concerning lust, greed, vanity, and revenge. <u>These shows</u> often have very devoted followings among viewers who watch them <u>faithfully</u> every day.

A) many
B) blend
C) with melodramatic plots
D) These
E) faithfully

8) Walt Disney World <u>is one of</u> the most visited tourist attractions in the United States. Its success <u>and prosperity</u> can be attributed to the <u>blend of</u> childhood fantasy and adult imagination. The park features rides and <u>attractions</u> that hold considerable appeal for <u>both</u> children and adults.

A) is one of
B) and prosperity
C) blend of
D) attractions
E) both

9) Jason was the best <u>baseball</u> player on the Delray Beach High School baseball team; in fact, he was known as the star <u>of the team</u>. He could play several positions on the field <u>with enthusiasm and skill</u>, but his strength was hitting balls <u>out of the park</u>. When Jason was at the plate, the coach expected him to score a home run <u>every time</u>.

A) baseball
B) of the team
C) with enthusiasm and skill
D) out of the park
E) every time

10) Many of the major cities in the United States are grappling with <u>a variety of</u> problems, such as crime, crumbling roadways, a shortage of <u>funding for</u> schools and healthcare, and a lack of jobs. There are <u>no easy</u> solutions to these problems, but mayors who have <u>strong</u> leadership abilities <u>work to</u> create good ideas to deal with them.

A) a variety of
B) funding for
C) no easy
D) strong
E) work to

ANSWERS: 1 D, 2 A, 3 E, 4 A, 5 A, 6 E, 7 E, 8 B, 9 A, 10) E

Recognize commonly confused or misused words or phrases
Students frequently encounter problems with **homonyms**—words that are spelled and pronounced the same as another but that have different meanings, such as *mean*, which can be a verb—"to intend"; an adjective—"unkind"; or a noun or adjective—"average."

A similar phenomenon that causes trouble is heteronyms (also sometimes called heterophones), which are words that are spelled the same but with different pronunciations and meanings. (In other words, homographs differ in pronunciation and technically, homographs are not homophones). For example, the homographs *desert* (abandon) and *desert* (arid region) are heteronyms (pronounced differently), but *mean* (intend) and *mean* (average) are not heteronyms because they are pronounced the same but are homonyms.

Another similar occurrence in English is the capitonym, a word spelled the same but with different meanings when it is capitalized. A capitonym may or may not have different pronunciations. Example: *polish* (to make shiny) and *Polish* (from Poland).

Some of the most troubling homonyms are those that are spelled differently but that sound the same. Examples: *its* (3rd person singular neuter pronoun) and *it's* ("it is"); *there*, *their* (3rd person plural pronoun), and *they're* ("they are"). Another common example is *to*, *too*, and *two*.

Some homonyms/homographs are particularly intriguing. *Fluke*, for instance, is a fish, a flatworm, the end parts of an anchor, the fins on a whale's tail, and a stroke of luck.

Common misused words:
Accept is a verb meaning "to receive or to tolerate." **Except** is usually a preposition meaning "excluding." Except is also a verb meaning "to exclude."

Advice is a noun meaning "recommendation." **Advise** is a verb meaning "to recommend."

Affect is usually a verb meaning "to influence." **Effect** is usually a noun meaning "result." Effect can also be a verb meaning "to bring about."

An **Allusion** is "an indirect reference." An **illusion** is "a misconception or false impression."

Add is a verb meaning "to put together." **Ad** is a noun that is the abbreviation for the word "advertisement."

Ain't is a common, nonstandard contraction for the contraction "aren't."

Allot is a verb meaning "to distribute." **A lot** can act as an adverb that means "often," "to a great degree," or "a large quantity." (Example: She shops a lot.)

Allowed is used as an adjective that means "permitted." **Aloud** is an adverb that means "audible."

Bare is an adjective that means "naked" or "exposed." It can also indicate a minimum. As a noun, **bear** is a large mammal. As a verb, **bear** means "to carry a heavy burden."

Capital refers to a city, **capitol** to "a building where lawmakers meet." **Capital** also refers to "wealth" or "resources."

A **chord** is a noun that refers to "a group of musical notes." **Cord** is a noun meaning "rope" or "a long electrical line."

Compliment is a noun meaning "a praising or flattering remark." **Complement** is a noun that means "something that completes or makes perfect."

Climactic is derived from climax, "the point of greatest intensity in a series or progression of events." **Climatic** is derived from climate; it refers to meteorological conditions.

Discreet is an adjective that means "tactful" or "diplomatic"; **discrete** is an adjective that means "separate" or "distinct."

Dye is a noun or verb used to indicate "artificially coloring something." **Die** is a verb that means "to pass away." Die is also a noun that means "a cube-shaped game piece."

Effect is a noun that means "outcome." **Affect** is a verb that means "to influence."

Elicit is a verb meaning "to bring out" or "to evoke." **Illicit** is an adjective meaning "unlawful."

Emigrate means "to leave one country or region to settle in another." **Immigrate** means "to enter another country and reside there."

Gorilla is a noun meaning "a large great ape." **Guerrilla** is "a member of a band of irregular soldiers."

Hoard is a verb that means "to accumulate" or "store up." **Horde** is "a large group."

Lead is a verb that means "to guide" or "toserve as the head of." It is also a noun that is a type of metal.

Medal is a noun that means "an award that is strung round the neck." **Meddle** is a verb that means "to involve oneself in a matter without right or invitation." **Metal** is "an element such as silver or gold." **Mettle** is a noun meaning "toughness" or "courage."

Morning is a noun indicating "the time between midnight and midday." **Mourning** is a verb or noun pertaining to "the period of grieving after a death."

Past is a noun meaning "a time before now" (past, present, and future). **Passed** is "the past tense of the verb 'to pass.'"

Piece is a noun meaning "portion." **Peace** is a noun meaning "the opposite of war or serenity."

Peak is a noun meaning "the tip" or "height to reach the highest point." **Peek** is a verb that means "to take a brief look." **Pique** is a verb meaning "to incite or raise interest."

Principal is a noun most commonly meaning "the chief or head," and it also means "a capital sum of money." **Principle** is a noun meaning "a basic truth or law."

Rite is a noun meaning "a special ceremony." **Right** is an adjective meaning "correct" or "the opposite direction of left." **Write** is a verb meaning "to compose in writing."

Than is a conjunction used in comparisons; **then** is an adverb denoting time. That pizza is more <u>than</u> I can eat. Tom laughed, and <u>then</u> we recognized him. To remember the correct use of these words, you can use the following:
Than is used to compare; both words have the letter *a* in them.
Then tells when; both are spelled the same, except for the first letter.

There is an adverb specifying place; it is also an expletive. Adverb: Sylvia is lying <u>there</u> unconscious. Expletive: <u>There</u> are two plums left. **Their** is a possessive pronoun. **They're** is a contraction of "they are." Fred and Jane finally washed <u>their</u> car. <u>They're</u> later than usual today.

To is a preposition; **too** is an adverb; **two** is a number.

Your is a possessive pronoun; **you're** is a contraction of "you are."

Strategies to help students conquer these demons: Practice using them in sentences; context is useful in understanding the difference; drill is necessary to overcome the misuses.

To teach language effectively, it is necessary to understand that as human beings acquire language, they realize that words have *denotative* and *connotative* meanings. Generally, denotative words point to things, and connotative words deal with mental suggestions that the words convey. The word *skunk* has a denotative meaning if the speaker can point to the actual animal as he speaks the word or intends the word to identify the animal. Skunk has a connotative meaning depending upon the tone of delivery, the socially acceptable attitudes about the animal, and the speaker's personal feelings about the animal.

Problem Phrases

Correct	Incorrect
Supposed to	Suppose to
Used to	Use to
Toward	Towards
Anyway	Anyways
Couldn't care less	Could care less
For all intents and purposes	For all intensive purposes
Come to see me	Come and see me
En route	In route
Regardless	Irregardless
Second, Third	Secondly, Thirdly

Other confusing words
Lie is an intransitive verb meaning to recline or rest on a surface. Its principal parts are *lie*, *lay*, and *lain*. **Lay** is a transitive verb meaning "to put or place." Its principal parts are *lay*, *laid*, and *laid*.

> Birds lay eggs.
> I lie down for bed around 10 PM.

Set is a transitive verb meaning "to put or to place." Its principal parts are *set*, *set*, and *set*. **Sit** is an intransitive verb meaning "to be seated." Its principal parts are *sit*, *sat*, and *sat*.

> I set my backpack down near the front door.
> They sat in the park until the sun went down.

Among is a preposition to be used with three or more items. **Between** is to be used with two items.

> Between you and me, I cannot tell the difference among those three Johnson sisters.

As is a subordinating conjunction used to introduce a subordinating clause. **Like** is a preposition and is followed by a noun or a noun phrase.

> As I walked to the lab, I realized that the recent experiment findings were much like those we found last year.

Can is a verb that means to be able. **May** is a verb that means to have permission. They are only interchangeable in cases of possibility.

> I can lift 250 pounds.
> May I go to Alex's house?

Skill 3.3   Identify errors in use of punctuation.

Commas
Commas indicate a brief pause. They are used to set off dependent clauses and long introductory word groups, to separate words in a series, to set off unimportant material that interrupts the flow of the sentence, and to separate independent clauses joined by conjunctions.

Error: After I finish my master's thesis I plan to work in Chicago.

Problem: A comma is needed after an introductory dependent word group containing a subject and verb.

Correction: *After I finish my master's thesis, I plan to work in Chicago.*

Error: I washed waxed and vacuumed my car today.

Problem: Commas should separate nouns, phrases, or clauses in a list, as well as two or more coordinate adjectives that modify one word. Although the word *and* is sometimes considered optional, it is often necessary to clarify the meaning.

Correction: *I washed, waxed, and vacuumed my car today.*

Error: She was a talented dancer but she is mostly remembered for her singing ability.

Problem: A comma is needed before a conjunction that joins two independent clauses (complete sentences).

Correction: *She was a talented dancer, but she is mostly remembered for her singing ability.*

Error: This incident is I think typical of what can happen when the community remains so divided.

Problem: Commas are needed between nonessential words or words that interrupt the main clause.

Correction: *This incident is, I think, typical of what can happen when the community remains so divided.*

Semicolons and colons
Semicolons are needed to separate two or more closely related independent clauses when a transitional adverb introduces the second clause. (These clauses may also be written as separate sentences, preferably by placing the adverb within the second sentence).

Error: I climbed to the top of the mountain, it took me three hours.

Problem: A comma alone cannot separate two independent clauses. Instead, a semicolon is needed to separate two related sentences.

Correction: *I climbed to the top of the mountain; it took me three hours.*

Error: In the movie, asteroids destroyed Dallas, Texas, Kansas City, Missouri, and Boston, Massachusetts.

Problem: Semicolons are needed to separate items in a series that already contain internal punctuation.

Correction: *In the movie, asteroids destroyed Dallas, Texas; Kansas City, Missouri; and Boston, Massachusetts.*

Colons are used to introduce lists and to emphasize what follows.

Error: Essays will receive the following grades, *A* for excellent, *B* for good, *C* for average, and *D* for unsatisfactory.

Problem: A colon is needed to emphasize the information or list that follows.

Correction: *Essays will receive the following grades: A for excellent, B for good, C for average, and D for unsatisfactory.*

Error: The school carnival included: amusement rides, clowns, food booths, and a variety of games.

Problem: The material preceding the colon and the list that follows is not a complete sentence. Do not separate a verb (or preposition) from the object.

Correction: *The school carnival included amusement rides, clowns, food booths, and a variety of games.*

Apostrophes

Apostrophes are used to show either contractions or possession.

Error: She shouldnt be permitted to smoke cigarettes in the building.

Problem: An apostrophe is needed in a contraction in place of the missing letter.

Correction: *She shouldn't be permitted to smoke cigarettes in the building.*

Error: My cousins motorcycle was stolen from his driveway.

Problem: An apostrophe is needed to show possession.

Correction: *My cousin's motorcycle was stolen from his driveway.* (Note: The use of the apostrophe before the letter "s" means that there is just one cousin. The plural form would read the following way: My cousins' motorcycle was stolen from their driveway.)

Error: The childrens new kindergarten teacher was also a singer.

Problem: An apostrophe is needed to show possession.

Correction: *The children's new kindergarten teacher was also a singer.*

Error: Children screams could be heard for miles.

Problem: An apostrophe and the letter -s are needed in the sentence
                 to show who is screaming.

Correction: *Children's screams could he heard for miles.*
                 (Note: Because the word *children* is already plural, the
                 apostrophe and -s must be added afterward to show
                 ownership.)

Quotation marks

In a quoted statement, that is either declarative or imperative, place the period inside the closing quotation marks.

> "The airplane crashed on the runway during takeoff."

If other words in the sentence follow the quotation, place a comma inside the closing quotations marks and a period at the end of the sentence.

> "The airplane crashed on the runway during takeoff," said the
> announcer.

In most instances in which a quoted title or expression occurs at the end of a sentence, the period is placed before either the single or double quotation marks.

> "The middle school readers were unprepared to understand Bryant's
> poem 'Thanatopsis.'"

> Early book-length adventure stories such as *Don Quixote* and *The Three
> Musketeers* were known as "picaresque novels."

There is an instance in which the final quotation mark would precede the period—if the content of the sentence were about a speech or quote so that the understanding of the meaning would be confused by the placement of the period.

> The first thing out of his mouth was "Hi, I'm home."
>   *-but-*
> The first line of his speech began: "I arrived home to an empty house".

In interrogatory or exclamatory sentences, the question mark or exclamation point should be positioned outside the closing quotation marks if the quote itself is a statement, command, or cited title.

> Who decided to lead us in the recitation of the "Pledge of Allegiance"?

> Why was Tillie shaking as she began her recitation, "Once upon a midnight dreary. . ."?

> I was embarrassed when Mrs. White said, "Your slip is showing"!

In declarative sentences, where the quotation is a question or an exclamation, place the question mark or exclamation point inside the quotation marks.

> The hall monitor yelled, "Fire! Fire!"

> "Fire! Fire!" yelled the hall monitor.

> Cory shrieked, "Is there a mouse in the room?" (In this instance, the question supersedes the exclamation.)

Quotations—whether words, phrases, or clauses—should be punctuated according to the rules of the grammatical function they serve in the sentence.

> The works of Shakespeare, "the Bard of Avon," have been contested as originating with other authors.

> "You'll get my money," the old man warned, "when 'hell freezes over'."

> Sheila cited the passage that began "Four score and seven years ago . . . ." (Note the ellipsis followed by an enclosed period.)

> "Old Ironsides" inspired the preservation of the U.S.S. Constitution.

Use quotation marks to enclose the titles of shorter works: songs, short poems, short stories, essays, and chapters of books. (See "Dashes and Italics" for punctuating longer titles.)

> "The Tell-Tale Heart"   "Casey at the Bat"   "America the Beautiful"

Dashes and Italics

Place **em dashes** to denote sudden breaks in thought.

Some periods in literature—the Romantic Age, for example—spanned different periods in different countries.

Use dashes instead of commas if commas are already used elsewhere in the sentence for amplification or explanation.

> The Fireside Poets included three Brahmans—James Russell Lowell, Henry David Wadsworth, and Oliver Wendell Holmes.

Use **italics** to punctuate the titles of long works of literature, names of periodical publications, musical scores, works of art, and motion picture, television, and radio programs. (When unable to write in italics, students should be instructed to underline in their own writing when italics would be appropriate.)

The Idylls of the King	*Hiawatha*	*The Sound and the Fury*
Mary Poppins	*Newsweek*	*The Nutcracker Suite*

Fragments

Fragments occur (1) if word groups standing alone are missing either a subject or a verb, and (2) if word groups containing a subject and verb and standing alone are actually made dependent because of the use of subordinating conjunctions or relative pronouns.

Error: The teacher waiting for the class to complete the assignment.

Problem: This sentence is not complete because an -ing word alone does not function as a verb. When a helping verb is added (for example, *was waiting*), it will become a sentence.

Correction: *The teacher was waiting for the class to complete the assignment.*

Error: Until the last toy was removed from the floor.

Problem: Words such as *until, because, although, when*, and *if* make a clause dependent and thus incapable of standing alone. An independent clause must be added to make the sentence complete.

Correction: *Until the last toy was removed from the floor, the kids could not go outside to play.*

Error: The city will close the public library. Because of a shortage of funds.

Problem: The problem is the same as above. The dependent clause must be joined to the independent clause.

Correction: *The city will close the public library because of a shortage of funds.*

Error: Anyone planning to go on the trip should bring the necessary items. Such as a backpack, boots, a canteen, and bug spray.

Problem: The second word group is a phrase and cannot stand alone because there is neither a subject nor a verb. The fragment can be corrected by adding the phrase to the sentence.

Correction: *Anyone planning to go on the trip should bring the necessary items, such as a backpack, boots, a canteen, and bug spray.*

PRACTICE EXERCISE: FRAGMENTS

Choose the option that corrects the underlined portion(s) of the sentence.
If no error exists, choose "No change is necessary."

1)   Despite the lack of funds in the <u>budget it</u> was necessary to rebuild the roads that were damaged from the recent floods.

     A) budget: it
     B) budget, it
     C) budget; it
     D) No change is necessary.

2)   After determining that the fire was caused by faulty <u>wiring, the</u> building inspector said the construction company should be fined.

     A) wiring. The
     B) wiring the
     C) wiring; the
     D) No change is necessary.

3)   Many years after buying a grand <u>piano Henry</u> decided he'd rather play the violin instead.

     A) piano: Henry
     B) piano, Henry
     C) piano; Henry
     D) No change is necessary.

4)   Computers are being used more and more <u>frequently. because</u> of their capacity to store information.

     A) frequently because
     B) frequently, because
     C) frequently; because
     D) No change is necessary.

5)   Doug washed the floors <u>everyday. to</u> keep them clean for the guests.

     A) everyday to
     B) everyday,
     C) everyday;
     D) No change is necessary.

ANSWER KEY: PRACTICE EXERCISE FOR FRAGMENTS

1. B   The clause that begins with *despite* is introductory and must be separated with the clause that follows by a comma. Option A is incorrect because a colon is used to set off a list or to emphasize what follows. In Option B, a comma incorrectly suggests that the two clauses are dependent.

2. D   A comma correctly separates the dependent clause *After...wiring* at the beginning of the sentence from the independent clause that follows. Option A incorrectly breaks the two clauses into separate sentences, Option B omits the comma, and Option C incorrectly suggests that the phrase is an independent clause.

3. B   The phrase *Henry decided...instead* must be joined to the independent clause. Option A incorrectly puts a colon before *Henry decided*, and Option C incorrectly separates the phrase as if it were an independent clause.

4. A   The second clause *because...information* is dependent and must be joined to the first independent clause. Option B is incorrect because as the dependent clause comes at the end of the sentence rather than at the beginning, a comma is not necessary. In Option C, a semicolon incorrectly suggests that the two clauses are independent.

5. A   The second clause *to keep...guests* is dependent and must be joined to the first independent clause. Option B is incorrect because as the dependent clause comes at the end of the sentence rather than at the beginning, a comma is not necessary. In Option C, a semicolon incorrectly suggests that the two clauses are independent.

Run-on sentences and comma splices

Comma splices appear when a comma joins two sentences. Fused sentences appear when two sentences are run together with no punctuation at all.

Error: Dr. Sanders is a brilliant scientist, his research on genetic disorders won him a Nobel Prize.

Problem: A comma alone cannot join two independent clauses (complete sentences). The two clauses can be joined by a semi-colon, joined by a conjunction and comma, or they can be separated into two sentences by a period.

Correction: *Dr. Sanders is a brilliant scientist; his research on genetic disorders won him a Nobel Prize.*
                             -OR-
                Dr. Sanders is a brilliant scientist. His research on genetic disorders won him a Nobel Prize.
                             -OR-
                Dr. Sanders is a brilliant scientist, and his research on genetic disorders won him a Nobel Prize.

Error: Paradise Island is noted for its beaches they are long, sandy, and beautiful.

Problem: The first independent clause ends with the word *beaches*, and the second independent clause is fused to the first. The fused sentence error can be corrected in several ways:

(1) one clause may be made dependent on another with a subordinating conjunction or a relative pronoun
(2) a semi-colon may be used to combine two equally important ideas
(3) the two independent clauses may be separated by a period
(4) the independent clauses may be joined by a conjunction and comma

Correction: *Paradise Island is noted for its beaches, which are long, sandy, and beautiful.*

-OR-

Paradise Island is noted for its beaches; they are long, sandy, and beautiful.

-OR -

Paradise Island is noted for its beaches. They are long, sandy, and beautiful.

-OR-

Paradise Island is noted for its beaches, for they are long, sandy, and beautiful.

Error: The number of hotels has increased, however, the number of visitors has grown also.

Problem: The first sentence ends with the word increased, and a comma is not strong enough to connect it to the second sentence. The adverbial transition *however* does not function the same way as a coordinating conjunction and cannot be used with commas to link two sentences. Several different corrections are available.

Correction: *The number of hotels has increased; however, the number of visitors has grown also.*
[Two separate but closely related sentences are created with the use of the semicolon.]

-OR-

The number of hotels has increased. However, the number of visitors has grown also.
[Two separate sentences are created.]

-OR-

Although the number of hotels has increased, the number of visitors has grown also.
[One idea is made subordinate to the other and separated with a comma.]

-OR-

The number of hotels has increased, but the number of visitors has grown also.

[The comma before the coordinating conjunction *but* is appropriate. The adverbial transition *however* does not function the same way as the coordinating conjunction *but* does.]

PRACTICE EXERCISE: FUSED SENTENCES AND COMMA SPLICES

Choose the option that corrects an error in the underlined portion(s). If no error exists, choose "No change is necessary."

1) Scientists are excited at the ability to clone a <u>sheep: however</u>, it is not yet known if the same can be done to humans.

   A) sheep, however,
   B) sheep. However,
   C) sheep, however;
   D) No change is necessary

2) Because of the rising cost of college <u>tuition the</u> federal government now offers special financial assistance, <u>such as loans</u>, to students.

   A) tuition, the
   B) tuition; the
   C) such as loans
   D) No change is necessary

• 3) As the number of homeless people continues to <u>rise, the major cities</u> such as <u>New York and Chicago</u>, are now investing millions of dollars in low-income housing.

   A) rise. The major cities
   B) rise; the major cities
   C) New York and Chicago
   D) No change is necessary

• 4) Unlike in <u>the 1950s, most</u> households find the husband and wife working full-time to make <u>ends meet in many</u> different career fields.

   A) the 1950s; most
   B) the 1950s most
   C) ends meet, in many
   D) No change is necessary

ANSWER KEY: PRACTICE EXERCISE FOR COMMA SPLICES AND FUSED SENTENCES

1) B   Option B correctly separates two independent clauses. The comma in Option A after the word *sheep* creates a run-on sentence. The semicolon in Option C does not separate the two clauses because it occurs at an inappropriate point.

2) A   The comma in Option A correctly separates the independent clause and the dependent clause. The semi-colon in Option B is incorrect because one of the clauses is independent. Option C requires a comma to prevent a run-on sentence.

3) C   Option C is correct because a comma creates a run-on. Option A is incorrect because the first clause is dependent. The semi-colon in Option B incorrectly divides the dependent clause from the independent clause.

4) D   Option D correctly separates the two clauses with a comma. Option A incorrectly uses a semi-colon to divide the clauses. The lack of a comma in Option B creates a run-on sentence. Option C puts a comma in an inappropriate place.

Skill 3.4   Identify errors in use of capitalization.

Capitalize all proper names of persons (including specific organizations or agencies of government); places (countries, states, cities, parks, and specific geographical areas); things (political parties, structures, historical and cultural terms, and calendar and time designations); and religious terms (any deity, revered person or group, and sacred writings).

> Percy Bysshe Shelley, Argentina, Mount Rainier National Park, Grand Canyon, League of Nations, the Sears Tower, Birmingham, Lyric Theater, Americans, Midwesterners, Democrats, Renaissance, Boy Scouts of America, Easter, God, Bible, Dead Sea Scrolls, Koran

Capitalize proper adjectives and titles used with proper names.

> California gold rush, President John Adams, French fries, Homeric epic, Romanesque architecture, Senator John Glenn

Note: Some words that represent titles and offices are not capitalized unless used with a proper name.

Capitalized	Not Capitalized
Congressman McKay	the congressman from Hawaii
Commander Alger	commander of the Pacific Fleet
Queen Elizabeth	the queen of England

Capitalize all main words in titles of works of literature, art, and music.

Error: Emma went to Dr. Peters for treatment since her own Doctor was on vacation.

Problem: The use of capital letters with *Emma* and *Dr .Peters* is correct since they are specific (proper) names; the title *Dr.* is also capitalized. However, the word *doctor* is not a specific name and should not be capitalized.

Correction: *Emma went to Dr. Peters for treatment since her own doctor was on vacation.*

Error: Our Winter Break does not start until next wednesday.

Problem: Days of the week are capitalized, but seasons are not capitalized.

Correction: *Our winter break does not start until next Wednesday.*

Error: The exchange student from Israel, who came to study biochemistry, spoke spanish very well.

Problem: Languages and the names of countries are always capitalized. Courses are also capitalized when one is referring to a specific course; courses in general are not capitalized.

Correction: *The exchange student from Israel, who came to study Biochemistry, spoke Spanish very well.*

PRACTICE EXERCISE: CAPITALIZATION AND PUNCTUATION (commas, colons, semicolons, apostrophes, and quotation marks)

Choose the option that corrects an error in the underlined portion(s). If no error exists, choose "No change is necessary."

1)   Greenpeace is an Organization that works to preserve the world's environment.

A) greenpeace
B) organization
C) worlds
D) No change is necessary.

2)   When our class travels to France next year, we will see the country's many famous landmarks.

A) france
B) year; we
C) countries
D) No change is necessary.

3)   New York City, the most heavily populated city in America has more than eight million people living there every day.

A) new york city
B) in America, has
C) Everyday
D) No change is necessary.

4)   The television show *The X-Files* has gained a huge following because it focuses on paranormal phenomena, extraterrestrial life, and the oddities of human existence.

A) Television
B) following, because
C) Human existence
D) No change is necessary.

5) Being a <u>Policeman</u> requires having many <u>qualities</u>: physical <u>agility</u>, good reflexes, and the ability to make quick decisions.

    A) policeman
    B) qualities;
    C) agility:
    D) No change is necessary.

6) "Tis <u>better to have loved and lost than never to have loved at all</u>," wrote <u>Tennyson,</u> the poet <u>who</u> demonstrates the value of love in a <u>mans</u> life.

    A) Better to have loved and lost, than never to have loved at all
    B) Tennyson who
    C) man's
    D) No change is necessary.

7) The <u>Boston americans</u> won the first <u>World Series</u> championship by defeating the Pittsburgh Pirates in <u>October 1903</u>.

    A) Boston americans
    B) World Series
    C) October,1903
    D) No change is necessary.

Error in book
#7

ANSWER KEY: PRACTICE EXERCISE FOR CAPITALIZATION AND PUNCTUATION

1. B   In the sentence, the word *organization* does not need to be capitalized because it is a general noun. In Option A, the name of the organization should be capitalized. In Option C, the apostrophe is used to show that one world is being protected, not more than one.

2. D   In Option A, France is capitalized because it is the name of a country. In Option B, the comma, not the semicolon, should separate a dependent clause from the main clause. In Option C, the use of an apostrophe and an -s indicate only one country is being visited.

3. B   In Option A, New York City is capitalized because it is the name of a place. In Option B, a comma is needed to separate the adjective clause ending with *America* from the verb *has*. In Option C, every *day* needs no capitalization and should not be joined as a compound word. (The word *everyday* is an adjective meaning *routine*.

4. D   In Option A, *television* does not need to be capitalized because it is a common noun. In Option B, a comma is necessary to separate an independent clause from the main clause. In Option C, *human existence* is a general term that does not need capitalization.

5. A   In Option A, *policeman* does not need capitalization because it is a common noun. In Option B, a colon, not a semicolon, is needed because the rest of the sentence is related to the main clause. In Option C, a comma, not a colon, is needed to separate the adjectives.

6. C   In Option A, a comma is needed to break the quote into distinct parts that give it greater clarity. In Option B, a comma is needed to separate the subject of the sentence from the relative clause. In Option C, an apostrophe is needed to show possession.

7. B   In Option A, Boston Americans must be capitalized because it is the name of a team. In Option B, World Series needs to be capitalized because it is the title of a sporting event. In Option C, no comma is needed because month and year need no distinction; they are general terms.

COMPETENCY 4.0   ESSAY

Skill 4.1   Write an essay that is appropriate for the assigned task and for the intended audience.

Tailoring language for a particular **audience** is an important skill. Writing to be read by a business associate will surely sound different from writing to be read by a younger sibling. Not only are the vocabularies different, but the formality/informality of the discourse will need to be adjusted as well.

Determining what the language should be for a particular audience, then, hinges on two things: **word choice** and **formality/informality**. The most formal language does not use contractions or slang. The most informal language will probably feature a more casual use of common sayings and anecdotes. Formal language will use longer sentences and will not sound like a conversation. The most informal language will use shorter sentences—not necessarily simple sentences but shorter constructions—and may sound like a conversation.

In both formal and informal writing, there exists a **tone**, the writer's attitude toward the material and/or readers. Tone may be playful, formal, intimate, angry, serious, ironic, outraged, baffled, tender, serene, depressed, etc. Both the subject matter and the audience dictate the overall tone of a piece of writing. Tone is also related to the actual words that make up the document, as we attach affective meanings, called **connotations,** to words. Gaining this conscious control over language makes it possible to use language appropriately in various situations and to evaluate its uses in literature and other forms of communication. By evoking the proper responses from readers/listeners, we can prompt them to take action.

The following questions are an excellent way to assess the audience and tone of a given piece of writing.

1. Who is your audience? (friend, teacher, business person, someone else)
2. How much does this person know about you and/or your topic?
3. What is your purpose? (to prove an argument, to persuade, to amuse, to register a complaint, to ask for a raise, etc.)
4. What emotions do you have about the topic? (nervous, happy, confident, angry, sad, no feelings at all)
5. What emotions do you want to register with your audience? (anger, nervousness, happiness, boredom, interest)
6. What persona do you need to create in order to achieve your purpose?
7. What choice of language is best suited to achieving your purpose with your particular subject? (slang, friendly but respectful, formal)
8. What emotional quality do you want to transmit to achieve your purpose? (matter-of-fact, informative, authoritative, inquisitive, sympathetic, or angry) And to what degree do you want to express this tone?

An essay is an extended discussion of a writer's point of view about a particular topic. This point of view may be supported by using such writing modes as examples, argument and persuasion, analysis, or comparison/contrast. In any case, a good essay is clear, coherent, well organized, and fully developed.

When an author sets out to write a passage, he/she usually has a purpose for doing so. That purpose may be to simply give information that might be interesting or useful to some reader or other; it may be to persuade the reader to a point of view or to move the reader to act in a particular way; it may be to tell a story; or it may be to describe something in such a way that an experience becomes available to the reader through one of the five senses. Following are the primary devices for expressing a particular purpose in a piece of writing:

- **Basic expository writing** simply gives information not previously known about a topic or is used to explain or define one. Facts, examples, statistics, cause and effect, direct tone, objective rather than subjective delivery, and non-emotional information are presented in a formal manner.

- **Descriptive writing** centers on person, place, or object, using concrete and sensory words to create a mood or impression, and arranging details in a chronological or spatial sequence.

- **Narrative writing** is developed using an incident, anecdote, or related series of events. Chronology, the 5 W's, topic sentence, and conclusion are essential ingredients.

- **Persuasive writing** implies the writer's ability to select vocabulary and arrange facts and opinions in such a way as to direct the beliefs or actions of the listener/reader. Persuasive writing may incorporate exposition and narration to illustrate the main idea.

- **Journalistic writing** is theoretically free of author bias. It is essential when relaying information about an event, person, or thing that it be factual and objective. Provide students with an opportunity to examine newspapers and create their own newspaper. Many newspapers have educational programs that are offered free to schools.

Topic Analysis

Even before you select a topic, determine what each prompt is asking you to discuss. This first decision is crucial. If you pick a topic you do not really understand or about which you have little to say, you will have difficulty developing your essay. So take a few moments to analyze each topic carefully *before* you begin to write.

Topic A: A modern invention that can be considered a wonder of the world

In general, the topic prompts have two parts:
the *SUBJECT* of the topic and
an *ASSERTION* about the subject.

The **subject** is *a modern invention*. In this prompt, the word *modern* indicates you should discuss something invented recently, The word *invention* indicates you are to write about something created by humans (not natural phenomena such as mountains or volcanoes). You may discuss an invention that has potential for harm, such as chemical warfare or the atomic bomb; or you may discuss an invention that has the potential for good, such as the computer, DNA testing, television, antibiotics, and so on.

The **assertion** (a statement of point of view) is that *the invention has such powerful or amazing qualities that it should be considered a wonder of the world*. The assertion states your point of view about the subject, and it limits the range for discussion. In other words, you would discuss particular qualities or uses of the invention, not just discuss how it was invented or whether it should have been invented at all.

Note also that this particular topic encourages you to use examples to show the reader that a particular invention is a modern wonder. Some topic prompts lend themselves to essays with an argumentative edge, one in which you take a stand on a particular issue and persuasively prove your point. Here, you undoubtedly could offer examples or illustrations of the many "wonders" and uses of the particular invention you chose.

Be aware that misreading or misinterpreting the topic prompt can lead to serious problems. Papers that do not address the topic occur when one reads too quickly or only half understands the topic. This may happen if you misread or misinterpret words. Misreading can also lead to a paper that addresses only part of the topic prompt rather than the entire topic.

Skill 4.2 Organize and develop ideas logically, making clear connections between them.

To develop a complete essay, spend a few minutes planning. Jot down your ideas, and quickly sketch an outline. Although you may feel under pressure to begin writing, you will write more effectively if you plan your major points.

Prewriting
Before actually writing, you will need to generate content and to develop a writing plan. Three prewriting techniques that can be helpful are:

Brainstorming

When brainstorming, quickly create a list of words and ideas that are connected to the topic. Let your mind roam free to generate as many relevant ideas as possible in a few minutes. For example, on the topic of computers you may write:

computer—modern invention
types—personal computers, micro-chips in calculators and watches
wonder—acts like an electronic brain
uses—science, medicine, offices, homes, schools
problems—too much reliance; the machines are not perfect

This list could help you focus on the topic, and it states the points you could develop in the body paragraphs. The brainstorming list keeps you on track and is well worth the few minutes it takes to jot down the ideas. While you have not ordered the ideas, seeing them on paper is an important step.

Questioning

Questioning helps you focus as you mentally ask a series of exploratory questions about the topic. You may use the most basic questions: **who, what, where, when, why, and how.**

"**What** is my subject?"
[computers]

"**What** types of computers are there?"
[personal computers, micro-chip computers]

"**Why** have computers been a positive invention?"
[act as an electronic brain in machinery and equipment; help solve complex scientific problems]

"**How** have computers been a positive invention?"
[used to make improvements in:
- science (space exploration, moon landings)
- medicine (MRIs, CT scans, surgical tools, research models)
- business (PCs, FAX, telephone equipment)
- education (computer programs for math, languages, science, social studies)
- personal use (family budgets, tax programs, healthy diet plans)]

"**How** can I show that computers are good?"
[citing numerous examples]

"**What** problems do I see with computers?"
[too much reliance; not yet perfect]

"**What** personal experiences would help me develop examples to respond to this topic?

       [my own experiences using computers]

Of course, you may not have time to write out the questions completely. You might just write the words *who, what, where, why,* and *how* and the major points next to each. An abbreviated list might look as follows:

What: computers/modern wonder/making life better

How: through technological improvements: lasers, calculators, CT scans, MRIs

Where: in science and space exploration, medicine, schools, offices

In a few moments, your questions should help you to focus on the topic and to generate interesting ideas and points to make in the essay. Later in the writing process, you can look back at the list to be sure you have made the key points you intended.

Clustering

Some visual thinkers find clustering an effective prewriting method. When clustering, you draw a box in the center of your paper and write your topic within that box. Then, you draw lines from the center box and connect it to small satellite boxes that contain related ideas. Note the cluster below on computers:

SAMPLE CLUSTER

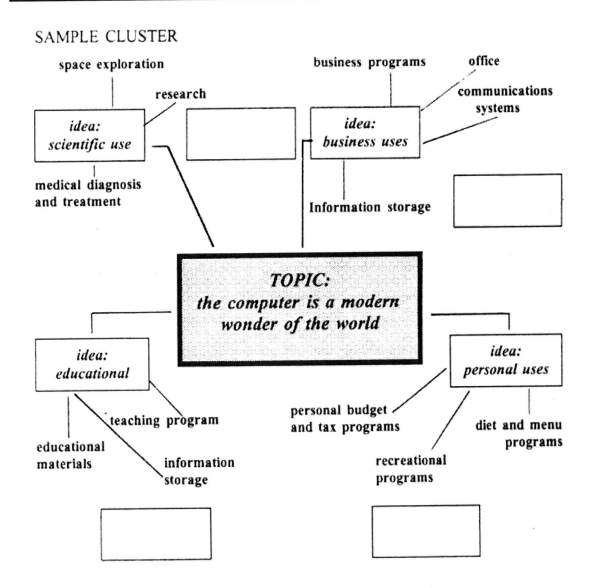

Skill 4.3   Provide and sustain a clear focus or thesis.

Writing the Thesis

After focusing on the topic and generating your ideas, form your thesis, the controlling idea of your essay. The thesis is your general statement to the reader that expresses your point of view and guides your essay's purpose and scope. The thesis should allow you either to explain your subject or to take an arguable position about it. A strong thesis statement is neither too narrow nor too broad.

Subject and Assertion of the Thesis

From the analysis of the general topic, you saw the topic in terms of its two parts: *subject* and *assertion*. On the exam, your thesis or viewpoint on a particular topic is stated in two important points:

the **subject** of the paper and the **assertion** about the subject

The **subject of the thesis** relates directly to the topic prompt but expresses the specific area you have chosen to discuss. (Remember, the exam topic will be general and will allow you to choose a particular subject related to the topic). For example, the computer is one modern invention.

The **assertion of the thesis** is your viewpoint, or opinion, about the subject. The assertion provides the motive or purpose for your essay, and it may be an arguable point or one that explains or illustrates a point of view.

For example, you may present an argument for or against a particular issue. You may contrast two people, objects, or methods to show that one is better than the other is. You may analyze a situation in all aspects and make recommendations for improvement. You may assert that a law or policy should be adopted, changed, or abandoned. You may also explain to your reader, as in the computer example, that a situation or condition exists; rather than argue a viewpoint, you would use examples to illustrate your assertion about the essay's subject.

Specifically, the **subject** of Topic A is *the computer*. The **assertion** is that *it is a modern wonder that has improved our lives and we rely on it.* Now you quickly have created a workable thesis in a few moments:

> *The computer is a modern wonder of the world that has improved our lives and that we have come to rely on.*

Guidelines for Writing Thesis Statements

The following guidelines are not a formula for writing thesis statements, but rather are general strategies for making your thesis statement clearer and more effective.

1.   State a *particular point* of *view* about the topic with both a *subject* and an *assertion*. The thesis should give the essay purpose and scope and thus provide the reader a guide. If the thesis is vague, your essay may be undeveloped because you do not have an idea to assert or a point to explain. Weak thesis statements are often framed as facts, questions, or announcements:

    a.   Avoid a fact statement as a thesis. While a fact statement may provide a subject, it generally does not include a point of view about the subject that provides the basis for an extended discussion. Example: *Recycling saved our community over $10,000 last year.* This fact statement provides a detail, *not* a point of view. Such a detail might be found within an essay, but it does not state a point of view.

    b.   Avoid framing the thesis as a vague question. In many cases, rhetorical questions do not provide a clear point of view for an extended essay. Example: *How do people recycle?* This question neither asserts a point of view nor helpfully guides the reader to understand the essay's purpose and scope.

    c.   Avoid the "announcer" topic sentence that merely states the topic you will discuss. Example: I *will discuss ways to recycle.* This sentence states the subject, but the scope of the essay is only suggested. Again, this statement does not assert a viewpoint that guides the essay's purpose. It merely "announces" that the writer will write about the topic.

2.   Start with a workable thesis. You might revise your thesis as you begin writing and discover your own point of view.

3.   If feasible and appropriate, perhaps state the thesis in multi-point form, expressing the scope of the essay. By stating the points in parallel form, you clearly lay out the essay's plan for the reader. Example: *To improve the environment, we can recycle our trash, elect politicians who see the environment as a priority, and support lobbying groups who work for environmental protection.*

4.   Because of the exam time limit, place your thesis in the first paragraph to key the reader to the essay's main idea.

Skill 4.4   Use supporting reasons, examples, and details to develop clearly and logically the ideas presented in the essay.

Creating a working outline
A good thesis gives structure to your essay and helps focus your thoughts. When forming your thesis, look at your prewriting strategy—clustering, questioning, or brainstorming. Then, decide quickly which two or three major areas you will discuss. Remember, you must limit *the scope* of the paper because of the time factor.

The **outline** lists those main areas or points as topics for each paragraph. Looking at the prewriting cluster on computers, you might choose several areas in which computers help us, for example in science and medicine, business, and education. You might also consider people's reliance on this "wonder" and include at least one paragraph about this reliance. A formal outline for this essay might look like the one below:

I.   Introduction and thesis
II. Computers used in science and medicine
II. Computers used in business
IV. Computers used in education
V.   People's reliance on computers
VI. Conclusion

Under time pressure, however, you may use a shorter organizational plan, such as abbreviated key words in a list. For example:

1. intro: wonders of the computer -OR- a. intro: wonders of computers—science
2. science   b. in the space industry
3. med   c. in medical technology
4. schools   d. conclusion
5. business
6. conclusion

Developing the essay
With a working thesis and outline, you can begin writing the essay. The essay should be in three main sections:

1) The **introduction** sets up the essay and leads to the thesis statement.
2) The **body paragraphs** are developed with concrete information leading from the **topic sentences**.
3) The **conclusion** ties the essay together.

Introduction

Put your thesis statement into a clear, coherent, opening paragraph. One effective device is to use a funnel approach, in which you begin with a brief description of the broader issue and then move to a clearly focused, specific thesis statement.

Consider the following introductions to the essay on computers. The length of each is an obvious difference. Read each, and consider the other differences.

Does each introduce the subject generally?
Does each lead to a stated thesis?
Does each relate to the topic prompt?

Introduction 1: *Computers are used every day. They have many uses. Some people who use them are workers, teachers, and doctors.*

Analysis: This introduction does give the general topic, computers used every day, but it does not explain what those uses are. This introduction does not offer a point of view in a clearly stated thesis, nor does it convey the idea that computers are a modem wonder.

Introduction 2: *Computers are used just about everywhere these days. I don't think there's an office around that doesn't use computers, and we use them a lot in all kinds of jobs. Computers are great for making life easier and work better. I don't think we'd get along without the computer.*

Analysis: This introduction gives the general topic about computers and mentions one area that uses computers. The thesis states that people could not get along without computers, but it does not state the specific areas the essay discusses. Note, too, the meaning is not helped by vague diction, such as *a lot* or *great.*

Introduction 3: *Each day, we either use computers or see them being used around us. We wake to the sound of a digital alarm operated by a micro-chip. Our cars run by computerized machinery. We use computers to help us learn. We receive phone calls and letters transferred from computers across continents. Our astronauts walked on the moon and returned safely, all because of computer technology. The computer is a wonderful electronic brain that we have come to rely on, and it has changed our world through advances in science, business, and education.*

Analysis: This introduction is the most thorough and fluent because it provides interest in the general topic and offers specific information about computers as a modern wonder. It also leads to a thesis that directs the reader to the scope of the discussion—advances in science, business, and education.

Topic Sentences

Just as the essay must have an overall focus reflected in the thesis statement, each paragraph must have a central idea reflected in the topic sentence. A good topic sentence also provides transition from the previous paragraph and relates to the essay's thesis. Good topic sentences, therefore, provide unity throughout the essay.

Consider the following potential topic sentences. Be sure that each provides transition and clearly states the subject of the paragraph.

Topic Sentence 1: *Computers are used in science.*

Analysis: This sentence simply states the topic: computers used in science. It does not relate to the thesis nor provide transition from the introduction. The reader still does not know how computers are used.

Topic Sentence 2: *Now I will talk about computers used in science.*

Analysis: Like the faulty "announcer" thesis statement, this "announcer" topic sentence is vague and merely names the topic.

Topic Sentence 3: *First, computers used in science have improved our lives.*

Analysis: The transition word *First* helps link the introduction and this paragraph. It adds unity to the essay. It, however, does not give specifics about the improvement computers have made in our lives.

Topic Sentence 4: *First used in scientific research and spaceflights, computers are now used extensively in the diagnosis and treatment of disease.*

Analysis: This sentence is the most thorough and fluent. It provides specific areas that will be discussed in the paragraph and it offers more than an announcement of the topic. The writer gives concrete information about the content of the paragraph that will follow.

Summary Guidelines for Writing Topic Sentences
1. Specifically relate the topic to the thesis statement.
2. State clearly and concretely the subject of the paragraph.
3. Provide some transition from the previous paragraph.
4. Avoid topic sentences that are facts, questions, or announcers.

Supporting Details

If you have a good thesis and a good outline, you should be able to construct a complete essay. Your paragraphs should contain concrete, interesting information and supporting details to support your point of view. As often as possible, create images in your reader's mind. Fact statements also add weight to your opinions, especially when you are trying to convince the reader of your viewpoint. Because every good thesis has an assertion, you should offer specifics, facts, data, anecdotes, expert opinions, and other details to *show* or *prove* that assertion. While *you* know what you mean, your *reader* does not. On the exam, you must explain and develop ideas as fully as possible in the time allowed.

In the following paragraph, the sentences in **bold print** provide a skeleton of a paragraph on the benefits of recycling. The sentences in bold are generalizations that, by themselves, do not explain the need to recycle. The sentences in *italics* add details to SHOW the general points in bold. Notice how the supporting details help you understand the necessity of recycling.

While one day recycling may become mandatory in all states, right now it is voluntary in many communities. *Those of us who participate in recycling are amazed by how much material is recycled.* **For many communities, the blue-box recycling program has had an immediate effect.** *By just recycling glass, aluminum cans, and plastic bottles, we have reduced the volume of disposable trash by one-third, thus extending the useful life of local landfills by over a decade. Imagine the difference if those dramatic results were achieved nationwide.* **The number of reusable items we thoughtlessly dispose of is staggering.** *For example, Americans dispose of enough steel every day to supply Detroit car manufacturers for three months. Additionally, we dispose of enough aluminum annually to rebuild the nation's air fleet. These statistics, available from the Environmental Protection Agency (EPA), should encourage all of us to watch what we throw away.* **Clearly, recycling in our homes and in our communities directly improves the environment.**

Notice how the author's supporting examples enhance the message of the paragraph and relate to the author's thesis noted above. If you only read the boldface sentences, you have a glimpse of the topic. This paragraph of illustration, however, is developed through numerous details creating specific images: *reduced the volume of disposable trash by one-third; extended the useful life of local landfills by over a decade; enough steel every day to supply Detroit car manufacturers for three months; enough aluminum to rebuild the nation's air fleet.* If the writer had merely written a few general sentences, as those shown in bold, you would not fully understand the vast amount of trash involved in recycling or the positive results of current recycling efforts.

End your essay with a brief straightforward **concluding paragraph** that ties together the essay's content and leaves the reader with a sense of its completion. The conclusion should reinforce the main points and offer some insight into the topic, provide a sense of unity for the essay by relating it to the thesis, and signal clear closure of the essay.

Skill 4.5   **Demonstrate facility in the use of language and the ability to use a variety of sentence structures.**

See Subarea I, Competency 3.0.

Skill 4.6   **Construct effective sentences that are generally free of errors in standard written English.**

See Subarea I, Competencies 1.0–3.0.

Sample Test: English

DIRECTIONS: *The passage below contains many errors. Read the passage. Then, answer each test item by choosing the option that corrects an error in the underlined portion(s). No more than one underlined error will appear in each item. If no error exists, choose "No change is necessary."*

Climbing to the top of Mount Everest is an adventure. One that everyone—whether physically fit or not—seems eager to try. The trail stretches for miles, the cold temperatures are usually frigid and brutal.
Climbers must endure several barriers on the way including other hikers, steep jagged rocks, and lots of snow. Plus, climbers often find the most grueling part of the trip is their climb back down, just when they are feeling greatly exhausted. Climbers who take precautions are likely to find the ascent less arduous than the unprepared. By donning heavy flannel shirts, gloves, and hats, climbers prevented hypothermia, as well as simple frostbite. A pair of rugged boots are also one of the necessities. If climbers are to avoid becoming dehydrated, there is beverages available for them to transport as well.

Once climbers are completely ready to begin their lengthy journey, they can comfortable enjoy the wonderful scenery. Wide rock formations dazzle the observers eyes with shades of gray and white, while the peak forms a triangle that seems to touch the sky. Each of the climbers are reminded of the splendor and magnificence of God's great Earth.

1) **Once climbers are completely prepared for their lengthy journey, they can comfortable enjoy the wonderful scenery.**
(Easy) (Skill 1.1)

   A. they're
   B. journey; they
   C. comfortably
   D. No change is necessary.

2) **Plus, climbers often find the most grueling part of the trip is their climb back down, just when they are feeling greatly exhausted.**
(Average Rigor) (Skill 1.3, 2.2, 3.3)

   A. his
   B. down; just
   C. were
   D. No change is necessary.

3) **A pair of rugged boots are also one of the necessities.**
(Rigorous) (Skill 1.3, 2.2, 3.3)

   A. necesities
   B. also, one
   C. is
   D. No change is necessary.

4) By donning heavy flannel shirts, boots, and <u>hats, climbers</u> <u>prevented</u> hypothermia, as well as simple frostbite.
(Average Rigor) (Skill 1.4)

    A. hats climbers
    B. can prevent
    C. hypothermia;
    D. No change is necessary.

5) <u>Climbers who</u> take precautions are likely to find the ascent <u>less difficult</u> <u>than</u> the unprepared.
(Average Rigor) (Skill 2.1, 3.3)

    A. Climbers, who
    B. least difficult
    C. then
    D. No change is necessary.

6) If climbers are to avoid <u>becoming</u> dehydrated, there <u>is</u> beverages available for <u>them</u> to transport as well.
(Easy) (Skill 2.2)

    A. becomming
    B. are
    C. him
    D. No change is necessary.

7) Each of the climbers <u>are</u> reminded of the splendor and <u>magnificence</u> of <u>God's</u> great Earth.
(Rigorous) (Skill 2.2)

    A. is
    B. magnifisence
    C. Gods
    D. No change is necessary.

8) Climbers must endure <u>several</u> barriers <u>on the way</u> <u>including</u> other <u>hikers</u>, steep jagged rocks, and lots of snow.
(Average Rigor) (Skill 3.3)

    A. on the way, including
    B. severel
    C. hikers'
    D. No change is necessary.

9) The <u>trail</u> stretches for <u>miles</u>, the cold temperatures are <u>usually</u> frigid and brutal.
(Rigorous) (Skill 3.3)

    A. trails
    B. miles;
    C. usual
    D. No change is necessary.

10) Wide rock formations dazzle the <u>observers eyes</u> with shades of gray and <u>white, while</u> the peak <u>forms</u> a triangle that seems to touch the sky.
(Rigorous) (Skill 3.3)

    A. observers' eyes
    B. white; while
    C. formed
    D. No change is necessary.

• 11) **Climbing to the top of Mount Everest is an <u>adventure. One</u> that everyone—<u>whether</u> physically fit or not—<u>seems</u> eager to try.**
(Rigorous) (Skill 3.3)

   A. adventure, one
   B. people, whether
   C. seem
   D. No change is necessary.

DIRECTIONS: *The passage below contains several errors. Read the passage. Then, answer each test item by choosing the option that corrects an error in the underlined portion(s). No more than one underlined error will appear in each item. If no error exists, choose "No change is necessary."*

Every job places different kinds of demands on their employees. For example, whereas such jobs as accounting and bookkeeping require mathematical ability; graphic design requires creative/artistic ability.

Doing good at one job does not usually guarantee success at another. However, one of the elements crucial to all jobs are especially notable—the chance to accomplish a goal.

The accomplishment of the employees vary according to the job. In many jobs, the employees become accustom to the accomplishments provided by the work they do every day.

In medicine, for example, every doctor tests him self by treating badly injured or critically ill people. In the operating room, a team of Surgeons, is responsible for operating on many of these patients. In addition to the feeling of accomplishment that the workers achieve, some jobs also give a sense of identity to the employees'. Professions such as law, education, and sales offers huge financial and emotional rewards. Politicians are public servants: who work for the federal and state governments. President bush is basically employed by the American people to make laws and run the country.

Finally; the contributions that employees make to their companies and to the world cannot be taken for granted. Through their work, employees are performing a service for their employers and are contributing something to the world.

12) **Doing <u>good</u> at one job does not <u>usually</u> guarantee <u>success</u> at another.**
(Rigorous) (Skill 1.1)

   A. well
   B. usualy
   C. succeeding
   D. No change is necessary.

13) **In medicine, for example, every doctor <u>tests</u> <u>him self</u> by treating badly injured and critically ill people.**
(Average Rigor) (Skill 1.3)

   A. test
   B. himself
   C. critical
   D. No change is necessary.

14) Every job <u>places</u> different kinds of demands on <u>their</u> <u>employees.</u>
(Rigorous) (Skill 1.3)

A. place
B. its
C. employes
D. No change is necessary.

15) The <u>accomplishment</u> of the <u>employees</u> <u>vary</u> according to the job.
(Rigorous) (Skill 1.4)

A. accomplishments
B. employee's
C. varies
D. No change is necessary.

16) <u>However,</u> one of the elements crucial to all jobs <u>are</u> especially <u>notable</u>—the accomplishment of a goal.
(Average Rigor) (Skill 2.2)

A. However
B. is
C. notable;
D. No change is necessary.

17) <u>Professions</u> such as law, <u>education,</u> and sales <u>offers</u> huge financial and emotional rewards.
(Rigorous) (Skill 2.2)

A. offer
B. education;
C. Profesions
D. No change is necessary.

18) In many jobs, the employees <u>become</u> <u>accustom</u> to the accomplishments <u>provided</u> by the work they do every day.
(Average Rigor) (Skill 3.2)

A. became
B. accustomed
C. provides
D. No change is necessary.

19) In the <u>operating room,</u> a team of <u>Surgeons, is</u> responsible for operating on many of <u>these</u> patients.
(Easy) (Skill 3.3)

A. operating room:
B. surgeons is
C. those
D. No change is necessary.

20) Politicians <u>are</u> public <u>servants: who</u> <u>work</u> for the federal and state governments.
(Easy) (Skill 3.3)

A. were
B. servants who
C. worked
D. No change is necessary.

* 21) <u>For example, whereas</u> such jobs as accounting and bookkeeping require mathematical <u>ability;</u> graphic design requires creative/artistic ability.
(Average Rigor) (Skill 3.3)

A. For example
B. whereas,
C. ability,
D. No change is necessary.

22) In addition to the feeling of accomplishment that the workers <u>achieve</u>, some jobs also <u>give</u> a sense of self-identity to the <u>employees'.</u>
(Average Rigor) (Skill 3.3)

A. acheive
B. gave
C. employees
D. No change is necessary.

23) <u>Finally;</u> the contributions that employees make to <u>their</u> companies and to the world cannot be <u>taken</u> for granted.
(Average Rigor) (Skill 3.3)

A. Finally,
B. their
C. took
D. No change is necessary.

24) President <u>bush</u> is basically employed <u>by</u> the American people to <u>make</u> laws and run the country.
(Easy) (Skill 3.4)

A. Bush
B. to
C. made
D. No change is necessary.

DIRECTIONS: *The passage below contains several errors. Read the passage. Then, answer each test item by choosing the option that corrects an error in the underlined portion(s). No more than one underlined error will appear in each item. If no error exists, choose "No change is necessary."*

The discovery of a body at Paris Point marina in Boca Raton shocked the residents of Palmetto Pines, a luxury condominium complex located next door to the marina.

The victim is a thirty-five-year-old woman who had been apparently bludgeoned to death and dumped in the ocean late last night. Many neighbors reported terrible screams, gunshots: as well as the sound of a car backfiring loudly to Boca Raton Police shortly after midnight. The woman had been spotted in the lobby of Palmetto Pines around ten thirty, along with an older man, estimated to be in his fifties, and a younger man, in his late twenties.

"Apparently, the victim had been driven to the complex by the older man and was seen arguing with him when the younger man intervened," said Sheriff Fred Adams, "all three of them left the building together and walked to the marina, where gunshots rang out an hour later." Deputies found five bullets on the sidewalk and some blood, along with a steel pipe that is assumed to be the murder weapon. Two men were seen fleeing the scene in a red Mercedes short after, rushing toward the Interstate.

The Palm Beach County Coroner, Melvin Watts, said he concluded the victim's skull had been crushed by a blunt tool, which resulted in a brain hemorrhage. As of now, there is no clear motive for the murder.

25) **Two men <u>were</u> seen fleeing the scene in a red Mercedes <u>short</u> after, <u>rushing</u> toward the Interstate.**
(Easy) (Skill 1.1)

A. are
B. shortly
C. rushed
D. No change is necessary.

26) **As of <u>now,</u> there <u>is</u> no clear motive for the murder.**
(Easy) (Skill 1.3, 2.2, 3.3)

A. now;
B. their
C. was
D. No change is necessary.

27) **Deputies found five bullets on the sidewalk and some <u>blood,</u> along with a steel pipe that is <u>assumed to be</u> the murder weapon.**
(Rigorous) (Skill 1.4)

A. blood;
B. assuming
C. to have been
D. No change is necessary.

28) **The victim <u>is</u> a thirty-five-year-old woman who had been apparently <u>bludgeoned</u> to death and dumped in the <u>ocean late</u> last night.**
(Rigorous) (Skill 2.2)

A. was
B. bludgoned
C. ocean: late
D. No change is necessary.

29) **Many <u>neighbors</u> reported terrible screams, <u>gunshots: as</u> well as the sound of a car backfiring <u>loudly</u> to Boca Raton Police shortly after midnight.**
(Average Rigor) (Skill 3.3)

A. nieghbors
B. gunshots, as
C. loud
D. No change is necessary.

30) "Apparently, the victim had been driven to the complex by the older man and was seen arguing with him when the younger man intervened," said Sheriff Fred Adams, "all three of them left the building together and walked to the marina, where gunshots rang out an hour later."
(Average Rigor) (Skill 3.3)

A. sheriff Fred Adams, "all
B. sheriff Fred Adams, "All
C. Sheriff Fred Adams. "All
D. No change is necessary.

31) The woman had been spotted in the lobby of Palmetto Pines around ten thirty, along with an older man, estimated to be in his fifties, and a younger man in his late twenties.
(Rigorous) (Skill 3.3)

A. has
B. thirty;
C. man estimated
D. No change is necessary.

32) The discovery of a body at Paris Point marina in Boca Raton shocked the residents of Palmetto Pines, a luxury condominium complex located next door to the marina.
(Easy) (Skill 3.4)

A. Marina
B. residence
C. condominnium
D. No change is necessary.

33) The Palm Beach county coroner, Kelvin Watts, said he concluded the victim's skull had been crushed by a blunt tool, which resulted in a brain hemorrhage.
(Rigorous) (Skill 3.4)

A. hemorrage
B. palm beach
C. County Coroner
D. No change is necessary.

DIRECTIONS: *For the underlined sentence(s), choose the option that expresses the meaning with the most fluency and the clearest logic within the context. If the underlined sentence should not be changed, choose Option A, which shows no change.*

34) **Selecting members of a President's cabinet can often be an aggravating process. <u>Either there are too many or too few qualified candidates for a certain position, and then they have to be confirmed by the Senate, where there is the possibility of rejection.</u>**
(Rigorous) (Skill 2.0)

A. Either there are too many or too few qualified candidates for a certain position, and then they have to be confirmed by the Senate, where there is the possibility of rejection.

B. Qualified candidates for certain positions face the possibility of rejection, when they have to be confirmed by the Senate.

C. The Senate has to confirm qualified candidates, who face the possibility of rejection.

D. Because the Senate has to confirm qualified candidates; they face the possibility of rejection.

35) **Treating patients for drug and/or alcohol abuse is a sometimes difficult process. <u>Even though there are a number of different methods for helping the patient overcome a dependency, there is no way of knowing which is best in the long run.</u>**
(Rigorous) (Skill 2.0)

A. Even though there are a number of different methods for helping the patient overcome a dependency, there is no way of knowing which is best in the long run.

B. Even though different methods can help a patient overcome a dependency, there is no way to know which is best in the long run.

C. Even though there is no way to know which way is best in the long run, patients can overcome their dependencies when they are helped.

D. There is no way to know which method will help the patient overcome a dependency in the long run, even though there are many different ones.

36) **Many factors account for the decline in the quality of public education.** Overcrowding, budget cutbacks, and societal deterioration which have greatly affected student learning.
(Rigorous) (Skill 3.3)

A. Overcrowding, budget cutbacks, and societal deterioration which have greatly affected student learning.

B. Student learning has been greatly affected by overcrowding, budget cutbacks, and societal deterioration.

C. Due to overcrowding, budget cutbacks, and societal deterioration, student learning has been greatly affected.

D. Overcrowding, budget cutbacks, and societal deterioration have affected students learning greatly.

DIRECTIONS: *Choose the sentence that logically and correctly expresses the comparison.*
(Easy) (Skill 2.1)

37) A. The Empire State Building in New York is taller than buildings in the city.

B. The Empire State Building in New York is taller than any other building in the city.

C. The Empire State Building in New York is tallest than other buildings in the city.

DIRECTIONS: *For the underlined sentence(s), choose the option that expresses the meaning with the most fluency and the clearest logic within the context. If the underlined sentence should not be changed, choose Option A, which shows no change.*

38) **John wanted to join his friends on the mountain-climbing trip. Seeing that the weather had become dark and stormy, John knew he would stay safe indoors.**
(Rigorous) (Skill 2.5)

A. Seeing that the weather had become dark and stormy, John knew he would stay safe indoors.

B. The weather had become dark and stormy, and John knew he would stay indoors, and he would be safe.

C. Because the weather had become dark and stormy, John knew he would stay indoors, where he would be safe.

D. Because the weather had become dark, as well as stormy, John knew he would stay safe indoors.

39) **A few hours later, the storm subsided, so John left the cabin to join his friends. Even though he was tired from the four-mile hike the day before, he climbed the mountain in a few hours.**
(Average Rigor) (Skill 2.5)

A. Even though he was tired from the four-mile hike the day before, he climbed the mountain in a few hours.

B. He was tired from the four-mile the day before; he climbed the mountain in a few hours.

C. He climbed the mountain in a few hours, John was tired from the four-mile hike the day before.

D. Seeing as he was tired from the day before, when he went on a four-mile hike, John climbed the mountain in a few hours.

DIRECTIONS: *Choose the most effective word within the context of the sentence.*

40) **Many of the clubs in Boca Raton are noted for their _____ elegance.**
(Average Rigor) (Skill 3.2)

A. vulgar
B. tasteful
C. ordinary

41) When a student is expelled from school, the parents are usually _____ in advance.
(Average Rigor) (Skill 3.2)

A. rewarded
B. congratulated
C. notified

42) Before appearing in court, the witness was _____ the papers requiring her to show up.
(Average Rigor) (Skill 3.2)

A. condemned
B. served
C. criticized

DIRECTIONS: *Choose the underlined word or phrase that is unnecessary within the context of the passage.*

43) The <u>expanding</u> number of television channels has <u>prompted</u> cable operators to raise their prices, <u>even though</u> many consumers do not want to pay a higher <u>increased</u> amount for their service.
(Easy) (Skill 3.2)

A. expanding
B. prompted
C. even though
D. increased

44) <u>Considered by many to be</u> one of the worst <u>terrorist</u> incidents <u>on American soil</u> was the bombing of the Oklahoma City Federal Building, which will be remembered <u>for years to come.</u>
(Average Rigor) (Skill 3.2)

A. Considered by many to be
B. terrorist
C. on American soil
D. for years to come

45) The <u>flu</u> epidemic struck <u>most of</u> the <u>respected</u> faculty and students of the Woolbright School, forcing the Boynton Beach School Superintendent to close it down <u>for two weeks.</u>
(Average Rigor) (Skill 3.2)

A. flu
B. most of
C. respected
D. for two weeks

DIRECTIONS: *Choose the most effective word or phrase within the context suggested by the sentence.*

46) Because George's _____ bothering him, he apologized for crashing his father's car.
(Average Rigor) (Skill 3.2)

A. feelings were
B. conscience was
C. guiltiness was

47) The charity art auction
    _____ every year at
    **Mizner Park has a wide
    selection of artists
    showcasing their work.**
    (Rigorous) (Skill 3.3)

    A. attended
    B. presented
    C. displayed

Answer Key: English

1.	C		25.	B
2.	D		26.	D
3.	C		27.	C
4.	B		28.	A
5.	D		29.	B
6.	B		30.	C
7.	A		31.	C
8.	A		32.	A
9.	B		33.	C
10.	A		34.	C
11.	A		35.	B
12.	A		36.	B
13.	B		37.	B
14.	B		38.	D
15.	A		39.	A
16.	B		40.	B
17.	A		41.	C
18.	B		42.	B
19.	B		43.	D
20.	B		44.	A
21.	C		45.	C
22.	C		46.	B
23.	A		47.	B
24.	A			

Rigor Table: English

	Easy 20%	Average 40%	Rigorous 40%
Questions (47)	1, 6, 19, 20, 23, 24, 30, 34, 40, 47	2, 4, 5, 8, 12, 16, 18, 21, 22, 27, 28, 36, 37, 38, 39, 41, 42, 43, 45	3, 7, 9, 10, 11, 12, 14, 15, 17, 25, 26, 29, 31, 32, 33, 35, 44, 46
TOTALS	10 (21.3%)	19 (40.4%)	18 (38.3%)

Rationales with Sample Questions: English

DIRECTIONS: *The passage below contains many errors. Read the passage. Then, answer each test item by choosing the option that corrects an error in the underlined portion(s). No more than one underlined error will appear in each item. If no error exists, choose "No change is necessary."*

Climbing to the top of Mount Everest is an adventure. One which everyone—whether physically fit or not—seems eager to try. The trail stretches for miles, the cold temperatures are usually frigid and brutal.

Climbers must endure several barriers on the way including other hikers, steep jagged rocks, and lots of snow. Plus, climbers often find the most grueling part of the trip is their climb back down, just when they are feeling greatly exhausted. Climbers who take precautions are likely to find the ascent less arduous than the unprepared. By donning heavy flannel shirts, gloves, and hats, climbers prevented hypothermia, as well as simple frostbite. A pair of rugged boots are also one of the necessities. If climbers are to avoid becoming dehydrated, there is beverages available for them to transport as well.

Once climbers are completely ready to begin their lengthy journey, they can comfortable enjoy the wonderful scenery. Wide rock formations dazzle the observers eyes with shades of gray and white, while the peak forms a triangle that seems to touch the sky. Each of the climbers are reminded of the splendor and magnificence of God's great Earth.

1) **Once climbers are completely prepared for <u>their</u> lengthy <u>journey, they</u> can <u>comfortable</u> enjoy the wonderful scenery.**
(Easy) (Skill 1.1)

    A. they're
    B. journey; they
    C. comfortably
    D. No change is necessary.

Answer: C. comfortably

The adverb form *comfortably* is needed to modify the verb phrase *can enjoy*. Option A is incorrect because the possessive plural pronoun is spelled *their*. Option B is incorrect because a semi-colon would make the first half of the item seem like an independent clause when the subordinating conjunction *once* makes that clause dependent.

2)   Plus, climbers often find the most grueling part of the trip is <u>their</u> climb back <u>down, just</u> when they <u>are</u> feeling greatly exhausted.
(Average Rigor) (Skill 1.3, 2.2, 3.3)

A. his
B. down; just
C. were
D. No change is necessary.

Answer: D. No change is necessary.

The present tense must be used consistently throughout; therefore, Option C is incorrect. Option A is incorrect because the singular pronoun *his* does not agree with the plural antecedent *climbers*. Option B is incorrect because a comma, not a semicolon, is needed to separate the dependent clause from the main clause.

3)   A pair of rugged boots <u>are</u> also one of the <u>necessities</u>.
(Rigorous) (Skill 1.3, 2.2, 3.3)

A. necesities
B. also, one
C. is
D. No change is necessary.

Answer: C. is

The word *necessities* is spelled correctly in the text. Option A is incorrect because the singular verb *is* must agree with the singular noun *pair* (a collective singular). Option B is incorrect because if *also* is set off with commas (potential correction), it should be set off on both sides.

4)   By donning heavy flannel shirts, boots, and <u>hats, climbers</u> <u>prevented</u> hypothermia, as well as simple frostbite.
(Average Rigor) (Skill 1.4)

A. hats climbers
B. can prevent
C. hypothermia;
D. No change is necessary.

Answer: B. can prevent

The verb *prevented* is in the past tense and must be changed to the present *can prevent* to be consistent. Option A is incorrect because a comma is needed after a long introductory phrase. Option C is incorrect because the semicolon creates a fragment of the phrase *as well as simple frostbite*.

5)   <u>Climbers who</u> take precautions are likely to find the ascent <u>less difficult</u> <u>than</u> the unprepared.
     (Average Rigor) (Skill 2.1, 3.3)

     A. Climbers, who
     B. least difficult
     C. then
     D. No change is necessary.

Answer: D. No change is necessary.

No change is needed. Option A is incorrect because a comma would make the phrase *who take precautions* seem less restrictive or less essential to the sentence. Option B is incorrect because *less* is appropriate when two items—the prepared and the unprepared—are compared. Option C is incorrect because the comparative adverb *than*, not *then*, is needed.

6)   If climbers are to avoid <u>becoming</u> dehydrated, there <u>is</u> beverages available for <u>them</u> to transport as well.
     (Easy) (Skill 2.2)

     A. becomming
     B. are
     C. him
     D. No change is necessary.

Answer: B. are

The plural verb *are* must be used with the plural subject *beverages*. Option A is incorrect because *becoming* is spelled correctly in the text. Option C is incorrect because the plural pronoun *them* is needed to agree with the referent *climbers*.

7)   Each of the climbers <u>are</u> reminded of the splendor and <u>magnificence</u> of <u>God's</u> great Earth.
     (Rigorous) (Skill 2.2)

     A. is
     B. magnifisence
     C. Gods
     D. No change is necessary.

Answer: A. is

The singular verb *is* agrees with the singular subject *each.* Option B is incorrect because *magnificence* is spelled correctly in the text. Option C is incorrect because an apostrophe is needed to show possession.

8) Climbers must endure <u>several</u> barriers <u>on the way including</u> other <u>hikers</u>, steep jagged rocks, and lots of snow.
(Average Rigor) (Skill 3.3)

    A. on the way, including
    B. severel
    C. hikers'
    D. No change is necessary.

Answer: A. on the way, including

Option B is incorrect because the word *several* is spelled correctly in the text. Option A is correct because a comma is needed to set off the modifying phrase. Option C is incorrect because no apostrophe is needed after *hikers* since possession is not involved.

9) The <u>trail</u> stretches for <u>miles</u>, the cold temperatures are <u>usually</u> frigid and brutal.
(Rigorous) (Skill 3.3)

    A. trails
    B. miles;
    C. usual
    D. No change is necessary.

Answer: B. miles;

A semicolon, not a comma, is needed to separate the first independent clause from the second independent clause. Option A is incorrect because the plural subject *trails* needs the singular verb *stretch*. Option C is incorrect because the adverb form *usually* is needed to modify the adjective *frigid.*

10) Wide rock formations dazzle the <u>observers eyes</u> with shades of gray and <u>white, while</u> the peak <u>forms</u> a triangle that seems to touch the sky.
(Rigorous) (Skill 3.3)

    A. observers' eyes
    B. white; while
    C. formed
    D. No change is necessary.

Answer: A. observers' eyes

An apostrophe is needed to show the plural possessive form *observers' eyes*. Option B is incorrect because the semicolon would make the second half of the item seem like an independent clause when the subordinating conjunction *while* makes that clause dependent. Option C is incorrect because *formed* is in the wrong tense.

11) Climbing to the top of Mount Everest is an <u>adventure. One</u> that everyone—<u>whether</u> physically fit or not—<u>seems</u> eager to try.
(Rigorous) (Skill 3.3)

    A. adventure, one
    B. people, whether
    C. seem
    D. No change is necessary.

Answer: A. adventure, one

A comma is needed between *adventure* and *one* to avoid creating a fragment of the second part. In Option B, a comma after *everyone* would not be appropriate when the dash is used on the other side of *not*. In Option C, the singular verb *seems* is needed to agree with the singular subject *everyone*.

DIRECTIONS: *The passage below contains several errors. Read the passage. Then, answer each test item by choosing the option that corrects an error in the underlined portion(s). No more than one underlined error will appear in each item. If no error exists, choose "No change is necessary."*

Every job places different kinds of demands on their employees. For example, whereas such jobs as accounting and bookkeeping require mathematical ability; graphic design requires creative/artistic ability. Doing good at one job does not usually guarantee success at another. However, one of the elements crucial to all jobs are especially notable—the chance to accomplish a goal.

The accomplishment of the employees vary according to the job. In many jobs, the employees become accustom to the accomplishments provided by the work they do every day.

In medicine, for example, every doctor tests him self by treating badly injured or critically ill people. In the operating room, a team of Surgeons, is responsible for operating on many of these patients. In addition to the feeling of accomplishment that the workers achieve, some jobs also give a sense of identity to the employees'. Professions such as law, education, and sales offers huge financial and emotional rewards. Politicians are public servants: who work for the federal and state governments. President bush is basically employed by the American people to make laws and run the country.

Finally; the contributions that employees make to their companies and to the world cannot be taken for granted. Through their work, employees are performing a service for their employers and are contributing something to the world.

12) **Doing <u>good</u> at one job does not <u>usually</u> guarantee <u>success</u> at another.**
(Rigorous) (Skill 1.1)

    A. well
    B. usualy
    C. succeeding
    D. No change is necessary.

Answer: A. well

The adverb *well* modifies the word *doing*. Option B is incorrect because *usually* is spelled correctly in the sentence. Option C is incorrect because *succeeding* is in the wrong tense.

13) In medicine, for example, every doctor <u>tests</u> <u>him self</u> by treating badly injured and critically ill people.
(Average Rigor) (Skill 1.3)

A. test
B. himself
C. critical
D. No change is necessary.

Answer: B. himself

The reflexive pronoun *himself* is needed. (Him self is nonstandard and never correct.) Option A is incorrect because the singular verb *test* is needed to agree with the singular subject *doctor*. Option C is incorrect because the adverb *critically* is needed to modify the verb *ill*.

14) Every job <u>places</u> different kinds of demands on <u>their</u> <u>employees</u>.
(Rigorous) (Skill 1.3)

A. place
B. its
C. employes
D. No change is necessary.

Answer: B. its

The singular possessive pronoun *its* must agree with its antecedent *job*, which is singular also. Option A is incorrect because *place* is a plural form and the subject, *job*, is singular. Option C is incorrect because the correct spelling of employees is given in the sentence.

15) The <u>accomplishment</u> of the <u>employees</u> <u>vary</u> according to the job.
(Rigorous) (Skill 1.4)

A. accomplishments
B. employee's
C. varies
D. No change is necessary.

Answer: A. accomplishments

The plural noun *accomplishments* is needed to agree with the plural noun *employees* and the plural verb *vary*. Option C is incorrect because *varies* is the correct form of the verb. Option B is incorrect because *employees* is not possessive.

16) <u>However,</u> one of the elements crucial to all jobs <u>are</u> especially n<u>otable</u>—the accomplishment of a goal.
(Average Rigor) (Skill 2.2)

    A. However
    B. is
    C. notable;
    D. No change is necessary.

Answer: B. is

The singular verb *is* is needed to agree with the singular subject *one*. Option A is incorrect because a comma is needed to set off the transitional word *however*. Option C is incorrect because an em dash, not a semicolon, is needed to set off this item.

17) <u>Professions</u> such as law, <u>education,</u> and sales <u>offers</u> huge financial and emotional rewards.
(Rigorous) (Skill 2.2)

    A. offer
    B. education;
    C. Profesions
    D. No change is necessary.

Answer: A. offer

Option A is correct because it shows correct subject-verb agreement. Option B is incorrect because a comma, not a semi-colon, is needed after *education*. In Option C, *Professions* is spelled correctly in the text.

18) In many jobs, the employees <u>become accustom</u> to the accomplishments <u>provided</u> by the work they do every day.
(Average Rigor) (Skill 3.2)

    A. became
    B. accustomed
    C. provides
    D. No change is necessary.

Answer: B. accustomed

The past participle *accustomed* is needed with the verb *become*. Option A is incorrect because the verb tense does not need to change to the past *became*. Option C is incorrect because *provides* is the wrong tense.

19) In the <u>operating room,</u> a team of <u>surgeons, is</u> responsible for operating on many of <u>these</u> patients.
(Easy) (Skill 3.3)

    A. operating room:
    B. surgeons is
    C. those
    D. No change is necessary.

Answer: B. surgeons is

Surgeons is not a proper name, so it does not need to be capitalized. A comma is not needed to break up *a team of surgeons* from the rest of the sentence. Option A is incorrect because a comma, not a colon, is needed to set off an item. Option C is incorrect because *those* is an incorrect pronoun.

20) Politicians <u>are</u> public <u>servants: who work</u> for the federal and state governments.
(Easy) (Skill 3.3)

    A. were
    B. servants who
    C. worked
    D. No change is necessary.

Answer: B. servants who

A colon is not needed to set off the introduction of the clause. In Option A, *were*, is the incorrect tense of the verb. In Option C, *worked*, is in the wrong tense.

21) <u>For example, whereas</u> such jobs as accounting and bookkeeping require mathematical <u>ability;</u> graphic design requires creative/artistic ability.
(Average Rigor) (Skill 3.3)

    A. For example
    B. whereas,
    C. ability,
    D. No change is necessary.

Answer: C. ability

An introductory dependent clause is set off with a comma, not a semicolon. Option A is incorrect because the transitional phrase *for example* should be set off with a comma. Option B is incorrect because the adverb *whereas* functions as *while* and does not take a comma after it.

22) In addition to the feeling of accomplishment that the workers <u>achieve</u>, some jobs also <u>give</u> a sense of self-identity to the <u>employees'</u>.
(Average Rigor) (Skill 3.3)

    A. acheive
    B. gave
    C. employees
    D. No change is necessary.

Answer: C. employees

Option C is correct because *employees* is not possessive. Option A is incorrect because *achieve* is spelled correctly in the sentence. Option B is incorrect because *gave* is the wrong tense.

23) <u>Finally;</u> the contributions that employees make to <u>their</u> companies and to the world cannot be <u>taken</u> for granted.
(Average Rigor) (Skill 3.3)

    A. Finally,
    B. their
    C. took
    D. No change is necessary.

Answer: A. Finally,

A comma is needed to separate *Finally* from the rest of the sentence. Finally is a preposition that usually heads a dependent sentence, hence a comma is needed. Option B is incorrect because *their* is misspelled. Option C is incorrect because *took* is the wrong form of the verb.

24) President <u>bush</u> is basically employed <u>by</u> the American people to <u>make</u> laws and run the country.
(Easy) (Skill 3.4)

    A. Bush
    B. to
    C. made
    D. No change is necessary.

Answer: A. Bush

Bush is a proper name and should be capitalized. In Option B, *to* does not fit with the verb *employed*. Option C uses the wrong form of the verb *make*.

TEACHER CERTIFICATION STUDY GUIDE

DIRECTIONS: *The passage below contains several errors. Read the passage. Then, answer each test item by choosing the option that corrects an error in the underlined portion(s). No more than one underlined error will appear in each item. If no error exists, choose "No change is necessary."*

The discovery of a body at Paris Point marina in Boca Raton shocked the residents of Palmetto Pines, a luxury condominium complex located next door to the marina.

The victim is a thirty-five-year-old woman who had been apparently bludgeoned to death and dumped in the ocean late last night. Many neighbors reported terrible screams, gunshots: as well as the sound of a car backfiring loudly to Boca Raton Police shortly after midnight. The woman had been spotted in the lobby of Palmetto Pines around ten thirty, along with an older man, estimated to be in his fifties, and a younger man, in his late twenties.

"Apparently, the victim had been driven to the complex by the older man and was seen arguing with him when the younger man intervened," said Sheriff Fred Adams, "all three of them left the building together and walked to the marina, where gunshots rang out an hour later." Deputies found five bullets on the sidewalk and some blood, along with a steel pipe that is assumed to be the murder weapon. Two men were seen fleeing the scene in a red Mercedes short after, rushing toward the Interstate.

The Palm Beach County Coroner, Melvin Watts, said he concluded the victim's skull had been crushed by a blunt tool, which resulted in a brain hemorrhage. As of now, there is no clear motive for the murder.

25)   Two men **were** seen fleeing the scene in a red Mercedes **short** after, **rushing** toward the Interstate.
(Easy) (Skill 1.1)

A. are
B. shortly
C. rushed
D. No change is necessary.

Answer: B. shortly

The adverb *shortly* is needed instead of the adjective short. Option A incorrectly uses the present tense *are* instead of the past tense *were*. Option C, *rushed*, is the wrong form of the verb.

26) As of <u>now,</u> <u>there</u> <u>is</u> no clear motive for the murder.
(Easy) (Skill 1.3, 2.2, 3.3)

A. now;
B. their
C. was
D. No change is necessary.

Answer: D. No change is necessary.

Option A is incorrect because a comma is needed to separate the independent clause from the dependent clause. Option B creates a misspelling. Option C uses the incorrect tense, *was*, which does not fit with the present tense phrase *as of now.*

27) Deputies found five bullets on the sidewalk and some <u>blood,</u> along with a steel pipe that is <u>assumed</u> <u>to be</u> the murder weapon.
(Rigorous) (Skill 1.4)

A. blood;
B. assuming
C. to have been
D. No change is necessary.

Answer: C. to have been

The past tense *to have been* is needed to maintain consistency. Option A incorrectly uses a semi-colon instead of a comma. Option B uses the wrong form of the verb *assumed.*

28) The victim <u>is</u> a thirty-five-year-old woman who had been apparently <u>bludgeoned</u> to death and dumped in the <u>ocean late</u> last night.
(Rigorous) (Skill 2.2)

A. was
B. bludgoned
C. ocean: late
D. No change is necessary.

Answer: A. was

The past tense *was* is needed to maintain consistency. Option B creates a misspelling. Option C incorrectly uses a colon when none is needed.

29) Many <u>neighbors</u> reported terrible screams, <u>gunshots: as</u> well as the sound of a car backfiring <u>loudly</u> to Boca Raton Police shortly after midnight.
(Average Rigor) (Skill 3.3)

A. neighbors
B. gunshots, as
C. loud
D. No change is necessary.

Answer: B. gunshots, as

Option B correctly uses a comma, not a colon, to separate the items. Option A creates a misspelling. Option C incorrectly changes the adverb into an adjective.

30) "Apparently, the victim had been driven to the complex by the older man and was seen arguing with him when the younger man intervened," said <u>Sheriff Fred Adams, "all</u> three of them left the building together and walked to the marina, where gunshots rang out an hour later."
(Average Rigor) (Skill 3.3)

A. sheriff Fred Adams, "all
B. sheriff Fred Adams, "All
C. Sheriff Fred Adams. "All
D. No change is necessary.

Answer: C. Sheriff Fred Adams. "All

The quote's source comes in the middle of two independent clauses, so a period should follow *Adams*. Option A is incorrect because titles, when they come before a name, must be capitalized. Punctuation is also faulty. Option B is incorrect because the word *Adams* ends a sentence; a comma is not strong enough to support two sentences.

31) The woman <u>had</u> been spotted in the lobby of Palmetto Pines around ten <u>thirty,</u> along with an older <u>man, estimated</u> to be in his fifties, and a younger man in his late twenties.
(Rigorous) (Skill 3.3)

    A. has
    B. thirty;
    C. man estimated
    D. No change is necessary.

Answer: C. man estimated

A comma is not needed to separate the item because *an older man estimated to be in his fifties* is one complete fragment. Option A incorrectly uses the present tense *has* instead of the past tense *had*. Option B incorrectly uses a semi-colon when a comma is needed.

32) The discovery of a body at Paris Point <u>marina</u> in Boca Raton shocked the <u>residents</u> of Palmetto Pines, a luxury <u>condominium</u> complex located next door to the marina.
(Easy) (Skill 3.4)

    A. Marina
    B. residence
    C. condominnium
    D. No change is necessary.

Answer: A. Marina

Marina is a name that needs to be capitalized. Options B and C create misspellings.

33) The <u>Palm Beach</u> <u>county</u> <u>coroner,</u> Kelvin Watts, said he concluded the victim's skull had been crushed by a blunt tool, which resulted in a brain <u>hemorrhage</u>.
(Rigorous) (Skill 3.4)

A. hemorrage
B. palm beach
C. County Coroner
D. No change is necessary.

Answer: C. County Coroner

Option A is incorrect because *hemorrhage* is spelled correctly in the text. Option B is incorrect because *Palm Beach* is a proper name and needs to be capitalized, as it is in the text. Option C is correct because *County Coroner* is a job title and must be capitalized.

DIRECTIONS: *For the underlined sentence(s), choose the option that expresses the meaning with the most fluency and the clearest logic within the context. If the underlined sentence should not be changed, choose Option A, which shows no change.*

34)   **Selecting members of a President's cabinet can often be an aggravating process. <u>Either there are too many or too few qualified candidates for a certain position, and then they have to be confirmed by the Senate, where there is the possibility of rejection.</u>**
(Rigorous) (Skill 2.0)

A. Either there are too many or too few qualified candidates for a certain position, and then they have to be confirmed by the Senate, where there is the possibility of rejection.

B. Qualified candidates for certain positions face the possibility of rejection, when they have to be confirmed by the Senate.

C. The Senate has to confirm qualified candidates, who face the possibility of rejection.

D. Because the Senate has to confirm qualified candidates; they face the possibility of rejection.

Answer: C. The Senate has to confirm qualified candidates, who face the possibility of rejection.

Option C is the most straightforward and concise sentence. Option A is too unwieldy with the wordy *Either...or* phrase at the beginning. Option B doesn't make clear the fact that candidates face rejection by the Senate. Option D illogically implies that candidates face rejection because they have to be confirmed by the Senate.

35)   Treating patients for drug and/or alcohol abuse is a sometimes difficult process. <u>Even though there are a number of different methods for helping the patient overcome a dependency, there is no way of knowing which is best in the long run.</u>
(Rigorous) (Skill 2.0)

A. Even though there are a number of different methods for helping the patient overcome a dependency, there is no way of knowing which is best in the long run.

B. Even though different methods can help a patient overcome a dependency, there is no way to know which is best in the long run.

C. Even though there is no way to know which way is best in the long run, patients can overcome their dependencies when they are helped.

D. There is no way to know which method will help the patient overcome a dependency in the long run, even though there are many different ones.

Answer: B. Even though different methods can help a patient overcome a dependency, there is no way to know which is best in the long run.

Option B is concise and logical. Option A tends to ramble with the use of *there are* and the verbs *helping* and *knowing*. Option C is awkwardly worded and repetitive in the first part of the sentence and vague in the second because it never indicates how the patients can be helped. Option D contains the unnecessary phrase *even though there are many different ones*.

36) **Many factors account for the decline in the quality of public education. _Overcrowding, budget cutbacks, and societal deterioration which have greatly affected student learning._** *(Rigorous) (Skill 3.3)*

   A. Overcrowding, budget cutbacks, and societal deterioration which have greatly affected student learning.

   B. ~~Student learning has been greatly affected by overcrowding, budget~~ cutbacks, and societal deterioration.

   C. Due to overcrowding, budget cutbacks, and societal deterioration, student learning has been greatly affected.

   D. Overcrowding, budget cutbacks, and societal deterioration have affected students learning greatly.

Answer: B. Student learning has been greatly affected by overcrowding, budget cutbacks, and societal deterioration.

Option B is concise and best explains the causes of the decline in student education. The unnecessary use of *which* in Option A makes the sentence feel incomplete. Option C has weak coordination between the reasons for the decline in public education and the fact that student learning has been affected. Option D incorrectly places the adverb *greatly* after learning, instead of before *affected.*

DIRECTIONS: *Choose the sentence that logically and correctly expresses the comparison.*
(Easy) (Skill 2.1)

37) A. The Empire State Building in New York is taller than buildings in the city.

   B. The Empire State Building in New York is taller than any other building in the city.

   C. The Empire State Building in New York is tallest than other buildings in the city.

Answer: B. The Empire State Building in New York is taller than any other building in the city.

Because the Empire State Building is a building in New York City, the phrase *any other* must be included. Option A is incorrect because the Empire State Building is implicitly compared to itself since it is one of the buildings. Option C is incorrect because *tallest i*s the incorrect form of the adjective.

DIRECTIONS: *For the underlined sentence(s), choose the option that expresses the meaning with the most fluency and the clearest logic within the context. If the underlined sentence should not be changed, choose Option A, which shows no change.*

38) **John wanted to join his friends on the mountain-climbing trip. <u>Seeing that the weather had become dark and stormy, John knew he would stay safe indoors.</u>**
(Rigorous) (Skill 2.5)

   A. Seeing that the weather had become dark and stormy, John knew he would stay safe indoors.

   B. The weather had become dark and stormy, and John knew he would stay indoors, and he would be safe.

   C. Because the weather had become dark and stormy, John knew he would stay indoors, where he would be safe.

   D. Because the weather had become dark, as well as stormy, John knew he would stay safe indoors.

Answer: D. Because the weather had become dark, as well as stormy, John knew he would stay safe indoors.

This sentence best subordinates the idea of dark and stormy weather to John's knowledge. Option A is incorrect because *seeing that* is an awkward construction. Option B does not subordinate any idea to any other. Option C is incorrect because the idea that John would be safe should not be subordinate to staying indoors.

39) **A few hours later, the storm subsided, so John left the cabin to join his friends. <u>Even though he was tired from the four-mile hike the day before, he climbed the mountain in a few hours.</u>**
(Average Rigor) (Skill 2.5)

    A. Even though he was tired from the four-mile hike the day before, he climbed the mountain in a few hours.

    ~~B. He was tired from the four-mile the day before; he climbed the~~ mountain in a few hours.

    C. He climbed the mountain in a few hours, John was tired from the four-mile hike the day before.

    D. Seeing as he was tired from the day before, when he went on a four-mile hike, John climbed the mountain in a few hours.

Answer: A. Even though he was tired from the four-mile hike the day before, he climbed the mountain in a few hours.

The idea that John was tired from the four-mile hike the day before is subordinate to the idea of John climbing the mountain. Options B and C do not subordinate the idea of John being tired from the four-mile hike to John climbing the mountain. In Option D, the modifying phrase *Seeing as... before* makes no logical sense in the context of the sentence.

DIRECTIONS: *Choose the most effective word within the context of the sentence.*

40) **Many of the clubs in Boca Raton are noted for their _____ elegance.**
(Average Rigor) (Skill 3.2)

    A. vulgar
    B. tasteful
    C. ordinary

Answer: B. tasteful

Tasteful means beautiful or charming, which would correspond to an elegant club. The words *vulgar* and *ordinary* have negative connotations.

41)   When a student is expelled from school, the parents are usually
       _____ in advance.
       (Average Rigor) (Skill 3.2)

       A. rewarded
       B. congratulated
       C. notified

Answer: C. notified

Notified means informed or told, which fits into the logic of the sentence. The words *rewarded* and *congratulated* are positive actions, which do not make sense regarding someone being expelled from school.

42)   Before appearing in court, the witness was _____ the papers
       requiring her to show up.
       (Average Rigor) (Skill 3.2)

       A. condemned
       B. served
       C. criticized

Answer: B. served

Served means given, which makes sense in the context of the sentence. *Condemned* and *criticized* do not make sense within the context of the sentence.

DIRECTIONS: *Choose the underlined word or phrase that is unnecessary within the context of the passage.*

43)   The <u>expanding</u> number of television channels has <u>prompted</u> cable
       operators to raise their prices, <u>even though</u> many consumers do not
       want to pay a higher <u>increased</u> amount for their service.
       (Easy) (Skill 3.2)

       A. expanding
       B. prompted
       C. even though
       D. increased

Answer: D. increased

The word *increased* is redundant with *higher* and should be removed. All the other words are necessary within the context of the sentence.

44) <u>Considered by many to be</u> one of the worst <u>terrorist</u> incidents <u>on American soil</u> was the bombing of the Oklahoma City Federal Building, which will be remembered <u>for years to come</u>.
(Average Rigor) (Skill 3.2)

      A. Considered by many to be
      B. terrorist
      C. on American soil
      D. for years to come

Answer: A. Considered by many to be

Considered by many to be is a wordy phrase and unnecessary in the context of the sentence. All other words are necessary within the context of the sentence.

45) The <u>flu</u> epidemic struck <u>most of</u> the <u>respected</u> faculty and students of the Woolbright School, forcing the Boynton Beach School Superintendent to close it down <u>for two weeks</u>.
(Average Rigor) (Skill 3.2)

      A. flu
      B. most of
      C. respected
      D. for two weeks

Answer: C. respected

The fact that the faculty might have been *respected* is not necessary to mention in the sentence. The other words and phrases are all necessary to complete the meaning of the sentence.

DIRECTIONS: *Choose the most effective word or phrase within the context suggested by the sentence.*

46) **Because George's _____ bothering him, he apologized for crashing his father's car.**
(Average Rigor) (Skill 3.2)

    A. feelings were
    B. conscience was
    C. guiltiness was

Answer: B. conscience was

Option B shows the correct word choice because a *conscience* would motivate someone to confess. Option A is incorrect because *feelings* is not as accurate as conscience. Option C is incorrect because *guiltiness* is less descriptive of George's motive for confession than conscience.

47) **The charity art auction _____ every year at Mizner Park has a wide selection of artists showcasing their work.**
(Rigorous) (Skill 3.3)

    A. attended
    B. presented
    C. displayed

Answer: B. presented

The word *presented* makes more sense in the context of the sentence than *attended* or *displayed*.

COMPETENCY 5.0   LITERAL COMPREHENSION

Skill 5.1   Identify summaries or paraphrases of the main idea or primary purpose of a reading selection.

The main idea of a passage or paragraph is the basic message, idea, point concept, or meaning that the author wants to convey to you, the reader. Understanding the main idea of a passage or paragraph is the key to understanding the more subtle components of the author's message. The main idea is what is being said about a topic or subject. Once you have identified the basic message, you will have an easier time answering other questions that test critical skills.

Main ideas are either *stated* or *implied*. A *stated main idea* is explicit: it is directly expressed in a sentence or two in the paragraph or passage. An *implied main idea* is suggested by the overall reading selection. In the first case, you need not pull information from various points in the paragraph or passage in order to form the main idea because the author already states it. If a main idea is implied, however, you must formulate, in your own words, a main idea statement by condensing the overall message contained in the material itself.

Sample Passage

Sometimes too much of a good thing can become a very bad thing indeed. In an earnest attempt to consume a healthy diet, dietary supplement enthusiasts have been known to overdose. Vitamin C, for example, long thought to help people ward off cold viruses, is currently being studied for its possible role in warding off cancer and other diseases that cause tissue degeneration. Unfortunately, an overdose of vitamin C—more than 10,000 mg—on a daily basis can cause nausea and diarrhea. Calcium supplements, commonly taken by women, are helpful in warding off osteoporosis. More than just a few grams a day, however, can lead to stomach upset and even kidney and bladder stones. Niacin, proven useful in reducing cholesterol levels, can be dangerous in large doses to those who suffer from heart problems, asthma, or ulcers.

The main idea expressed in this paragraph is

    A. Supplements taken in excess can be a bad thing indeed.
    B. Dietary supplement enthusiasts have been known to overdose.
    C. Vitamins can cause nausea, diarrhea, and kidney or bladder stones.
    D. People who take supplements are preoccupied with their health.

Answer A is a paraphrase of the first sentence and provides a general framework for the rest of the paragraph: excess supplement intake is bad. The rest of the paragraph discusses the consequences of taking too many vitamins. Options B and C refer to major details and Option D introduces the idea of preoccupation, which is not included in this paragraph.

Skill 5.2   Identify summaries or paraphrases of supporting ideas.

See Skill 4.4.

Skill 5.3   Recognize how a reading selection is organized.

The **organization** of a written work includes two factors: the order in which the writer has chosen to present the different parts of the discussion or argument and the relationships he or she constructs between these parts.

Written ideas need to be presented in a **logical order** so that a reader can follow the information easily and quickly. There are many different ways to order a series of ideas, but they all share one thing—to lead the reader along a desired path, while avoiding backtracking and skipping around, in order to give a clear, strong presentation of the writer's main idea. The following are *some* of the ways in which a paragraph may be organized:

Sequence of events—In this type of organization, the details are presented in the order in which they have occurred. Paragraphs that describe a process or procedure, give directions, or outline a given period (such as a day or a month) are often arranged chronologically.

Statement support—In this type of organization, the main idea is stated, and the rest of the paragraph explains or proves it. This is also referred to as relative or order of importance. This type of order is organized in four ways: most to least, least to most, most-least-most, and least-most-least.

Comparison-Contrast—The compare-contrast pattern is used when a paragraph describes the differences or similarities of two or more ideas, actions, events, or things. Usually, the topic sentence describes the basic relationship between the ideas or items, and the rest of the paragraph explains this relationship.

Classification—In this type of organization, the paragraph presents grouped information about a topic. The topic sentence usually states the general category, and the rest of the sentences show how various elements of the category have a common base and how they differ from the common base.

Cause and Effect—This pattern describes how two or more events are connected. The main sentence usually states the primary cause(s) and the primary effect(s) and how they are connected. The rest of the sentences explain the connection—how one event caused the next.

Spatial/Place—In this type of organization, certain descriptions are organized according to the location of items in relation to each other and to a larger context. The orderly arrangement guides the reader's eye as he or she mentally envisions the scene or place being described.

Example, Clarification and Definition—These types of organization show, explain, or elaborate on the main idea. This can be done by showing specific cases, examining meaning multiple times, or describing one term extensively. Many times, all of these organizations follow the basic P.I.E. sequence:

P—the point, or main idea, of the paragraph
I—the information (data, details, facts) that supports the main idea
E—the explanation or analysis of the information and how it proves, is related to, or connects to the main idea

Skill 5.4   Recognize how the ideas in a selection are related to one another.

The relationship between sentences is the link that conceptually ties one sentence to another. The relationship may be explicit, in which case, a transition or clue word helps identify the connection. The relation may be implicit, in which case, you must closely examine the elements found in each sentence and often in the material between the sentences.

Most sentences cannot meaningfully stand alone. To read a passage without recognizing how each sentence is linked to those around it is to lose the passage's meaning.

Sentences can be connected to one another in many ways.

Addition—One sentence is "tacked on" to another without making one sentence depend upon the other. Both are equally important.

> *Joanna recently purchased a new stereo system, computer, and home alarm system. She **also** put a down payment on a new automobile.*

Clarification—One sentence restates the point of an earlier one but in different terms.

> *The national debt is growing continually. **In fact**, by next year it may be ten trillion dollars.*

Comparison/Contrast—Connection is one of similarity or difference.

> *Shelley's strained relationship with his father led the poet to a life of rebellion.* **Likewise**, *Byron's Bohemian lifestyle may be traced to his ambivalence towards authority.*

Example—One sentence works to make another more concrete or specific.

> *Sarah has always been an optimistic person. She believes that when she graduates from college, she will get the job of her choice. (implicit)*

Location/Spatial Order—The relationship between sentences shows the placement of objects or items relative to each other in space.

> *The park was darkened by the school building's shadow. However, the sun still splashed the front window with light. (implicit)*

Cause/Effect—One event (cause) brings about the second event (effect).

> *General Hooker failed to anticipate General Lee's bold maneuver.* **As a result**, *Hooker's army was nearly routed by a smaller force.*

Summary—A summary sentence surveys and captures the most important points of the previous sentence(s).

> *Every Fourth of July, Ralph brings his whole family to the local parade; every Memorial Day, he displays the flag; and every November 4, he votes.* **Overall, he is** *a patriotic American.*

Time—The relationship describes the passage of time or various states of completion of events.

> *The car slid down the embankment.* **Shortly thereafter**, *curious onlookers had backed up traffic five miles.*

Skill 5.5 **Recognize how key phrases and transition words are used in a reading selection.**

Even if the sentences that make up a given paragraph or passage are arranged in logical order, the document as a whole can still seem choppy, the various ideas disconnected. **Transitions**, words that signal relationships between ideas, can help improve the flow of a document. Transitions can help achieve clear and effective presentation of information by establishing connections between sentences, paragraphs, and sections of a document. With transitions, each sentence builds on the ideas in the last, and each paragraph has clear links to the preceding one. As a result, the reader receives clear directions on how to piece together the writer's ideas in a logically coherent argument. By signaling how to organize, interpret, and react to information, transitions allow writers to explain their ideas effectively and elegantly. Below is a list of common transitional expressions.

Common Transitions

Logical Relationship	Transitional Expression
Similarity	also, in the same way, just as ... so too, likewise, similarly
Exception/Contrast	but, however, in spite of, on the one hand ... on the other hand, nevertheless, nonetheless, notwithstanding, in contrast, on the contrary, still, yet, although
Sequence/Order	first, second, third, ... next, then, finally, until
Time	after, afterward, at last, before, currently, during, earlier, immediately, later, meanwhile, now, presently, recently, simultaneously, since, subsequently, then
Example	for example, for instance, namely, specifically, to illustrate
Emphasis	even, indeed, in fact, of course, truly
Place/Position	above, adjacent, below, beyond, here, in front, in back, nearby, there
Cause and Effect	accordingly, consequently, hence, so, therefore, thus, as a result, because, consequently, hence, if...then, in short
Additional Support or Evidence	additionally, again, also, and, as well, besides, equally important, further, furthermore, in addition, moreover, then

Conclusion/Summary	finally, in a word, in brief, in conclusion, in the end, in the final analysis, on the whole, thus, to conclude, to summarize, in sum, in summary
Statement Support	Most important, more significant, primarily, most essential
Addition	Again, also, and, besides, equally important, finally, furthermore, in addition, last, likewise, moreover, too
Clarification	Actually, clearly, evidently, in fact, in other words, obviously, of course, indeed

The following example shows good logical order and transitions, with the transition words being highlighted:

No one really knows how Valentine's Day started. There are several legends, **however**, which are often told. The **first** attributes Valentine's Day to a Christian priest who lived in Rome during the third century under the rule of Emperor Claudius. Rome was at war, and **apparently**, Claudius felt that married men did not fight as well as bachelors. **Consequently**, Claudius banned marriage for the duration of the war. **But** Valentinus, the priest, risked his life to marry couples secretly in violation of Claudius' law. The **second** legend is **even more** romantic. **In this story**, Valentinus is a prisoner, having been condemned to death for refusing to worship pagan deities. **While** in jail, he fell in love with his jailer's daughter, who happened to be blind. Daily, he prayed for her sight to return and miraculously, it did. On February 14, the day that he was condemned to die, he was allowed to write the young woman a note. **In this farewell letter**, he promised eternal love and signed at the bottom of the page the now famous words, "Your Valentine."

Skill 5.6   Identify the meanings of words as they are used in the context of a reading selection.

Context clues help readers determine the meanings of words with which they are not familiar. The context of a word is the sentence or sentences that surround the word.

Read the following sentences and attempt to determine the meanings of the words in bold print.

> The **luminosity** of the room was so incredible that there was no need for lights.
>
> > If there was no need for lights, then one must assume that the word *luminosity* has something to do with giving off light. The definition of *luminosity* is "the emission of light."
>
> Jamie could not understand Joe's feelings. His mood swings made understanding him somewhat of an **enigma.**
>
> > The fact that he could not be understood made him somewhat of a puzzle. The definition of *enigma* is "a mystery or puzzle."

Familiarity with word **roots** (the basic elements of words) and with **prefixes** can help one determine the meanings of unknown words.

Following is a partial list of roots and prefixes. It might be useful to review these.

Root	Meaning	Example
aqua	water	aqualung
astro	stars	astrology
bio	life	biology
carn	meat	carnivorous
circum	around	circumnavigate
geo	earth	geology
herb	plant	herbivorous
mal	bad	malicious
neo	new	neonatal
tele	distant	telescope

Prefix	Meaning	Example
un-	not	unnamed
re-	again	reenter
il-	not	illegible
pre-	before	preset
mis-	incorrectly	misstate
in-	not	informal
anti-	against	antiwar
de-	opposite	derail
post-	after	postwar
ir-	not	irresponsible

Word forms
Sometimes a very familiar word can appear as a different part of speech, as in the examples below.

> You may have heard that *fraud* involves a criminal misrepresentation, so when it appears as the adjective form *fraudulent* (He was suspected of fraudulent activities.), you can make an educated guess.

> You probably know that something out-of-date is *obsolete;* therefore, when you read about "built-in *obsolescence,*" you can detect the meaning of the unfamiliar word.

The context for a word is the written passage that surrounds it. Sometimes the writer offers synonyms—words that have nearly the same meaning. Context clues can appear within the sentence itself, within the preceding and/or following sentence(s), or in the passage as a whole.

Sentence clues
Often, a writer will actually **define** a difficult or particularly important word for you the first time it appears in a passage. Phrases such as *that is, such as, which is,* or *is called* might announce the writer's intention to give just the definition you need. Occasionally, a writer will simply use a synonym (a word that means the same thing) or near-synonym joined by the word *or.* Look at the following examples:

> The <u>credibility</u>, *that is to say the believability, of the witness was called into question by evidence of previous perjury.*
> *Nothing would <u>assuage</u> or lessen the child's grief.*

Punctuation at the sentence level is often a clue to the meaning of a word. Commas, parentheses, quotation marks, and dashes tell the reader that the writer is offering a definition.

> *A tendency toward <u>hyperbole</u>, extravagant exaggeration, is a common flaw among persuasive writers.*

> *Political <u>apathy</u>—lack of interest—can lead to the death of the state.*

A writer might simply give an **explanation** in other words that you can understand in the same sentence:

> *The <u>xenophobic</u> townspeople were suspicious of every foreigner.*

Writers also explain a word in terms of its opposite at the sentence level:

> *His <u>incarceration</u> was ended, and he was elated to be out of jail.*

Adjacent sentence clues

The context for a word goes beyond the sentence in which it appears. At times, the writer uses adjacent (adjoining) sentences to present an explanation or definition:

> *The 200 dollars for the car repair would have to come out of the <u>contingency</u> fund. Fortunately, Angela's father had taught her to keep some money set aside for just such emergencies.*

> Analysis: The second sentence offers a clue to the definition of *contingency* as used in this sentence: "emergencies." Therefore, a fund for contingencies would be money tucked away for unforeseen and/or urgent events.

Entire passage clues

On occasion, you must look at an entire paragraph or passage to figure out the definition of a word or term. In the following paragraph, notice how the word *nostalgia* undergoes a form of extended definition throughout the selection rather than in just one sentence.

> The word nostalgia *links Greek words for "away from home" and "pain." If you are feeling* nostalgic, *then you are probably in some physical distress or discomfort, suffering from a feeling of alienation and separation from loved ones or loved places.* Nostalgia *is that awful feeling you remember the first time you went away to camp or spent the weekend with a friend's family—homesickness, or some condition even more painful than that. However, in common use,* nostalgia *has come to have associations that are more sentimental. A few years back, for example, a* nostalgic *craze had to do with the 1950s. We resurrected poodle skirts and saddle shoes, built new restaurants to look like old ones, and tried to make chicken à la king just as Mother probably never made it. In TV situation comedies, we recreated a pleasant world that probably never existed and relished our* nostalgia, *longing for a homey, comfortable, lost time.*

COMPETENCY 6.0   CRITICAL AND INFERENTIAL COMPREHENSION

Skill 6.1   Determine the strengths and weaknesses of arguments in a reading selection.

On the test, the terms **valid** and **invalid** have special meaning. If an argument is valid, it is reasonable. It is objective (not biased) and can be supported by evidence. If an argument is invalid, it is not reasonable. It is not objective. In other words, one can find evidence of bias.

Read the following passage:

> Most dentists agree that Bright Smile Toothpaste is the best for fighting cavities. It tastes good and leaves your mouth minty fresh.

Is this a valid or invalid argument?

(A) valid
(B) invalid

It is invalid (B). It mentions that *most* dentists agree. What about those who do not agree? The author is clearly exhibiting bias in leaving those who disagree out.

Read the following passage:

> It is difficult to decide who will make the best presidential candidate, Senator Johnson or Senator Keeley. They have both been involved in scandals and have both gone through messy divorces while in office.

Is this argument valid or invalid?

(A) valid
(B) invalid

(A) is the correct choice. The author appears to be listing facts. He does not seem to favor one candidate over the other.

An argument is a generalization that is proven or supported with facts. If the facts are not accurate, the generalization remains unproven. Using inaccurate "facts" to support an argument is called a *fallacy* in reasoning. Some factors to consider in judging whether the facts used to support an argument are accurate are as follow:

1. Are the facts current, or are they out-of-date? For example, if the proposition is "birth defects in babies born to drug-using mothers are increasing," then the data must include the latest available.
2. Another important factor to consider in judging the accuracy of a fact is its source. Where was the data obtained, and is that source reliable?
3. The calculations on which the facts are based may be unreliable. It is a good idea to run one's own calculations before using a piece of derived information.

Even facts that are true and have a sharp impact on the argument may not be relevant to the case at hand, as in the following:

1. Health statistics from an entire state may have no relevance, or little relevance, to a particular county or zip code. Statistics from an entire country cannot be used to prove very much about a particular state or county.
2. An analogy can be useful in making a point, but the comparison must match up in all characteristics, or it will not be relevant. Analogies should be used very carefully. They are often just as likely to destroy an argument, as they are to strengthen one.

The importance or significance of a fact may not be sufficient to strengthen an argument. For example, of the millions of immigrants in the U.S., using a single family to support a solution to the immigration problem will not make much difference overall even though those single-example arguments are often used to support one approach or another. They may achieve a positive reaction, but they will not prove that one solution is better than another is. If enough cases were cited from a variety of geographical locations, the information might be significant.

> Sometimes more than three arguments are too many. On the other hand, it is not unusual to hear public speakers, particularly politicians, who will cite a long litany of facts to support their positions.

A very good example of the omission of facts in an argument is the résumé of an applicant for a job. The applicant is arguing that he/she should be chosen for a particular job. The application form will ask for information about past employment, and unfavorable dismissals from jobs in the past may just be omitted. Employers are usually suspicious of periods when the applicant has not listed an employer.

A writer makes choices about which facts will be used and which will be discarded in developing an argument. Those choices may exclude anything that is not supportive of the point of view the arguer is taking. It is always a good idea for the reader to do some research to spot the omissions and to ask whether they may have an impact on acceptance of the point of view presented in the argument.

No judgment is either black or white. If the argument seems too neat or too compelling, facts that might be relevant probably have not been included.

Skill 6.2   Determine the relevance of evidence presented in the reading selection to the assertions made in the selection.

The main idea of a passage may contain a wide variety of supporting information, but it is important that each sentence be related to the main idea. When a sentence contains information that bears little or no connection to the main idea, it is said to be **irrelevant**. It is important to assess continually whether or not a sentence contributes to the overall task of supporting the main idea. When a sentence is deemed irrelevant, it is best either to omit it from the passage or to make it relevant by one of the following strategies:

1. Adding detail—Sometimes a sentence can seem out of place if it does not contain enough information to link it to the topic. Adding specific information can show how the sentence relates to the main idea.

2. Adding an example—This is especially important in passages in which information is being argued or compared or contrasted. Examples can support the main idea and give the document overall credibility.

3. Using diction effectively—It is important to understand connotation, avoid ambiguity, and avoid too much repetition when selecting words.

4. Adding transitions—Transitions are extremely helpful for making sentences relevant because they are specifically designed to connect one idea to another. They can also reduce a paragraph's choppiness.

The following passage has several irrelevant sentences that are highlighted in bold:

The New City Planning Committee is proposing a new capitol building to represent the multicultural face of New City. **The current mayor is a Democrat.** The new capitol building will be on 10th Street across from the grocery store and next to the recreational center. It will be within walking distance to the subway and bus depot, as the designers want to emphasize the importance of public transportation. Aesthetically, the building will have a contemporary design, featuring a brushed-steel exterior and large, floor-to-ceiling windows. **It is important for employees to have a connection with the outside world even when they are in their offices.** Inside the building, the walls will be moveable. This will not only facilitate a multitude of creative floor plans, but it will also create a focus on open communication and flow of information. **It sounds a bit gimmicky to me.** Finally, the capitol will feature a large outdoor courtyard full of lush greenery and serene fountains. **Work will now seem like Club Med to those who work at the New City capitol building!**

Skill 6.3 Judge if material presented is fact or opinion.

Facts are verifiable statements. Opinions are statements that must be supported in order to be accepted, such as beliefs, values, judgments, or feelings. Facts are objective statements used to support subjective opinions. For example, "Jane is a bad girl" is an opinion. However, "Jane hit her sister with a baseball bat" is a fact upon which the opinion is based. Judgments are opinions, decisions, or declarations based on observation or reasoning that express approval or disapproval. Facts report what has happened or exists and come from observation, measurement, or calculation. Facts can be tested and verified whereas opinions and judgments cannot. They can only be supported with facts.

Most statements cannot be so clearly distinguished. "I believe that Jane is a bad girl" is a fact. The speaker knows what he/she believes. However, it obviously includes a judgment that could be disputed by another person who might believe otherwise. Judgments are not usually so firm. They are, rather, plausible opinions that provoke thought or lead to factual development.

Mickey Mantle replaced Joe DiMaggio, a Yankees centerfielder, in 1952.

This is a fact. If necessary, evidence can be produced to support this.

First-year players are more ambitious than seasoned players are.

This is an opinion. There is no proof to support that everyone feels this way.

PRACTICE QUESTIONS

1. The Inca were a group of Indians who ruled an empire in South America.

    (A) fact
    (B) opinion

2. The Inca were clever.

    (A) fact
    (B) opinion

3. The Inca built very complex systems of bridges.

    (A) fact
    (B) opinion

ANSWERS:

1. (A) is the correct answer. Research can prove this true.
2. (B) is the correct answer. It is doubtful that all people who have studied the Inca agree with this statement. Therefore, no proof is available.
3. (A) is the correct answer. As with question number one, research can prove this true.

Skill 6.4   Draw inferences and implications from the directly stated content of a reading selection.

An **inference** is sometimes called an "educated guess" because it requires going beyond the strictly obvious to create additional meaning by taking the text one logical step further. Inferences and conclusions are based on the content of the passage—that is, on what the passage says or how the writer says it—and are derived by reasoning.

Inference is an essential and automatic component of most reading. Examples include making educated guesses about the meaning of unknown words, the author's main idea, or the existence of bias. Such is the essence of inference. You use your own ability to reason in order to figure out what the writer implies. As a reader, then, you must often logically extend meaning that is only implied.

Consider the following example. Assume you are an employer, and you are reading over the letters of reference submitted by a prospective employee for the position of clerk/typist in your real estate office. The position requires the applicant to be neat, careful, trustworthy, and punctual. You come across this letter of reference submitted by an applicant:

To Whom It May Concern:

> *Todd Finley has asked me to write a letter of reference for him. I am well qualified to do so because he worked for me for three months last year. His duties included answering the phone, greeting the public, and producing some simple memos and notices on the computer. Although Todd initially had few computer skills and little knowledge of telephone etiquette, he did acquire some during his stay with us. Todd's manner of speaking, both on the telephone and with the clients who came to my establishment, could be described as casual. He was particularly effective when communicating with peers. Please contact me by telephone if you wish to have further information about my experience with Todd.*

Here the writer implies, rather than openly states, the main idea. This letter calls attention to itself because there is a problem with its tone. A truly positive letter would say something such as, "I have the distinct honor of recommending Todd Finley." Here, however, the letter simply verifies that Todd worked in the office. Second, the praise is obviously lukewarm. For example, the writer says that Todd "was particularly effective when communicating with peers." An educated guess translates that statement into a nice way of saying Todd was not serious about his communication with clients.

Skill 6.5   Determine the author's attitude toward the material discussed.

The *tone* of a written passage is the author's attitude toward the subject matter. The tone (mood, feeling) is revealed through the qualities of the writing itself and is a direct product of such stylistic elements as language and sentence structure. The tone of the written passage is much like a speaker's voice; instead of being spoken, however, it is the product of words on a page.

Often, writers have an emotional stake in the subject, and their purpose, either explicitly or implicitly, is to convey those feelings to the reader. In such cases, the writing is generally subjective; that is, it stems from opinions, judgments, values, ideas, and feelings. Both sentence structure (syntax) and word choice (diction) are instrumental tools in creating tone.

Tone may be thought of generally as positive, negative, or neutral. Below is a statement about snakes that demonstrates this.

> *Many species of snakes live here. Some of those species, both poisonous and non-poisonous, have habitats that coincide with those of human residents of the state.*

The voice of the writer in this statement is neutral. The sentences are declarative (not exclamations, fragments, or questions). The adjectives are few and nondescript—*many, some, poisonous* (balanced with *non-poisonous).*

Nothing much in this brief paragraph would alert the reader to the feelings of the writer about snakes. The paragraph has a neutral, objective, detached, impartial tone.

Then again, if the writer's attitude towards snakes involves admiration, or even affection, the tone would generally be positive:

> *These snakes are a tenacious bunch. When they find their habitats invaded by humans, they cling to their home territories as long as they can, as if vainly attempting to fight off the onslaught of the human hordes.*

An additional message emerges in this paragraph—the writer quite clearly favors snakes over people. The writer uses adjectives such as *tenacious* to describe his/her feelings about snakes. The writer also humanizes the reptiles, making them brave, beleaguered creatures. Obviously, the writer is more sympathetic to snakes than to people in this paragraph.

If the writer's attitude toward snakes involves active dislike and fear, then the tone would also reflect that attitude by being negative:

> *Countless species of snakes, some more dangerous than others, still lurk on the urban fringes of towns and cities. They will often invade domestic spaces, terrorizing people and their pets.*

Here, obviously, the snakes are the villains. They *lurk,* they *invade,* and they *terrorize.* The tone of this paragraph might be said to be distressed about snakes.

In the same manner, a writer can use language to portray characters as good or bad. A writer uses positive and negative adjectives, as seen above, to convey the manner of a character.

Skill 6.6   Draw conclusions about the material in a selection.

In order to draw **inferences** and make **conclusions**, a reader must use prior knowledge and apply it to the current situation. A conclusion or inference is never stated. You must rely on common sense.

PRACTICE QUESTIONS

Read the following passages and select an answer.

1.   Tim Sullivan had just turned fifteen. As a birthday present, his parents had given him a guitar and a certificate for ten guitar lessons. He had always shown a love of music and a desire to learn an instrument. Tim began his lessons, and before long, he was making up his own songs. At the music studio, Tim met Josh, who played the piano, and Roger, whose instrument was the saxophone. They all shared the same dream—to start a band—and each was praised by his teacher as having real talent.

From this passage, one can infer that:

(A) Tim, Roger, and Josh are going to start their own band.
(B) Tim is going to give up his guitar lessons.
(C) Tim, Josh, and Roger will no longer be friends.
(D) Josh and Roger are going to start their own band.

2.   The Smith family waited patiently around carousel number 7 for their luggage to arrive. They were exhausted after their five-hour trip and were anxious to get to their hotel. After about an hour, they realized that they no longer recognized any of the other passengers' faces. Mrs. Smith asked the person who appeared to be in charge if they were at the right carousel.

The man replied, "Yes, this is it, but we finished unloading that baggage almost half an hour ago."

From the man's response, we can infer that:

(A) The Smiths were ready to go to their hotel.
(B) The Smith's luggage was lost.
(C) The man had their luggage.
(D) They were at the wrong carousel.

ANSWERS

1. (A) is the correct choice. Given the facts that Tim wanted to be a musician and start his own band, after meeting others who shared the same dreams, we can infer that they joined in an attempt to make their dreams become a reality.

2. Since the Smiths were still waiting for their luggage, we know that they were not yet ready to go to their hotel. From the man's response, we know that they were not at the wrong carousel and that he did not have their luggage. Therefore, though not directly stated, it appears that their luggage was lost. Choice (B) is the correct answer.

Sample Test: Reading

Read the following paragraph and answer the questions that follow.

This writer has often been asked to tutor hospitalized children with cystic fibrosis. While undergoing all the precautionary measures to see these children (i.e. scrubbing thoroughly and donning sterilized protective gear for the child's protection), she has often wondered why their parents subject these children to the pressures of schooling and trying to catch up on what they have missed because of hospitalization, which is a normal part of cystic fibrosis patients' lives. These children undergo so many tortuous treatments a day that it seems cruel to expect them to learn as normal children do, especially with their life expectancies being as short as they are.

1. **What is the main idea of this passage?**
    (Average Rigor) (Skill 5.1)

    A. There is much preparation involved in visiting a patient with cystic fibrosis.
    B. Children with cystic fibrosis are incapable of living normal lives.
    C. Certain concessions should be made for children with cystic fibrosis.
    D. Children with cystic fibrosis die young.

2. **What is the author's purpose?**
    (Average Rigor) (Skill 5.1)

    A. To inform
    B. To entertain
    C. To describe
    D. To narrate

3. **What type of organizational pattern is the author using?**
    (Rigorous) (Skill 5.3)

    A. Classification
    B. Explanation
    C. Comparison and contrast
    D. Cause and effect

4. **What kind of relationship is found within the last sentence, which starts with "These children undergo ..." and ends with "... as short as they are"?**
    (Rigorous) (Skill 5.3)

    A. Comparison and Contrast
    B. Statement Support
    C. Spatial/Place
    D. Classification

5. **What is meant by the word "precautionary" in the second sentence?**
    (Average Rigor) (Skill 5.6)

    A. Careful
    B. Protective
    C. Medical
    D. Sterilizing

6. How is the author so familiar with the procedures used when visiting a child with cystic fibrosis?
(Easy) (Skill 6.1)

A. She has read about it.
B. She works in a hospital.
C. She is the parent of one.
D. She often tutors them.

7. Does the author present an argument that is valid or invalid concerning the schooling of children with cystic fibrosis?
(Rigorous) (Skill 6.1)

A. Valid
B. Invalid

8. The author states that it is "cruel" to expect children with cystic fibrosis to learn as "normal" children do. Is this a fact or an opinion?
(Rigorous) (Skill 6.3)

A. Fact
B. Opinion

9. What is the author's tone?
(Rigorous) (Skill 6.5)

A. Sympathetic
B. Cruel
C. Disbelieving
D. Cheerful

10. Is there evidence of bias in this paragraph?
(Rigorous) (Skill 6.5)

A. Yes
B. No

Read the following passage and answer the questions that follow.

Disciplinary practices have been found to affect diverse areas of child development, such as the acquisition of moral values, obedience to authority, and performance at school. Even though the dictionary has a specific definition of the word "discipline," it is still open to interpretation by people of different cultures.

There are four types of disciplinary styles: assertion of power, withdrawal of love, reasoning, and permissiveness. Assertion of power involves the use of force to discourage unwanted behavior. Withdrawal of love involves making the love of a parent conditional on a child's good behavior. Reasoning involves persuading the child to behave one way rather than another. Permissiveness involves allowing the child to do as he or she pleases and face the consequences of his/her actions.

11. What is the author's purpose in writing this?
(Easy) (Skill 5.1)

A. To describe
B. To narrate
C. To entertain
D. To inform

12. **What is the main idea of this passage?**
(Average Rigor) (Skill 5.1)

   A. Different people have different ideas of what discipline is.
   B. Permissiveness is the most widely-used disciplinary style.
   C. Most people agree on their definition of discipline.
   D. There are four disciplinary styles.

13. **Name the four types of disciplinary styles.**
(Easy) (Skill 5.2)

   A. Reasoning, power assertion, morality, and permissiveness
   B. Morality, reasoning, permissiveness, and withdrawal of love
   C. Withdrawal of love, permissiveness, assertion of power, and reasoning
   D. Permissiveness, morality, reasoning, and power assertion

14. **What does the technique of reasoning involve?**
(Easy) (Skill 5.2)

   A. Persuading the child to behave in a certain way
   B. Allowing the child to do as he/she pleases
   C. Using force to discourage unwanted behavior
   D. Making love conditional on good behavior

15. **What organizational structure is used in the first sentence of the second paragraph?**
(Rigorous) (Skill 5.3)

   A. Addition
   B. Cause and effect
   C. Clarification
   D. Example

16. **What is the overall organizational pattern of this passage?**
(Rigorous) (Skill 5.3)

   A. Statement Support
   B. Cause and effect
   C. Classification
   D. Summary

17. **What is the meaning of the word "diverse" in the first sentence?**
(Easy) (Skill 5.6)

   A. Many
   B. Related to children
   C. Disciplinary
   D. Moral

18. **The author states "assertion of power involves the use of force to discourage unwanted behavior." Is this a fact or an opinion?**
(Average Rigor) (Skill 6.3)

A. ~~Fact~~
B. Opinion

19. **Is this passage biased?**
(Average Rigor) (Skill 6.5)

A. Yes
B. No

20. **What is the author's tone?**
(Average Rigor) (Skill 6.5)

A. Disbelieving
B. Angry
C. Informative
D. Optimistic

21. **From reading this passage, we can conclude that**
(Rigorous) (Skill 6.6)

A. The author is a teacher.
B. The author has many children.
C. The author has written a book about discipline.
D. The author has done a lot of research on discipline.

Read the following passage and answer the questions that follow.

One of the most difficult problems plaguing American education is the assessment of teachers. No one denies that teachers should be answerable for what they do, but what exactly does that mean? The Oxford American Dictionary defines accountability as the obligation to give a reckoning or explanation for one's actions.

Does a student have to learn for teaching to have taken place? Historically, teaching has not been defined in this restrictive manner; the teacher was thought to be responsible for the quantity and quality of material covered and the way in which it was presented. However, some definitions of teaching now imply that students must learn in order for teaching to have taken place.

As a teacher who tries my best to keep current on all the latest teaching strategies, I believe that those teachers who do not bother even to pick up an educational journal every once in a while should be kept under close watch. There are many teachers out there who have been teaching for decades and who refuse to change their ways even if research has proven that their methods are outdated and ineffective. There is no place in the profession of teaching for these types of individuals. It is time that the American educational system clean house, for the sake of our children.

22. **What is the main idea of the passage?**
(Average Rigor) (Skill 5.1)

   A.   Teachers should not be answerable for what they do.
   B.   Teachers who do not do their job should be fired.
   C.   The author is a good teacher.
   D.   Assessment of teachers is a serious problem in society today.

23. **What is the author's purpose in writing this?**
(Average Rigor) (Skill 5.1)

   A.   To entertain
   B.   To narrate
   C.   To describe
   D.   To persuade

24. **Where does the author get her definition of "accountability"?**
(Easy) (Skill 5.2)

   A.   Webster's Dictionary
   B.   Encyclopedia Britannica
   C.   Oxford Dictionary
   D.   World Book Encyclopedia

25. **The author states that teacher assessment is a problem for**
(Easy) (Skill 5.2)

   A.   Elementary schools
   B.   Secondary schools
   C.   American education
   D.   Families

26. **What is the author's overall organizational pattern?**
(Rigorous) (Skill 5.3)

   A.   Classification
   B.   Cause and effect
   C.   Definition
   D.   Comparison and contrast

27. **What is the organizational pattern of the second paragraph?**
(Rigorous) (Skill 5.3)

   A.   Cause and effect
   B.   Classification
   C.   Sequence of Events
   D.   Explanation

28. **What is meant by the word "plaguing" in the first sentence?**
(Easy) (Skill 5.6)

   A.   Causing problems
   B.   Causing illness
   C.   Causing anger
   D.   Causing failure

29. What is the meaning of the word "reckoning" in the third sentence?
(Average Rigor) (Skill 5.6)

A. Thought
B. Answer
C. Obligation
D. Explanation

30. Is this a valid argument?
(Rigorous) (Skill 6.1)

A. Yes
B. No

31. Teachers who do not keep current on educational trends should be fired. Is this a fact or an opinion?
(Average Rigor) (Skill 6.3)

A. Fact
B. Opinion

32. The author's tone is one of
(Average Rigor) (Skill 6.5)

A. Disbelief
B. Excitement
C. Support
D. Concern

33. Is there evidence of bias in this passage?
(Rigorous) (Skill 6.5)

A. Yes
B. No

34. From the passage, one can infer that
(Rigorous) (Skill 6.6)

A. The author considers herself a good teacher.
B. Poor teachers will be fired.
C. Students have to learn for teaching to take place.
D. The author will be fired.

Read the following paragraph and answer the questions that follow.

Mr. Smith gave instructions for the painting to be hung on the wall. Then, it leaped forth before his eyes: the little cottages on the river, the white clouds floating over the valley, and the green of the towering mountain ranges that were seen in the distance. The painting was so vivid that it seemed almost real. Mr. Smith was now certain that the painting had been worth money.

35. What is the main idea of this passage?
(Average Rigor) (Skill 5.1)

A. The painting that Mr. Smith purchased is expensive.
B. Mr. Smith purchased a painting.
C. Mr. Smith was pleased with the quality of the painting he had purchased.
D. The painting depicted cottages and valleys.

36. The author's purpose is to
     (Rigorous) (Skill 5.1)

     A. Inform
     B. Entertain
     C. Persuade
     D. Narrate

37. What does the author mean
     by the expression "it leaped
     forth before his eyes"?
     (Average Rigor) (Skill 5.6)

     A. The painting fell off
         the wall.
     B. The painting appeared
         so real it was almost
         three-dimensional.
     C. The painting struck
         Mr. Smith in the face.
     D. Mr. Smith was
         hallucinating.

38. What is the meaning of the
     word "vivid" in the third
     sentence?
     (Average Rigor) (Skill 5.6)

     A. Lifelike
     B. Dark
     C. Expensive
     D. Big

39. Is this passage biased?
     (Average Rigor) (Skill 6.5)

     A. Yes
     B. No

40. From the last sentence, one
     can infer that
     (Rigorous) (Skill 6.6)

     A. The painting was
         expensive.
     B. The painting was
         cheap.
     C. Mr. Smith was
         considering purchasing
         the painting.
     D. Mr. Smith thought the
         painting was too
         expensive and decided
         not to purchase it.

Answer Key: Reading

1.	C		21.	D
2.	C		22.	D
3.	B		23.	D
4.	B		24.	C
5.	B		25.	C
6.	D		26.	C
7.	B		27.	D
8.	B		28.	A
9.	A		29.	D
10.	A		30.	B
11.	D		31.	B
12.	A		32.	D
13.	C		33.	A
14.	A		34.	A
15.	D		35.	C
16.	C		36.	D
17.	A		37.	B
18.	A		38.	A
19.	B		39.	B
20.	C		40.	A

Rigor Table: Reading

	Easy 20%	Average 40%	Rigorous 40%
Questions (40)	6, 11, 13, 14, 17, 24, 25, 28	1, 2, 5, 12, 18, 19, 20, 22, 23, 29, 31, 32, 35, 37, 38, 39	3, 4, 7, 8, 9, 10, 15, 16, 21, 26, 27, 30, 33, 34, 36, 40
TOTALS	8 (20.0%)	16 (40.0%)	16 (40.0%)

Rationales with Sample Questions: Reading

Read the following paragraph, and answer the questions that follow.

This writer has often been asked to tutor hospitalized children with cystic fibrosis. While undergoing all the precautionary measures to see these children (i.e. scrubbing thoroughly and donning sterilized protective gear for the child's protection), she has often wondered why their parents subject these children to the pressures of schooling and trying to catch up on what they have missed because of hospitalization, which is a normal part of cystic fibrosis patients' lives. These children undergo so many tortuous treatments a day that it seems cruel to expect them to learn as normal children do, especially with their life expectancies being as short as they are.

• 1.   **What is the main idea of this passage?**
        (Average Rigor) (Skill 5.1)

        A.   There is much preparation involved in visiting a patient with cystic fibrosis.
        B.   Children with cystic fibrosis are incapable of living normal lives.
        C.   Certain concessions should be made for children with cystic fibrosis.
        D.   Children with cystic fibrosis die young.

Answer: C. Certain concessions should be made for children with cystic fibrosis.

The correct answer is C. The author states that she wonders, "why parents subject these children to the pressures of schooling" and that "it seems cruel to expect them to learn as normal children do." In making these statements, she appears to be expressing the belief that these children should not have to do what "normal" children do. They have enough to deal with— their illness itself.

2.   **What is the author's purpose?**
      (Average Rigor) (Skill 5.1)

      A.   To inform
      B.   To entertain
      C.   To describe
      D.   To narrate

Answer: C. To describe

The correct answer is C. The author is simply describing her experience in working with children with cystic fibrosis.

3. **What type of organizational pattern is the author using?**
   (Rigorous) (Skill 5.3)

   A. Classification
   B. Explanation
   C. Comparison and contrast
   D. Cause and effect

Answer: B. Explanation

The correct answer is B. The author mentions tutoring children with cystic fibrosis in her opening sentence and goes on to "explain" some of the issues that are involved with her job.

4. **What kind of relationship is found within the last sentence, which starts with "These children undergo..." and ends with "...as short as they are"?**
   (Rigorous) (Skill 5.3)

   A. Comparison and Contrast
   B. Statement Support
   C. Spatial/Place
   D. Classification

Answer: B. Statement Support

The correct answer is B. In mentioning that their life expectancies are short, she supports her belief that it is cruel to expect them to learn as normal children do.

5. **What is meant by the word "precautionary" in the second sentence?**
   (Average Rigor) (Skill 5.6)

   A. Careful
   B. Protective
   C. Medical
   D. Sterilizing

Answer: B. Protective

The correct answer is B. The writer uses expressions such as "protective gear" and "child's protection" to emphasize this.

6.	How is the author so familiar with the procedures used when visiting a child with cystic fibrosis?
(Easy) (Skill 6.1)

	A.	She has read about it.
	B.	She works in a hospital.
	C.	She is the parent of one.
	D.	She often tutors them.

Answer: D. She often tutors them.

The correct answer is D. The writer states this fact in the opening sentence.

7.	Does the author present an argument that is valid or invalid concerning the schooling of children with cystic fibrosis?
(Rigorous) (Skill 6.1)

	A.	Valid
	B.	Invalid

Answer: B. Invalid

The correct answer is B. Even though the writer's argument makes good sense to most readers, it is biased and it lacks real evidence.

8.	The author states that it is "cruel" to expect children with cystic fibrosis to learn as "normal" children do. Is this a fact or an opinion?
(Rigorous) (Skill 6.3)

	A.	Fact
	B.	Opinion

Answer: B. Opinion

The correct answer is B. The fact that she states that it "seems" cruel indicates there is no evidence to support this belief.

9. **What is the author's tone?**
    (Rigorous) (Skill 6.5)

    A. Sympathetic
    B. Cruel
    C. Disbelieving
    D. Cheerful

Answer: A. Sympathetic

The correct answer is A. The author states that "it seems cruel to expect them to learn as normal children do," thereby indicating that she feels sorry for them.

10. **Is there evidence of bias in this paragraph?**
    (Rigorous) (Skill 6.5)

    A. Yes
    B. No

Answer: A. Yes

The correct answer is A. The writer clearly feels sorry for these children and gears her writing in that direction.

Read the following passage, and answer the questions that follow.

Disciplinary practices have been found to affect diverse areas of child development, such as the acquisition of moral values, obedience to authority, and performance at school. Even though the dictionary has a specific definition of the word "discipline," it is still open to interpretation by people of different cultures.

There are four types of disciplinary styles: assertion of power, withdrawal of love, reasoning, and permissiveness. Assertion of power involves the use of force to discourage unwanted behavior. Withdrawal of love involves making the love of a parent conditional on a child's good behavior. Reasoning involves persuading the child to behave one way rather than another. Permissiveness involves allowing the child to do as he or she pleases and face the consequences of his/her actions.

11.   **What is the author's purpose in writing this?**
       (Easy) (Skill 5.1)

       A.   To describe
       B.   To narrate
       C.   To entertain
       D.   To inform

Answer: D. To inform

The correct answer is D. The author is providing the reader with information about disciplinary practices.

12.   **What is the main idea of this passage?**
       (Average Rigor) (Skill 5.1)

       A.   Different people have different ideas of what discipline is.
       B.   Permissiveness is the most widely used disciplinary style.
       C.   Most people agree on their definition of discipline.
       D.   There are four disciplinary styles.

Answer: A. Different people have different ideas of what discipline is.

The correct answer is A. Choice C is not true; the opposite is stated in the passage. Choice B could be true, but we have no evidence of this. Choice D is just one of the many facts listed in the passage.

13.   Name the four types of disciplinary styles.
         (Easy) (Skill 5.2)

     A.   Reasoning, power assertion, morality, and permissiveness
     B.   Morality, reasoning, permissiveness, and withdrawal of love
     C.   Withdrawal of love, permissiveness, assertion of power, and reasoning
     D.   Permissiveness, morality, reasoning, and power assertion

Answer: C. Withdrawal of love, permissiveness, assertion of power, and reasoning.

The correct answer is C. This is directly stated in the second paragraph.

14.   What does the technique of reasoning involve?
         (Easy) (Skill 5.2)

     A.   Persuading the child to behave in a certain way
     B.   Allowing the child to do as he/she pleases
     C.   Using force to discourage unwanted behavior
     D.   Making love conditional on good behavior

Answer: A. Persuading the child to behave in a certain way.

The correct answer is A. This fact is directly stated in the second paragraph.

• 15.   What organizational structure is used in the first sentence of the second paragraph?
         (Rigorous) (Skill 5.3)

     A.   Addition
     B.   Cause and effect
     C.   Clarification
     D.   Example

Answer: D. Example

The correct answer is D. The author simply states and gives examples of the types of disciplinary styles.

16. **What is the overall organizational pattern of this passage?**
(Rigorous) (Skill 5.3)

    A.   Statement Support
    B.   Cause and effect
    C.   Classification
    D.   Summary

Answer: C. Classification

The correct answer is C. The author has taken a subject, in this case discipline, and developed it point by point.

17. **What is the meaning of the word "diverse" in the first sentence?**
(Easy) (Skill 5.6)

    A.   Many
    B.   Related to children
    C.   Disciplinary
    D.   Moral

Answer: A. Many

The correct answer is A. Any of the other choices would be redundant in this sentence.

18. **The author states "assertion of power involves the use of force to discourage unwanted behavior." Is this a fact or an opinion?**
(Average Rigor) (Skill 6.3)

    A.   Fact
    B.   Opinion

Answer: A. Fact

The correct answer is A. The author appears to have done extensive research on this subject.

19.   Is this passage biased?
       (Average Rigor) (Skill 6.5)

       A.   Yes
       B.   No

Answer: B. No

The correct answer is B. If the reader were so inclined, he could research discipline and find this information.

20.   **What is the author's tone?**
       (Average Rigor) (Skill 6.5)

       A.   Disbelieving
       B.   Angry
       C.   Informative
       D.   Optimistic

Answer: C. Informative

The correct answer is C. The author appears to be simply stating the facts.

21.   **From reading this passage, we can conclude that**
       (Rigorous) (Skill 6.6)

       A.   The author is a teacher.
       B.   The author has many children.
       C.   The author has written a book about discipline.
       D.   The author has done a lot of research on discipline.

Answer: D. The author has done a lot of research on discipline.

The correct answer is D. Given all the facts mentioned in the passage, this is the only inference one can make.

Read the following passage, and answer the questions that follow.

One of the most difficult problems plaguing American education is the assessment of teachers. No one denies that teachers should be answerable for what they do, but what exactly does that mean? The Oxford American Dictionary defines accountability as the obligation to give a reckoning or explanation for one's actions.

Does a student have to learn for teaching to have taken place? Historically, teaching has not been defined in this restrictive manner; the teacher was thought to be responsible for the quantity and quality of material covered and the way in which it was presented. However, some definitions of teaching now imply that students must learn in order for teaching to have taken place.

As a teacher who tries my best to keep current on all the latest teaching strategies, I believe that those teachers who do not bother even to pick up an educational journal every once in a while should be kept under close watch. There are many teachers out there who have been teaching for decades and who refuse to change their ways even if research has proven that their methods are outdated and ineffective. There is no place in the profession of teaching for these types of individuals. It is time that the American educational system clean house, for the sake of our children.

22. **What is the main idea of the passage?**
    (Average Rigor) (Skill 5.1)

    A. Teachers should not be answerable for what they do.
    B. Teachers who do not do their job should be fired.
    C. The author is a good teacher.
    D. Assessment of teachers is a serious problem in society today.

Answer: D. Assessment of teachers is a serious problem in society today.

The correct answer is D. Most of the passage is dedicated to elaborating on why teacher assessment is such a problem.

23. **What is the author's purpose in writing this?**
(Average Rigor) (Skill 5.1)

    A.   To entertain
    B.   To narrate
    C.   To describe
    D.   To persuade

Answer: D. To persuade

The correct answer is D. The author does some describing, but the majority of her statements seem to be geared towards convincing the reader that teachers who are lazy or who do not keep current should be fired.

24. **Where does the author get her definition of "accountability"?**
(Easy) (Skill 5.2)

    A.   Webster's Dictionary
    B.   Encyclopedia Britannica
    C.   Oxford Dictionary
    D.   World Book Encyclopedia

Answer: C. Oxford Dictionary

The correct answer is C. This is directly stated in the third sentence of the first paragraph.

25. **The author states that teacher assessment is a problem for**
(Easy) (Skill 5.2)

    A.   Elementary schools
    B.   Secondary schools
    C.   American education
    D.   Families

Answer: C. Oxford Dictionary

26.   **What is the author's overall organizational pattern?**
        (Rigorous) (Skill 5.3)

      A.   Classification
      B.   Cause and effect
      C.   Definition
      D.   Comparison and contrast

~~Answer: C. Definition~~

The correct answer is C. The author identifies teacher assessment as a problem and spends the rest of the passage defining why it is considered a problem.

27.   **What is the organizational pattern of the second paragraph?**
        (Rigorous) (Skill 5.3)

      A.   Cause and effect
      B.   Classification
      C.   Sequence of Events
      D.   Explanation

Answer: D. Explanation

The correct answer is D. The author goes on to explain further what she meant by "...what exactly does that mean?" in the first paragraph.

28.   **What is meant by the word "plaguing" in the first sentence?**
        (Easy) (Skill 5.6)

      A.   Causing problems
      B.   Causing illness
      C.   Causing anger
      D.   Causing failure

Answer: A. Causing problems

The correct answer is A. The first paragraph makes this definition clear.

29. **What is the meaning of the word "reckoning" in the third sentence?**
(Average Rigor) (Skill 5.6)

    A.   Thought
    B.   Answer
    C.   Obligation
    D.   Explanation

Answer: D. Explanation

The correct answer is D. The meaning of this word is directly stated in the same sentence.

30. **Is this a valid argument?**
(Rigorous) (Skill 6.1)

    A.   Yes
    B.   No

Answer: B. No

The correct answer is B. In the third paragraph, the author appears to be resentful of lazy teachers.

31. **Teachers who do not keep current on educational trends should be fired. Is this a fact or an opinion?**
(Average Rigor) (Skill 6.3)

    A.   Fact
    B.   Opinion

Answer: B. Opinion

The correct answer is B. There may be those who feel they can be good teachers by using old methods.

32. **The author's tone is one of**
(Average Rigor) (Skill 6.5)

    A.   Disbelief
    B.   Excitement
    C.   Support
    D.   Concern

Answer: D. Concern

The correct answer is D. The author appears concerned with the future of education.

33. **Is there evidence of bias in this passage?**
(Rigorous) (Skill 6.5)

    A.   Yes
    B.   No

Answer: A. Yes

The correct answer is A. The entire third paragraph is the author's opinion on the matter.

34. **From the passage, one can infer that**
(Rigorous) (Skill 6.6)

    A.   The author considers herself a good teacher.
    B.   Poor teachers will be fired.
    C.   Students have to learn for teaching to take place.
    D.   The author will be fired.

Answer: A. The author considers herself a good teacher.

The correct answer is A. The first sentence of the third paragraph alludes to this.

Read the following paragraph, and answer the questions that follow.

Mr. Smith gave instructions for the painting to be hung on the wall. Then, it leaped forth before his eyes: the little cottages on the river, the white clouds floating over the valley, and the green of the towering mountain ranges that were seen in the distance. The painting was so vivid that it seemed almost real. Mr. Smith was now certain that the painting had been worth money.

35. **What is the main idea of this passage?**
(Average Rigor) (Skill 5.1)

   A.   The painting that Mr. Smith purchased is expensive.
   B.   Mr. Smith purchased a painting.
   C.   Mr. Smith was pleased with the quality of the painting he had purchased.
   D.   The painting depicted cottages and valleys.

Answer: C. Mr. Smith was pleased with the quality of the painting he had purchased.

The correct answer is C. Every sentence in the paragraph alludes to this fact.

36. **The author's purpose is to**
(Rigorous) (Skill 5.1)

   A.   Inform
   B.   Entertain
   C.   Persuade
   D.   Narrate

Answer: D. Narrate

The correct answer is D. The author is simply narrating or telling the story of Mr. Smith and his painting.

37.   **What does the author mean by the expression "it leaped forth before his eyes"?**
      (Average Rigor) (Skill 5.6)

      A.   The painting fell off the wall.
      B.   The painting appeared so real it was almost three-dimensional.
      C.   The painting struck Mr. Smith in the face.
      D.   Mr. Smith was hallucinating.

Answer: B. The painting appeared so real it was almost three-dimensional.

The correct answer is B. This is almost directly stated in the third sentence.

38.   **What is the meaning of the word "vivid" in the third sentence?**
      (Average Rigor) (Skill 5.6)

      A.   Lifelike
      B.   Dark
      C.   Expensive
      D.   Big

Answer: A. Lifelike

The correct answer is A. The second half of the same sentence reinforces this.

39.   **Is this passage biased?**
      (Average Rigor) (Skill 6.5)

      A.   Yes
      B.   No

Answer: B. No

The correct answer is B. The author appears to be just telling what happened when Mr. Smith had his new painting hung on the wall.

40. **From the last sentence, one can infer that**
    (Rigorous) (Skill 6.6)

    A.   The painting was expensive.
    B.   The painting was cheap.
    C.   Mr. Smith was considering purchasing the painting.
    D.   Mr. Smith thought the painting was too expensive and decided not to purchase it.

Answer: A. The painting was expensive.

The correct answer is A. Choice B is incorrect because, had the painting been cheap, chances are that Mr. Smith would not have considered his purchase. Choices C and D are ruled out by the fact that the painting had already been purchased. The author makes this clear when she says, "...the painting had been worth the money."

SUBAREA III. **MATHEMATICS**

COMPETENCY 7.0   CONCEPTUAL KNOWLEDGE

Skill 7.1   Understand the foundational ideas of numbers, number properties, and operations defined on numbers (whole numbers, fractions, and decimals).

Rational numbers can be expressed as the ratio of two integers, $\frac{a}{b}$ where b ≠ 0, for example $\frac{2}{3}, -\frac{4}{5}, 5 = \frac{5}{1}$.

The rational numbers include integers, fractions and mixed numbers, and terminating and repeating decimals. Every rational number can be expressed as a repeating or terminating decimal and can be shown on a number line.

Integers are positive and negative whole numbers and zero.

...−6, −5, −4, −3, −2, −1, 0, 1, 2, 3, 4, 5, 6,...

Whole numbers are natural numbers and zero.

0, 1, 2, 3, 4, 5, 6...

Natural numbers are the counting numbers.

1, 2, 3, 4, 5, 6...

Irrational numbers are real numbers that cannot be written as the ratio of two integers. These are infinite non-repeating decimals.

Examples: $\sqrt{5} = 2.2360$,   pi = π = 3.1415927...

A **fraction** is an expression of numbers in the form of x/y, where **x** is the numerator and **y** is the denominator, which cannot be zero.

Example: $\frac{3}{7}$ 3 is the numerator; 7 is the denominator

If the fraction has common factors for the numerator and denominator, divide both by the common factor to reduce the fraction to its lowest form.

Example:

$$\frac{13}{39} = \frac{1 \times 13}{3 \times 13} = \frac{1}{3}$$ Divide by the common factor 13

A **mixed** number has an integer part and a fractional part.

Example: $2\frac{1}{4}, \ -5\frac{1}{6}, \ 7\frac{1}{3}$

Percent = per 100 (written with the symbol %). Thus, $10\% = \frac{10}{100} = \frac{1}{10}$.

Decimals = deci = part of ten. To find the decimal equivalent of a fraction, use the denominator to divide the numerator, as shown in the following example.

Example: Find the decimal equivalent of $\frac{7}{10}$.

Since 10 cannot divide into 7 evenly,

$$\frac{7}{10} = 0.7$$

Skill 7.2   Demonstrate an understanding of order among whole numbers, fractions, and decimals.

For example:

Symbol for inequality: In the symbols > (greater than) or < (less than), the open side of the symbol always faces the larger of the two numbers, and the point of the symbol always faces the smaller number.

Example: Compare 15 and 20 on the number line.

Since 20 is further away from the zero than 15 is, 20 is greater than 15, or 20 > 15.

Example: Compare $\dfrac{3}{7}$ and $\dfrac{5}{10}$.

To compare fractions, they should have the same least common denominator (LCD). The LCD in this example is 70.

$$\frac{3}{7} = \frac{3 \times 10}{7 \times 10} = \frac{30}{70} \qquad\qquad \frac{5}{10} = \frac{5 \times 7}{10 \times 7} = \frac{35}{70}$$

Since the denominators are equal, compare only the numerators. $30 < 35$, so:

$$\frac{3}{7} < \frac{5}{10}$$

Skill 7.3 **Demonstrate an understanding that a number can be represented in more than one way.**

The **exponent form** is a shortcut method to write repeated multiplication. Basic form: b^n, where b is called the base and n is the exponent. b and n are both real numbers. b^n implies that the base b is multiplied by itself n times.

Examples: $3^4 = 3 \times 3 \times 3 \times 3 = 81$

$2^3 = 2 \times 2 \times 2 = 8$

$(-2)^4 = (-2) \times (-2) \times (-2) \times (-2) = 16$

$-2^4 = -(2 \times 2 \times 2 \times 2) = -16$

Key exponent rules:

For 'a' nonzero, and 'm' and 'n' real numbers:

1) $a^m \cdot a^n = a^{(m+n)}$ Product rule

2) $\dfrac{a^m}{a^n} = a^{(m-n)}$ Quotient rule

3) $\dfrac{a^{-m}}{a^{-n}} = \dfrac{a^n}{a^m}$

When 10 is raised to any power, the exponent tells the numbers of zeroes in the product.

Example: $10^7 = 10,000,000$

Caution: Unless the negative sign is inside the parentheses and the exponent is outside the parentheses, the exponent does not affect the sign.

$(-2)^4$ implies that -2 is multiplied by itself 4 times.

-2^4 implies that 2 is multiplied by itself 4 times, and then the answer becomes negative.

Scientific notation is a more convenient method for writing very large and very small numbers. It employs two factors. The first factor is a number between 1 and 10. The second factor is a power of 10. This notation is "shorthand" for expressing large numbers (such as the weight of 100 elephants) or small numbers (such as the weight of an atom in pounds).

Recall that:

$10^n = (10)^n$ Ten multiplied by itself n times.

$10^0 = 1$ Any nonzero number raised to power of zero is 1.

$10^1 = 10$

$10^2 = 10 \times 10 = 100$

$10^3 = 10 \times 10 \times 10 = 1000$ (kilo)

$10^{-1} = 1/10$ (deci)

$10^{-2} = 1/100$ (centi)

$10^{-3} = 1/1000$ (milli)

$10^{-6} = 1/1,000,000$ (micro)

Example: Write 46,368,000 in scientific notation.

1)   Introduce a decimal point and decimal places.

        46,368,000 = 46,368,000.0000

2)   Make a mark between the two digits that give a number between

        −9.9 and 9.9.
        4 ∧ 6,368,000.0000

3)   Count the number of digit places between the decimal point and the ∧ mark. This number is the nth power of ten.

        So, $46,368,000 = 4.6368 \times 10^7$

Example: Write 0.00397 in scientific notation.

1)   Decimal place is already in place.

2)   Make a mark between 3 and 9 to obtain one number between −9.9 and 9.9.

3)   Move decimal place to the mark (3 hops).

0.003 ∧ 97

Motion is to the right, so n of 10^n is negative.

Therefore, $0.00397 = 3.97 \times 10^{-3}$

Converting decimals, fractions, and percents

A **decimal** can be converted to a **percent** by multiplying by 100 or by merely moving the decimal point two places to the right. A **percent** can be converted to a **decimal** by dividing by 100 or by moving the decimal point two places to the left.

Examples: 0.375 = 37.5%
             0.7 = 70%
             0.04 = 4%
             3.15 = 315%
             84% = 0.84
             3% = 0.03
             60% = 0.6
             110% = 1.1
             $\frac{1}{2}$% = 0.5% = 0.005

A **percent** can be converted to a **fraction** by placing it over 100 and reducing to simplest terms.

Example: Convert 0.056 to a fraction.

Multiply 0.056 by $\frac{1000}{1000}$ to get rid of the decimal point:

$$0.056 \times \frac{1000}{1000} = \frac{56}{1000} = \frac{7}{125}$$

Example: Find 23% of 1000.

$$= \frac{23}{100} \times \frac{1000}{1} = 23 \times 10 = 230$$

Example: Convert 6.25% to a decimal and to a fraction.

$$6.25\% = 0.0625 = 0.0625 \times \frac{10000}{10000} = \frac{625}{10000} = \frac{1}{16}$$

An example of a type of problem involving fractions is the conversion of recipes. For example, if a recipe serves eight people and we want to make enough to serve only four, we must determine how much of each ingredient to use. The conversion factor, the number we multiply each ingredient by, is:

$$\text{Conversion Factor} = \frac{\text{Number of Servings Needed}}{\text{Number of Servings in Recipe}}$$

Example: Consider the following recipe.

3 cups flour
$\frac{1}{2}$ tsp. baking powder
2/3 cups butter
2 cups sugar
2 eggs

If the above recipe serves 8, how much of each ingredient do we need to serve only 4 people?

First, determine the conversion factor.

$$\text{Conversion Factor} = \frac{4}{8} = \frac{1}{2}$$

Next, multiply each ingredient by the conversion factor.

$3 \times \frac{1}{2} =$ $\quad\quad$ $1\frac{1}{2}$ cups flour

$\frac{1}{2} \times \frac{1}{2} =$ $\quad\quad$ $\frac{1}{4}$ tsp. baking powder

$\frac{2}{3} \times \frac{1}{2} = \frac{2}{6} =$ $\quad\quad$ $\frac{1}{3}$ cups butter

$2 \times \frac{1}{2} =$ $\quad\quad$ 1 cup sugar

$2 \times \frac{1}{2} =$ $\quad\quad$ 1 egg

Skill 7.4 Demonstrate an understanding of how numbers are named, place value, and order of magnitude of numbers.

Whole Number Place Value

Consider the number 792. We can assign a place value to each digit.

Reading from left to right, the first digit (7) represents the hundreds place. The hundreds place tells us how many sets of one hundred the number contains. Thus, there are seven sets of one hundred in the number 792.

The second digit (9) represents the tens place. The tens place tells us how many sets of ten the number contains. Thus, there are nine sets of ten in the number 792.

The last digit (2) represents the ones place. The ones place tells us how many ones the number contains. Thus, there are two sets of one in the number 792.

Therefore, there are seven sets of 100, plus nine sets of 10, plus two ones in the number 792.

Decimal Place Value

More complex numbers have additional place values to both the left and right of the decimal point. Consider the number 374.8.

Reading from left to right, the first digit (3) is in the hundreds place and tells us the number contains three sets of one hundred.

The second digit (7) is in the tens place and tells us the number contains seven sets of ten.

The third digit, 4, is in the ones place and tells us the number contains four ones.

Finally, the number after the decimal (8) is in the tenths place and tells us the number contains eight tenths.

Skill 7.5 Demonstrate an understanding of the properties of the basic operations.

Properties are rules that apply for addition, subtraction, multiplication, or division of real numbers. These properties are:

Commutative: You can change the order of the terms or factors as follows:

For addition: $a + b = b + a$
For multiplication: $ab = ba$

Since addition is the inverse operation of subtraction and multiplication is the inverse operation of division, subtraction and division do not need separate laws.

Example: $5 + -8 = -8 + 5 = -3$

Example: $-2 \times 6 = 6 \times -2 = -12$

Associative: You can regroup the terms as you like.

For addition: $a + (b + c) = (a + b) + c$
For multiplication: $a(bc) = (ab)c$

This rule does not apply for division and subtraction.

Example: $(-2 + 7) + 5 = -2 + (7 + 5)$
$5 + 5 = -2 + 12 = 10$

Example: $(3 \times -7) \times 5 = 3 \times (-7 \times 5)$
$-21 \times 5 = 3 \times -35 = -105$

Identity: Finding a number so that when added to a term results in that number (additive identity); finding a number such that when multiplied by a term results in that number (multiplicative identity).

For addition: $a + 0 = a$ (zero is additive identity)
For multiplication: $a \cdot 1 = a$ (one is multiplicative)

Example: $17 + 0 = 17$

Example: $-34 \times 1 = -34$
The product of any number and one is that number.

Inverse: Finding a number such that when added to the number it results in zero or when multiplied by the number results in 1.

For addition: $a + (-a) = 0$
For multiplication: $a \cdot (1/a) = 1$

$(-a)$ is the additive inverse of a; $1/a$, also called the reciprocal, is the multiplicative inverse of a.

Example: $25 + -25 = 0$

Example: $5 \times \dfrac{1}{5} = 1$ The product of any number and its reciprocal is one.

Distributive: This technique allows us to operate on terms applied to parentheses without first performing operations within the parentheses. This is especially helpful when we cannot combine terms within the parentheses.

$a (b + c) = ab + ac$

Example: $6 \times (-4 + 9) = (6 \times -4) + (6 \times 9)$
$6 \times 5 = -24 + 54 = 30$

To multiply a sum by a number, multiply each addend by the number, then add the products.

Follow **the Order of Operations** when evaluating algebraic expressions. Follow these steps in order:

1. Simplify inside grouping characters such as parentheses, brackets, square root, fraction bar, etc.

2. Multiply out expressions with exponents.

3. Do multiplication or division, from left to right.

4. Do addition or subtraction, from left to right.

Example: $3^3 - 5(b + 2)$

$= 3^3 - 5b - 10$

$= 27 - 5b - 10 = 17 - 5b$

Example: $2 - 4 \times 2^3 - 2(4 - 2 \times 3)$

$= 2 - 4 \times 2^3 - 2(4 - 6) = 2 - 4 \times 2^3 - 2(-2)$

$= 2 - 4 \times 2^3 + 4 = 2 - 4 \times 8 + 4$

$= 2 - 32 + 4 = 6 - 32 = -26$

COMPETENCY 8.0   PROCEDURAL KNOWLEDGE

Skill 8.1   Perform computations and identify numbers or information or operations needed to solve a problem.

Addition of whole numbers

Example: At the end of a day of shopping, a shopper had $24 remaining in his wallet. He spent $45 on various goods. How much money did the shopper have at the beginning of the day?

The total amount of money the shopper started with is the sum of the amount spent and the amount remaining at the end of the day.

$$
\begin{array}{r}
24 \\
+\ 45 \\
\hline
69
\end{array}
$$
→   The original total was $69.

Example: A race took the winner 1 hr. 58 min. 12 sec. on the first half of the race and 2 hr. 9 min. 57 sec. on the second half of the race. How much time did the entire race take?

$$
\begin{array}{r}
1 \text{ hr. } 58 \text{ min. } 12 \text{ sec.} \\
+\ 2 \text{ hr. }\ \ 9 \text{ min. } 57 \text{ sec.} \\
\hline
3 \text{ hr. } 67 \text{ min. } 69 \text{ sec.} \\
+\ 1 \text{ min–60 sec.}
\end{array}
$$
   Add these numbers

   Change 60 seconds to 1 min.

$$
\begin{array}{r}
3 \text{ hr. }\ 68 \text{ min. }\ 9 \text{ sec.} \\
+\ 1 \text{ hr.–60 min.} \\
\hline
4 \text{ hr. }\ \ \ 8 \text{ min. }\ 9 \text{ sec.}
\end{array}
$$
   Change 60 minutes to 1 hr.

←final answer

Subtraction of Whole Numbers

Example: At the end of his shift, a cashier has $96 in the cash register. At the beginning of his shift, he had $15. How much money did the cashier collect during his shift?

The total collected is the difference of the ending amount and the starting amount.

$$
\begin{array}{r}
96 \\
-\ 15 \\
\hline
81
\end{array}
$$
→   The total collected was $81.

Multiplication of whole numbers

Multiplication is one of the four basic number operations. In simple terms, multiplication is the addition of a number to itself a certain number of times. For example, 4 multiplied by 3 is equal to 4 + 4 + 4 or 3 + 3 + 3 +3. Another way of conceptualizing multiplication is to think in terms of groups. For example, if we have 4 groups of 3 students, the total number of students is 4 multiplied by 3. We call the solution to a multiplication problem the product.

The basic algorithm for whole number multiplication begins with aligning the numbers by place value with the number containing more places on top.

$$\begin{array}{r} 172 \\ \times\ \ 43 \end{array} \longrightarrow$$ Note that we placed 172 on top because it has more places than 43 does.

Next, we multiply the ones place of the second number by each place value of the top number sequentially.

$$\begin{array}{r} (2) \\ 172 \\ \times\ \ 43 \\ \hline 516 \end{array} \longrightarrow$$ {3 x 2 = 6, 3 x 7 = 21, 3 x 1 = 3}
Note that we had to carry a 2 to the hundreds column because 3 x 7 = 21. Note also that we add, not multiply, carried numbers to the product.

Next, we multiply the number in the tens place of the second number by each place value of the top number sequentially. Because we are multiplying by a number in the tens place, we place a zero at the end of this product.

$$\begin{array}{r} (2) \\ 172 \\ \times\ \ 43 \\ \hline 516 \\ 6880 \end{array} \longrightarrow$$ {4 x 2 = 8, 4 x 7 = 28, 4 x 1 = 4}

Finally, to determine the final product, we add the two partial products.

$$\begin{array}{r} 172 \\ \times\ \ 43 \\ \hline 516 \\ +\ 6880 \\ \hline 7396 \end{array} \longrightarrow$$ The product of 172 and 43 is 7396.

Example: A student buys 4 boxes of crayons. Each box contains 16 crayons. How many total crayons does the student have?

The total number of crayons is 16 x 4.

$$
\begin{array}{r}
16 \\
\times\ 4 \\
\hline
64
\end{array}
$$

→ Total number of crayons equals 64.

Division of whole numbers

Division, the inverse of multiplication, is another of the four basic number operations. When we divide one number by another, we determine how many times we can multiply the divisor (number divided by) before we exceed the number we are dividing (dividend). For example, 8 divided by 2 equals 4 because we can multiply 2 four times to reach 8 (2 x 4 = 8 or 2 + 2 + 2 + 2 = 8). Using the grouping conceptualization we used with multiplication, we can divide 8 into 4 groups of 2 or 2 groups of 4. We call the answer to a division problem the quotient.

If the divisor does not divide evenly into the dividend, we express the leftover amount either as a remainder or as a fraction with the divisor as the denominator. For example, 9 divided by 2 equals 4 with a remainder of 1 or $4\frac{1}{2}$.

The basic algorithm for division is long division. We start by representing the quotient as follows:

$14\overline{)293}$ → 14 is the divisor and 293 is the dividend.

This represents 293 ÷ 14.

Next, we divide the divisor into the dividend starting from the left.

$14\overline{)293}^{\,2}$ → 14 divides into 29 two times with a remainder.

Next, we multiply the partial quotient by the divisor, subtract this value from the first digits of the dividend, and bring down the remaining dividend digits to complete the number.

$$
\begin{array}{r}
2 \\
14\overline{)293} \\
-28 \\
\hline
13
\end{array}
$$

$\longrightarrow$ 2 x 14 = 28, 29 – 28 = 1 and bringing down the 3 yields 13.

Finally, we divide again (the divisor into the remaining value) and repeat the preceding process. The number left after the subtraction represents the remainder.

$$
\begin{array}{r}
20 \\
14\overline{)293} \\
-28 \\
\hline
13 \\
-0 \\
\hline
13
\end{array}
$$

$\longrightarrow$ The final quotient is 20 with a remainder of 13. We can also represent this quotient as $20\frac{13}{14}$.

Example: Each box of apples contains 24 apples. How many boxes must a grocer purchase to supply a group of 252 people with one apple each?

The grocer needs 252 apples. Because he must buy apples in groups of 24, we divide 252 by 24 to determine how many boxes he needs to buy.

$$
\begin{array}{r}
10 \\
24\overline{)252} \\
-24 \\
\hline
12 \\
-0 \\
\hline
12
\end{array}
$$

$\longrightarrow$ The quotient is 10 with a remainder of 12.

Thus, the grocer needs 10 boxes plus 12 more apples. Therefore, the minimum number of boxes the grocer can purchase is 11.

Example: At his job, John gets paid $20 for every hour he works. If John made $940 in a week, how many hours did he work?

This is a division problem. To determine the number of hours John worked, we divide the total amount made ($940) by the hourly rate of pay ($20). Thus, the number of hours worked equals 940 divided by 20.

$$\begin{array}{r} 47 \\ 20\overline{)940} \\ -80 \\ \hline 140 \\ -140 \\ \hline 0 \end{array}$$

⟶ 20 divides into 940, 47 times with no remainder.

John worked 47 hours.

Addition and Subtraction of Decimals

When adding and subtracting decimals, we align the numbers by place value as we do with whole numbers. After adding or subtracting each column, we bring the decimal down, placing it in the same location as in the numbers added or subtracted.

Example: Find the sum of 152.3 and 36.342.

$$\begin{array}{r} 152.300 \\ +\ \ 36.342 \\ \hline 188.642 \end{array}$$

Note that we placed two zeroes after the final place value in 152.3 to clarify the column addition.

Example: Find the difference of 152.3 and 36.342.

$$\begin{array}{r} 2\ 9\ 10 \\ 152.300 \\ -\ \ 36.342 \\ \hline 58 \end{array} \quad \longrightarrow \quad \begin{array}{r} (4)11(12) \\ 152.300 \\ -\ \ 36.342 \\ \hline 115.958 \end{array}$$

Note how we borrowed to subtract from the zeroes in the hundredths and thousandths places of 152.300.

Multiplication of Decimals

When multiplying decimal numbers, we multiply exactly as with whole numbers and place the decimal in from the left the total number of decimal places contained in the two numbers multiplied. For example, when multiplying 1.5 and 2.35, we place the decimal in the product 3 places in from the left (3.525).

Example: Find the product of 3.52 and 4.1.

$$
\begin{array}{r}
3.52 \\
\times\ 4.1 \\
\hline
352 \\
+\ 14080 \\
\hline
14432
\end{array}
$$

3.52 ⟶ Note that there are three total decimal places in the two numbers.

14432 ⟶ We place the decimal three places in from the left.

Thus, the final product is 14.432.

Example: A shopper has 5 one-dollar bills, 6 quarters, 3 nickels, and 4 pennies in his pocket. How much money does he have?

$$
5 \times \$1.00 = \$5.00 \qquad
\begin{array}{r}
\overset{3}{\$0.25} \\
\times\ 6 \\
\hline
\$1.50
\end{array}
\qquad
\begin{array}{r}
\$0.05 \\
\times\ 3 \\
\hline
\$0.15
\end{array}
\qquad
\begin{array}{r}
\$0.01 \\
\times\ 4 \\
\hline
\$0.04
\end{array}
$$

Note the placement of the decimals in the multiplication products. Thus, the total amount of money in the shopper's pocket is:

$$
\begin{array}{r}
\$5.00 \\
1.50 \\
0.15 \\
+\ 0.04 \\
\hline
\$6.69
\end{array}
$$

Division of Decimals

When dividing decimal numbers, we first remove the decimal in the divisor by moving the decimal in the dividend the same number of spaces to the right. For example, when dividing 1.45 into 5.3 we convert the numbers to 145 and 530 and perform normal whole number division.

Example: Find the quotient of 5.3 divided by 1.45.
Convert to 145 and 530.

Divide.

$$\begin{array}{r} 3 \\ 145\overline{)530} \\ -435 \\ \hline 95 \end{array}$$ $\longrightarrow$ $$\begin{array}{r} 3.65 \\ 145\overline{)530} \\ -435 \\ \hline 950 \\ -870 \\ \hline 800 \end{array}$$ $\longrightarrow$ Note that we insert the decimal to continue division.

Because one of the numbers divided contained one decimal place, we round the quotient to one decimal place. Thus, the final quotient is 3.7.

Addition and subtraction of fractions

GCF is the abbreviation for the **greatest common factor**. The GCF is the largest number that is a factor of all the numbers given in a problem. The GCF can be no larger than the smallest number given in the problem. If no other number is a common factor, then the GCF will be the number 1.

To find the GCF, list all possible factors of the smallest number given (include the number itself). Starting with the largest factor (which is the number itself), determine if it is also a factor of all the other given numbers. If so, that is the GCF. If that factor doesn't work, try the same method on the next smaller factor. Continue until a common factor is found. That is the GCF. Note: There can be other common factors besides the GCF.

Example: Find the GCF of 12, 20, and 36.

The smallest number in the problem is 12. The factors of 12 are 1, 2, 3, 4, 6 and 12. 12 is the largest factor, but it does not divide evenly into 20. Neither does 6, but 4 will divide into both 20 and 36 evenly.

Therefore, 4 is the GCF.

Example: Find the GCF of 14 and 15.

Factors of 14 are 1, 2, 7 and 14. 14 is the largest factor, but it does not divide evenly into 15. Neither does 7 or 2. Therefore, the only factor common to both 14 and 15 is the number 1, the GCF.

LCM is the abbreviation for **least common multiple**. The least common multiple of a group of numbers is the smallest number that all of the given numbers will divide into. The LCM will always be the largest of the given numbers or a multiple of the largest number.

Example: Find the LCM of 20, 30 and 40.

The largest number given is 40, but 30 will not divide evenly into 40. The next multiple of 40 is 80 (2 x 40), but 30 will not divide evenly into 80 either. The next multiple of 40 is 120. 120 is divisible by both 20 and 30, so 120 is the LCM .

Example: Find the LCM of 96, 16 and 24.

The largest number is 96. 96 is divisible by both 16 and 24, so 96 is the LCM.

Example: Elly Mae can feed the animals in 15 minutes. Jethro can feed them in 10 minutes. How long will it take them if they work together?

If Elly Mae can feed the animals in 15 minutes, then she could feed $1/15$ of them in 1 minute, $2/15$ of them in 2 minutes, $x/15$ of them in x minutes. In the same fashion, Jethro could feed $x/10$ of them in x minutes. Together, they complete 1 job. The equation is:

$$\frac{x}{15} + \frac{x}{10} = 1$$

Multiply each term by the LCD of 30:

$$2x + 3x = 30$$
$$x = 6 \text{ minutes}$$

Addition and subtraction of fractions

<u>Key Points</u>

1. You need a common denominator in order to add and subtract reduced and improper fractions.

Example: $\dfrac{1}{3} + \dfrac{7}{3} = \dfrac{1+7}{3} = \dfrac{8}{3} = 2\dfrac{2}{3}$

Example: $\dfrac{4}{12} + \dfrac{6}{12} - \dfrac{3}{12} = \dfrac{4+6-3}{12} = \dfrac{7}{12}$

2. Adding an integer and a fraction of the <u>same</u> sign results directly in a mixed fraction.

Example: $2 + \dfrac{2}{3} = 2\dfrac{2}{3}$

Example: $-2 - \dfrac{3}{4} = -2\dfrac{3}{4}$

3. Adding an integer and a fraction with different signs involves the following steps.

-get a common denominator
-add or subtract as needed
-change to a mixed fraction if possible

Example: $2 - \dfrac{1}{3} = \dfrac{2 \times 3 - 1}{3} = \dfrac{6 - 1}{3} = \dfrac{5}{3} = 1\dfrac{2}{3}$

Example: Add $7\dfrac{3}{8} + 5\dfrac{2}{7}$

Add the whole numbers; add the fractions and combine the two results:

$$7\dfrac{3}{8} + 5\dfrac{2}{7} = (7 + 5) + (\dfrac{3}{8} + \dfrac{2}{7})$$

$$= 12 + \dfrac{(7 \times 3) + (8 \times 2)}{56} \quad \text{(LCM of 8 and 7)}$$

$$= 12 + \dfrac{21 + 16}{56} = 12 + \dfrac{37}{56} = 12\dfrac{37}{56}$$

Example: Perform the operation.

$$\frac{2}{3} - \frac{5}{6}$$

We first find the LCM of 3 and 6, which is 6.

$$\frac{2 \times 2}{3 \times 2} - \frac{5}{6} \rightarrow \frac{4 - 5}{6} - \frac{-1}{6} \qquad \text{(Using method A)}$$

Example: $-7\frac{1}{4} + 2\frac{7}{8}$

$$-7\frac{1}{4} + 2\frac{7}{8} = (-7 + 2) + (\frac{-1}{4} + \frac{7}{8})$$

$$= (-5) + \frac{(-2 + 7)}{8} = (-5) + (\frac{5}{8})$$

$$= (-5) + \frac{5}{8} = \frac{-5 \times 8}{1 \times 8} + \frac{5}{8} = \frac{-40 + 5}{8}$$

$$= \frac{-35}{8} = -4\frac{3}{8}$$

Divide 35 by 8 to get 4, remainder 3.

Caution: Common error would be

$$-7\frac{1}{4} + 2\frac{7}{8} = -7\frac{2}{8} + 2\frac{7}{8} = -5\frac{9}{8} \qquad \text{Wrong.}$$

It is correct to add –7 and 2 to get –5, but adding $\frac{2}{8} + \frac{7}{8} = \frac{9}{8}$

is wrong. It should have been $\frac{-2}{8} + \frac{7}{8} = \frac{5}{8}$. Then,

$$-5 + \frac{5}{8} = -4\frac{3}{8} \quad \text{as before.}$$

Multiplication of fractions

Using the following example: $3\dfrac{1}{4}\times\dfrac{5}{6}$

1. Convert each number to an improper fraction.

$$3\dfrac{1}{4}=\dfrac{(12+1)}{4}=\dfrac{13}{4}\qquad \dfrac{5}{6}\ \text{is already in reduced form.}$$

2. Reduce (cancel) common factors of the numerator and denominator if they exist.

$$\dfrac{13}{4}\times\dfrac{5}{6}\qquad \text{No common factors exist.}$$

3. Multiply the numerators by each other and the denominators by each other.

$$\dfrac{13}{4}\times\dfrac{5}{6}=\dfrac{65}{24}$$

4. If possible, reduce the fraction back to its lowest term.

$$\dfrac{65}{24}\qquad \text{Cannot be reduced further.}$$

5. Convert the improper fraction back to a mixed fraction by using long division.

$$\dfrac{65}{24}=24\overline{)65}\ \ \dfrac{\ \ 2}{}\quad\begin{array}{r}48\\\hline 17\end{array}\qquad =2\dfrac{17}{24}$$

Summary of sign changes for multiplication:

a. $(+)\times(+)=(+)$

b. $(-)\times(+)=(-)$

c. $(+)\times(-)=(-)$

d. $(-)\times(-)=(+)$

Example: $7\dfrac{1}{3} \times \dfrac{5}{11} = \dfrac{22}{3} \times \dfrac{5}{11}$ Reduce like terms (22 and 11)

$$= \dfrac{2}{3} \times \dfrac{5}{1} = \dfrac{10}{3} = 3\dfrac{1}{3}$$

Example: $-6\dfrac{1}{4} \times \dfrac{5}{9} = \dfrac{-25}{4} \times \dfrac{5}{9}$

$$= \dfrac{-125}{36} = -3\dfrac{17}{36}$$

Example: $\dfrac{-1}{4} \times \dfrac{-3}{7}$ Negative times a negative equals positive.

$$= \dfrac{1}{4} \times \dfrac{3}{7} = \dfrac{3}{28}$$

Division of fractions:

1. Change mixed fractions to improper fraction.

2. Change the division problem to a multiplication problem by using the reciprocal of the number after the division sign.

3. Find the sign of the final product.

4. Cancel if common factors exist between the numerator and the denominator.

5. Multiply the numerators together and the denominators together.

6. Change the improper fraction to a mixed number.

Example: $3\dfrac{1}{5} \div 2\dfrac{1}{4} = \dfrac{16}{5} \div \dfrac{9}{4}$

$$= \dfrac{16}{5} \times \dfrac{4}{9}$$ Reciprocal of $\dfrac{9}{4}$ is $\dfrac{4}{9}$.

$$= \dfrac{64}{45} = 1\dfrac{19}{45}$$

Example:
$$7\frac{3}{4} \div 11\frac{5}{8} = \frac{31}{4} \div \frac{93}{8}$$

$$= \frac{31}{4} \times \frac{8}{93} \quad \text{Reduce like terms.}$$

$$= \frac{1}{1} \times \frac{2}{3} = \frac{2}{3}$$

Example:
$$\left(-2\frac{1}{2}\right) \div 4\frac{1}{6} = \frac{-5}{2} \div \frac{25}{6}$$

$$= \frac{-5}{2} \times \frac{6}{25} \quad \text{Reduce like terms.}$$

$$= \frac{-1}{1} \times \frac{3}{5} = \frac{-3}{5}$$

Example:
$$\left(-5\frac{3}{8}\right) \div \left(\frac{-7}{16}\right) = \frac{-43}{8} \div \frac{-7}{16}$$

$$= \frac{-43}{8} \times \frac{-16}{7} \quad \text{Reduce like terms.}$$

$$= \frac{43}{1} \times \frac{2}{7} \quad \text{Negative times a negative equals a positive.}$$

$$= \frac{86}{7} = 12\frac{2}{7}$$

Skill 8.2   Estimate the result of a calculation and determine the reasonableness of an estimate.

Rounding numbers is a form of estimation that is very useful in many mathematical operations. For example, when estimating the sum of two three-digit numbers, it is helpful to round the two numbers to the nearest hundred prior to addition. We can round numbers to any place value.

Rounding Whole Numbers

To round whole numbers, first find the place value you want to round to (the rounding digit). Look at the digit directly to the right. If the digit is less than 5, do not change the rounding digit and replace all numbers after the rounding digit with zeros. If the digit is greater than or equal to 5, increase the rounding digit by 1, and replace all numbers after the rounding digit with zeros.

Example: Round 517 to the nearest ten.

1 is the rounding digit because it occupies the tens place.

517 rounded to the nearest ten = 520; because 7 > 5, we add 1 to the rounding digit.

Example: Round 15,449 to the nearest hundred.

The first 4 is the rounding digit because it occupies the hundreds place.

15,449 rounded to the nearest hundred = 15,400; because 4 < 5, we do not add to the rounding digit.

Rounding Decimals

Rounding decimals is identical to rounding whole numbers except that you simply drop all the digits to the right of the rounding digit.

Example: Round 417.3621 to the nearest tenth.

3 is the rounding digit because it occupies the tenth place.

417.3621 rounded to the nearest tenth = 417.4; because 6 > 5, we add one to the rounding digit.

Skill 8.3   Solve problems involving ratio, proportion, and percent.

A **ratio** is a comparison of two numbers. If a class had 11 boys and 14 girls, the ratio of boys to girls could be written one of three ways:

$$11{:}14 \quad \text{or} \quad 11 \text{ to } 14 \quad \text{or} \quad \frac{11}{14}$$

The ratio of girls to boys is:

$$14{:}11, \quad 14 \text{ to } 11 \quad \text{or} \quad \frac{14}{11}$$

Ratios can be reduced when possible. A ratio of 12 cats to 18 dogs would reduce to 2:3, 2 to 3 or $\frac{2}{3}$.

Note: Read ratio questions carefully. Given a group of 6 adults and 5 children, the ratio of children to the entire group would be 5:11.

A **proportion** is an equation in which a fraction is set equal to another. To solve the proportion, multiply each numerator times the other fraction's denominator. Set these two products equal to each other and solve the resulting equation. This is called **cross-multiplying** the proportion.

Example: $\dfrac{4}{15} = \dfrac{x}{60}$ is a proportion.

To solve this, cross-multiply.

$$15x = 240$$
$$x = 16$$

Example: $\dfrac{x+3}{3x+4} = \dfrac{2}{5}$ is a proportion.

To solve, cross-multiply.

$$5(x+3) = 2(3x+4)$$
$$5x + 15 = 6x + 8$$
$$7 = x$$

TEACHER CERTIFICATION STUDY GUIDE

Proportions can be used to solve word problems whenever relationships are compared. Some situations include scale drawings and maps, similar polygons, speed, time and distance, cost, and comparison shopping.

Example 1: Which is the better buy—6 items for $1.29 or 8 items for $1.69?

Find the unit price.

$$\frac{6}{1.29} = \frac{1}{x}$$
$$6x = 1.29$$
$$x = 0.215$$

$$\frac{8}{1.69} = \frac{1}{x}$$
$$8x = 1.69$$
$$x = 0.21125$$

Thus, 8 items for $1.69 is the better buy.

Example 2: A car travels 125 miles in 2.5 hours. How far will it go in 6 hours?

Write a proportion comparing the distance and time.

$$\frac{miles}{hours} = \frac{125}{2.5} = \frac{x}{6}$$
$$2.5x = 750$$
$$x = 300$$

Thus, the car can travel 300 miles in 6 hours.

Example 3: The scale on a map is $\frac{3}{4}$ inch = 6 miles. What is the actual distance between two cities if they are $1\frac{1}{2}$ inches apart on the map?

Write a proportion comparing the scale to the actual distance.

$$\frac{\frac{3}{4}}{\frac{3}{2}} = \frac{6}{x}$$
$$\frac{3}{4}x = \left(\frac{3}{2}\right)(6)$$
$$\frac{3}{4}x = 9$$
$$3x = 36$$
$$x = 12$$

Thus, the actual distance between the cities is 12 miles.

PPST I: BASIC SKILLS   194

Operating with Percents

Example: 5 is what percent of 20?

This is the same as converting $\dfrac{5}{20}$ to % form.

$$\frac{5}{20} \times \frac{100}{1} = \frac{5}{1} \times \frac{5}{1} = 25\%$$

Example: There are 64 dogs in the kennel, 48 are collies. What percent are collies?

Restate the problem.   48 is what percent of 64?
Write an equation. $48 = n \times 64$
Solve. $\dfrac{48}{64} = n$

$n = \dfrac{3}{4}$ = 75%

75% of the dogs are collies.

Example: The auditorium was filled to 90% capacity. There were 558 seats occupied. What is the capacity of the auditorium?

Restate the problem.   90% of what number is 558?
Write an equation. $0.9n = 558$
Solve. $n = \dfrac{558}{.9}$
                              $n = 620$

The capacity of the auditorium is 620 people.

Example: A pair of shoes costs $42.00. Sales tax is 6%. What is the total cost of the shoes?

Restate the problem.   What is 6% of 42?
Write an equation. $n = 0.06 \times 42$
Solve. $n = 2.52$

Add the sales tax to the cost. $42.00 + $2.52 = $44.52

The total cost of the shoes, including sales tax, is $44.52.

Skill 8.4   Interpret numbers used to express simple probability.

In probability, the **sample space** is a list of all possible outcomes of an experiment. For example, the sample space of tossing two coins is the set {HH, HT, TT, TH}; the sample space of rolling a six-sided die is the set {1, 2, 3, 4, 5, 6}; and the sample space of measuring the height of students in a class is the set of all real numbers {R}. **Probability** measures the chances of an event occurring. The probability of an event that *must* occur, a certain event, is **one.** When no outcome is favorable, the probability of an impossible event is **zero.**

$$P(\text{event}) = \frac{\text{number of favorable outcomes}}{\text{number of possible outcomes}}$$

Skill 8.5   Assign a probability to a possible outcome.

Example: Given one die with faces numbered 1–6, the probability of tossing an even number on one throw of the die is $\frac{3}{6}$ or $\frac{1}{2}$ since there are three favorable outcomes (even faces) and six possible outcomes (faces).

Example: If we roll a fair die.

a) Find the probability of rolling an even number.
b) Find the probability of rolling a number less than three.

a) The sample space is

S = {1, 2, 3, 4, 5, 6} and the event representing even numbers is

E = {2, 4, 6}

Hence, the probability of rolling an even number is

$$p(E) = \frac{n(E)}{n(S)} = \frac{3}{6} = \frac{1}{2} \text{ or } 0.5$$

b) We represent the event of rolling a number less than three by

A = {1, 2}

Hence, the probability of rolling a number less than three is

$$p(A) = \frac{n(A)}{n(S)} = \frac{2}{6} = \frac{1}{3} \text{ or } 0.33$$

Example: A class has thirty students. Out of the thirty students, twenty-four are males. Assuming all the students have the same chance of being selected, find the probability of selecting a female. (Only one person is selected.)

The number of females in the class is

$$30 - 24 = 6$$

Hence, the probability of selecting a female is

$$p(\text{female}) = \frac{6}{30} = \frac{1}{5} \text{ or } 0.2$$

If A and B are **independent** events, then the outcome of event A does not affect the outcome of event B or vice versa. We use the multiplication rule to find joint probability.

$$P(A \text{ and } B) = P(A) \times P(B)$$

Example: The probability that a patient is allergic to aspirin is 0.30. If the probability of a patient having a window in his/her room is 0.40, find the probability that the patient is allergic to aspirin and has a window in his/her room.

Defining the events: A = the patient being allergic to aspirin
                     B = the patient has a window in his/her room

Events A and B are independent, hence
$p(A \text{ and } B) = p(A) \cdot p(B)$
$= (0.30) \ (0.40)$
$= 0.12 \text{ or } 12\%$

Example: Given a jar containing 10 marbles—3 red, 5 black, and 2 white—what is the probability of drawing a red marble and then a white marble if the marble is returned to the jar after choosing?
$3/10 \ X \ 2/10 = 6/100 = 3/50$

When the outcome of the first event affects the outcome of the second event, the events are **dependent.** Any two events that are not independent are dependent. This is also known as conditional probability.

$$\text{Probability of } (A \text{ and } B) = P(A) \times P(B \text{ given } A)$$

Example: Two cards are drawn from a deck of 52 cards without replacement; that is, the first card is not returned to the deck before the second card is drawn. What is the probability of drawing a diamond?

A = drawing a diamond first
B = drawing a diamond second
P(A) = drawing a diamond first
P(B) = drawing a diamond second

P(A) = 13/52 = ¼   P(B) = 12/52 = 4/17
(PA+B) = ¼ X 4/17 = 1/17

Example: A class of ten students has six males and four females. If two students are selected to represent the class, find the probability that

a) the first is a male and the second is a female
b) the first is a female and the second is a male
c) both are females
d) both are males

Defining the events: F = a female is selected to represent the class.
M = a male is selected to represent the class.
F/M = a female is selected after a male has been selected.
M/F = a male is selected after a female has been selected.

a) Since F and M are dependent events, it follows that
P(M and F) = P(M) · P(F/M)
$$= \frac{6}{10} \times \frac{4}{9} = \frac{3}{5} \times \frac{4}{9} = \frac{12}{45}$$

P(F/M) = $\frac{4}{9}$ instead of $\frac{4}{10}$ since the selection of a male first changed the sample space from ten to nine students.

b) P(F and M) = P(F) · P(M/F)
$$= \frac{4}{10} \times \frac{6}{9} = \frac{2}{5} \times \frac{2}{3} = \frac{4}{15}$$

c) $P(\text{F and F}) = p(F) \cdot p(F/F)$

$$= \frac{4}{10} \times \frac{3}{9} = \frac{2}{5} \times \frac{1}{3} = \frac{2}{15}$$

d)   P(both are males) = p(M and M)

$$= \frac{6}{10} \times \frac{5}{9} = \frac{30}{90} = \frac{1}{3}$$

Skill 8.6   Solve simple equations and inequalities.

An equation consists of two statements linked by an equal sign.

Left Hand Side (LHS) = Right Hand Side (RHS)

Example: $2x = 6$
(LHS) (RHS)

This statement is only true if we substitute 3 for x.

$2 x 3 = 6$ (True).

Therefore, 3 is a solution for the equation.

Example: Is 2 a solution of $2x - 6 = 6x + 1$?

Substituting 2 for x:
$2(2) - 6 = 6(2) + 1 \rightarrow 4 - 6 = 12 + 1 \rightarrow -2 = 13$ (False).
2 is not a solution.

Procedure for solving algebraic equations

Example: $3(x + 3) = -2x + 4$ Solve for x.

1) Expand to eliminate all parentheses.

$3x + 9 = -2x + 4$

2) Multiply each term by the LCD to eliminate all denominators.

3) Combine like terms on each side when possible.

4) Use the properties to put all variables on one side and all constants on the other side.

$\rightarrow 3x + 9 - 9 = -2x + 4 - 9$ (Subtract nine from both sides)

$\rightarrow 3x = -2x - 5$

$\rightarrow 3x + 2x = -2x + 2x - 5$ (Add 2x to both sides)

$\rightarrow 5x = -5$

$\rightarrow \dfrac{5x}{5} = \dfrac{-5}{5}$ (Divide both sides by 5)

$\rightarrow x = -1$

Example: Solve: $3(2x + 5) - 4x = 5(x + 9)$
$6x + 15 - 4x = 5x + 45$
$2x + 15 = 5x + 45$
$-3x + 15 = 45$
$-3x = 30$
$x = -10$

The solution **set of linear equations** is all the ordered pairs of real numbers that satisfy both equations, thus the intersection of the lines. There are two methods for solving linear equations: **linear combinations** and **substitution**.

In the **substitution** method, we solve an equation for either variable. Then, we substitute that solution in the other equation to find the remaining variable.

Example:

(1) $2x + 8y = 4$
(2) $x - 3y = 5$

(2a) $x = 3y + 5$ Solve equation (2) for x

(1a) $2(3y + 5) + 8y = 4$ Substitute x in equation (1)
        $6y + 10 + 8y = 4$ Solve.
        $14y = -6$
        $y = \frac{-3}{7}$ Solution

(2) $x - 3y = 5$
      $x - 3(\frac{-3}{7}) = 5$ Substitute the value of y.

      $x = \frac{26}{7} = 3\frac{5}{7}$ Solution

Thus, the solution set of the system of equations is $(3\frac{5}{7}, \frac{-3}{7})$.

In the **linear combinations** method, we replace one or both of the equations with an equivalent equation so that we can combine (add or subtract) the two equations to eliminate one variable.

Example:

(1) $4x + 3y = -2$
(2) $5x - y = 7$

(1) $4x + 3y = -2$
(2a) $15x - 3y = 21$ Multiply equation (2) by 3

$19x = 19$ Combining (1) and (2a)
$x = 1$ Solve.

To find y, substitute the value of x in equation 1 (or 2).

(1) $4x + 3y = -2$
      $4(1) + 3y = -2$
      $4 + 3y = -2$
      $3y = -2$
      $y = -2$

Thus, the solution is $x = 1$ and $y = -2$ or the ordered pair $(1, -2)$.

Example: Solve for x and y.

$$4x + 6y = 340$$
$$3x + 8y = 360$$

To solve by addition-subtraction:

Multiply the first equation by 4: $4(4x + 6y = 340)$
Multiply the other equation by -3: $-3(3x + 8y = 360)$
By doing this, the equations can be added to each other to eliminate one variable and solve for the other variable.

$$16x + 24y = 1360$$
$$\underline{-9x - 24y = -1080}$$
$$7x = 280$$
$$x = 40$$

Solving for y, $y = 30$

We use the same procedure used for solving linear equations, but we represent the answer in graphical form on the number line or in interval form.

Example: Solve the inequality, show its solution using interval form, and graph the solution on the number line.

$$\frac{5x}{8} + 3 \geq 2x - 5$$

$$8\left(\frac{5x}{8}\right) + 8(3) \geq 8(2x) - 5(8) \qquad \text{Multiply by LCD = 8.}$$

$$5x + 24 \geq 16x - 40$$

$$5x + 24 - 24 - 16x \geq 16x - 16x - 40 - 24$$

Subtract 16x and 24 from both sides of the equation.

$$-11x \geq -64$$

$$\frac{-11x}{-11} \leq \frac{-64}{-11}$$

$$x \leq \frac{64}{11} \ ; \ x \leq 5\frac{9}{11}$$

Solution in interval form: $\left(-\infty, 5\frac{9}{11}\right]$

Note: "] " means $5\frac{9}{11}$ is included in the solution.

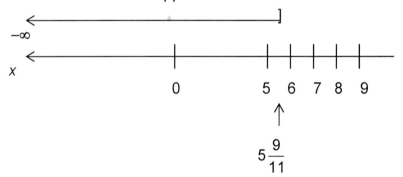

Example: Solve the following inequality and express your answer in both interval and graphical form.

$$3x - 8 < 2(3x - 1)$$

$$3x - 8 < 6x - 2 \qquad \text{Distributive property}$$

$$3x - 6x - 8 + 8 < 6x - 6x - 2 + 8$$

Add 8 and subtract $6x$ from both sides of the equation.

$$-3x < 6$$

$$\frac{-3x}{-3} > \frac{6}{-3} \qquad \text{Note the change in direction of the equality.}$$

$$x > -2$$

Graphical form:

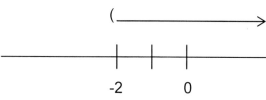

or

Interval form: $(-2, \infty)$

Recall that using a parentheses or an open circle implies the point is not included in the answer and using a bracket or a closed circle implies the point is included in the answer.

Example: Solve: $6x + 21 < 8x + 31$
$\qquad\qquad\qquad -2x + 21 < 31$

$\qquad\qquad\qquad -2x < 10$

$\qquad\qquad\qquad x > -5$

Note that the inequality sign has changed.

Absolute value equations and equalities

If a and b are real numbers, and k is a non-negative real number, the solution of

$$|ax + b| = k \text{ is } ax + b = k \text{ or } ax + b = -k$$

$$|ax + b| > k \text{ is } ax + b > k \text{ or } ax + b < -k$$

Example: $|2x + 3| = 9$ solve for x.

$2x + 3 = 9$	or	$2x + 3 = -9$
$2x + 3 - 3 = 9 - 3$	or	$2x + 3 - 3 = -9 - 3$
$2x = 6$	or	$2x = -12$
$\dfrac{2x}{2} = \dfrac{6}{2}$	or	$\dfrac{2x}{2} = \dfrac{-12}{2}$
$x = 3$	or	$x = -6$

Therefore, the solution is $x = \{3, -6\}$

Example: Solve $|7x + 3| < 25$

$$-25 < (7x + 3) < 25$$
$$(-25 - 3) < (7x) < (25 - 3)$$

Subtract 3 from all sides.

$$-28 < 7x < 22$$
$$-4 < x < \frac{22}{7}$$

Divide all terms by 7.

Solution in interval form is $\left(-4, \dfrac{22}{7}\right)$

Solution in graphical form:

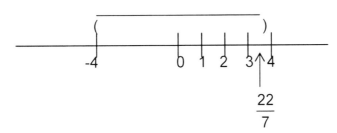

COMPETENCY 9.0   REPRESENTATIONS OF QUANTITATIVE INFORMATION

Skill 9.1   Read _and_ interpret visual displays of quantitative information, such as bar graphs, line graphs, pie charts, pictographs, tables, stemplots, scatterplots, schedules, and diagrams.

To make a **bar graph** or a **pictograph**, we determine the scale for the graph. Then we determine the length of each bar on the graph or determine the number of pictures needed to represent each item of information. We need to be sure to include an explanation of the scale in the legend.

Example: A class had the following grades:
4 A's, 9 B's, 8 C's, 1 D, 3 F's.
Graph these on a pictograph and a bar graph.

Pictograph

Grade	Number of Students
A	☺☺☺☺
B	☺☺☺☺☺☺☺☺☺
C	☺☺☺☺☺☺☺☺
D	☺
F	☺☺☺

Bar graph

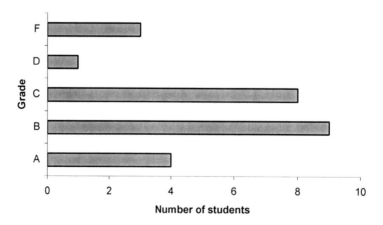

To make a **line graph**, we determine appropriate scales for both the vertical and horizontal axes (based on the information we are graphing). Describe what each axis represents and mark the scale periodically on each axis. Graph the individual points of the graph and connect the points on the graph from left to right.

Example: Graph the following information using a line graph.

The number of National Merit finalists/school year

	90–91	91–92	92–93	93–94	94–95	95–96
Central	3	5	1	4	6	8
Wilson	4	2	3	2	3	2

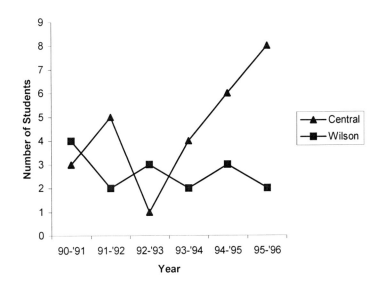

To make a **circle graph**, we total all the information that is to be included on the graph. We then determine the central angle to be used for each sector of the graph using the following formula:

$$\frac{\text{information}}{\text{total information}} \times 360° = \text{degrees in central} \square$$

We lay out the central angles to these sizes, label each section, and include its percent.

Example: Graph this information on a circle graph:

Monthly expenses:

Rent, $400
Food, $150
Utilities, $75
Clothes, $75
Church, $100
Misc., $200

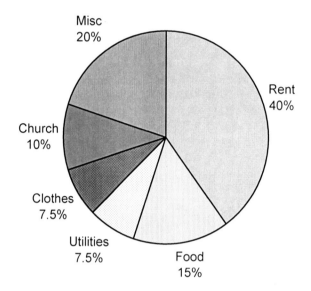

Scatter plots compare two characteristics of the same group of things or people and usually consist of a large body of data. They show how much one variable affects another. The relationship between the two variables is their **correlation**. The closer the data points come to making a straight line when plotted, the closer the correlation.

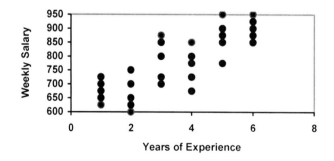

Stem and leaf plots are visually similar to line plots. The **stems** are the digits in the greatest place value of the data values, and the **leaves** are the digits in the next greatest place value. Stem and leaf plots are best suited for small sets of data and are especially useful for comparing two sets of data. The following is an example using test scores:

4	9
5	4 9
6	1 2 3 4 6 7 8 8
7	0 3 4 6 6 6 7 7 7 8 8 8 8
8	3 5 5 7 8
9	0 0 3 4 5
10	0 0

We use **histograms** to summarize information from large sets of data that we can naturally group into intervals. The vertical axis indicates **frequency** (the number of times any particular data value occurs), and the horizontal axis indicates data values or ranges of data values. The number of data values in any interval is the **frequency of the interval**.

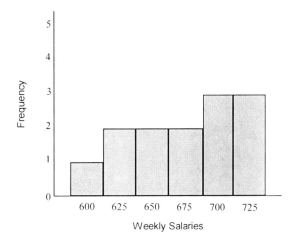

Skill 9.2 Determine an average, a range, a mode, or a median.

The arithmetic **mean** (or average) of a set of numbers is the *sum* of the numbers given *divided* by the number of items being averaged.

Example: Find the mean. Round to the nearest tenth.

24.6, 57.3, 44.1, 39.8, 64.5
The sum is 230.3 ÷ 5 = 46.06, rounded to 46.1

The **median** of a set is the middle number. To calculate the median, we must arrange the terms in order. If there is an even number of terms, the median is the mean of the two middle terms.

Example: Find the median.

12, 14, 27, 3, 13, 7, 17, 12, 22, 6, 16

Rearrange the terms.

3, 6, 7, 12, 12, 13,14,16,17, 22, 27

Since there are eleven numbers, the middle would be the sixth number or 13.

The **mode** of a set of numbers is the number that occurs with the greatest frequency. A set can have no mode if each term appears exactly one time. Similarly, there can also be more than one mode.

Example: Find the mode.

26, 15, 37, **26**, 35, **26**, 15

15 appears twice, but 26 appears 3 times, therefore, the mode is 26.

The **range** is the difference between the highest and lowest value of data items.

Example: Given the ungrouped data below, calculate the mean and range.

| 15 | 22 | 28 | 25 | 34 | 38 |
| 18 | 25 | 30 | 33 | 19 | 23 |

Mean ($\overline{X}$) = 25.8333333
Range: 38 − 15 = 23

Percentiles divide data into 100 equal parts. A person whose score falls in the 65th percentile has outperformed 65 percent of all those who took the test. This does not mean that the score was 65 out of 100 nor does it mean that 65 percent of the questions answered were correct. It means that the grade was higher than 65 percent of all those who took the test.

Stanine, "standard nine," scores combine the understandability of percentages with the properties of the normal curve of probability. Stanines divide the bell curve into nine sections, the largest of which stretches from the 40th to the 60th percentile and is the "Fifth Stanine" (the average of taking into account error possibilities).

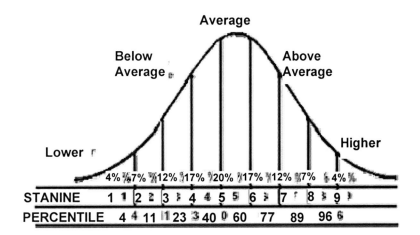

Quartiles divide the data into four parts. First, find the median of the data set (Q2), then find the median of the upper (Q3) and lower (Q1) halves of the data set. If there are an odd number of values in the data set, include the median value in both halves when finding quartile values. For example, given the data set {1, 4, 9, 16, 25, 36, 49, 64, 81}, first find the median value, which is 25. This is the second quartile. Since there are an odd number of values in the data set (9), we include the median in both halves.

To find the quartile values, we much find the medians of {1, 4, 9, 16, 25} and {25, 36, 49, 64, 81}. Since each of these subsets has an odd number of elements (5), we use the middle value. Thus, the first quartile value is 9 and the third quartile value is 49. If the data set has an even number of elements, average the middle two values. The quartile values are always either one of the data points, or exactly halfway between two data points.

Example: Given the following set of data, find the percentile of the score 104.

70, 72, 82, 83, 84, 87, 100, 104, 108, 109, 110, 115

Find the percentage of scores below 104.

7/12 of the scores are less than 104. This is 58.333%; therefore, the score of 104 is in the 58th percentile.

Example: Find the first, second and third quartile for the data listed.

6, 7, 8, 9, 10, 12, 13, 14, 15, 16, 18, 23, 24, 25, 27, 29, 30, 33, 34, 37

Quartile 1: The 1st Quartile is the median of the lower half of the data set, which is 11.

Quartile 2: The median of the data set is the 2nd Quartile, which is 17.

Quartile 3: The 3rd Quartile is the median of the upper half of the data set, which is 28.

Skill 9.3 Identify trends and patterns in data and draw inferences and conclusions.

A **trend** line on a line graph shows the correlation between two sets of data. A trend may show positive correlation (both sets of data get bigger together), negative correlation (one set of data gets bigger while the other gets smaller), or no correlation.

An **inference** is a statement that is derived from reasoning. When reading a graph, inferences help with interpretation of the data that is being presented. From this information, a **conclusion** and even **predictions** about what the data actually means is possible.

Example: Katherine and Tom were both doing poorly in math class. Their teacher had a conference with each of them in November. The following graph shows their math test scores during the school year.

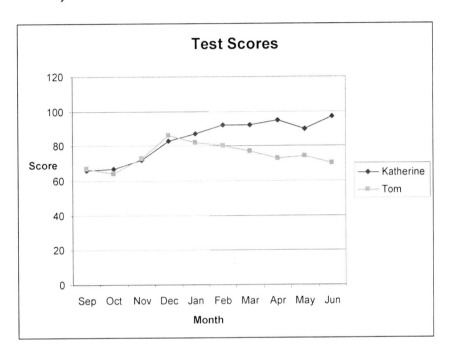

What kind of trend does this graph show?

This graph shows that there is a positive trend in Katherine's test scores and a negative trend in Tom's test scores.

What inferences can you make from this graph?

We can infer that Katherine's test scores rose steadily after November. Tom's test scores spiked in December but then began to fall again and became negatively trended.

What conclusion can you draw based upon this graph?

We can conclude that Katherine took her teacher's meeting seriously and began to study in order to do better on the exams. It seems as though Tom tried harder for a bit, but his test scores eventually slipped back down to the level where he began.

Skill 9.4 Demonstrate an understanding of the relationship between numerical values in a table, the symbolic rule relating table values, and the corresponding graphical representation of the table and the rule.

We can use a table, graph, or rule to show a relationship between two quantities. In this example, the rule y= 9x describes the relationship between the total amount earned, y, and the total amount of $9 sunglasses sold, x.

A table using this data would appear as:

number of sunglasses sold	1	5	10	15
total dollars earned	9	45	90	135

Each *(x, y)* relationship between a pair of values is called the coordinate pair and can be plotted on a graph. The coordinate pairs (1, 9), (5, 45), (10, 90), and (15,135), are plotted on the graph below.

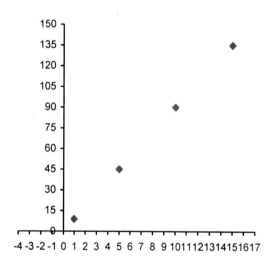

The graph shows a linear relationship. A linear relationship is one in which two quantities are proportional to each other. Doubling *x* also doubles *y*. On a graph, a straight line depicts a linear relationship.

We can analyze the function or relationship between two quantities to determine how one quantity depends on the other. For example, the function below shows a relationship between y and x:

$$y = 2x+1$$

The function, y = 2x + 1, is written as a symbolic rule. The table below shows the same relationship:

x	0	2	3	6	9
y	1	5	7	13	19

We can write a relationship in words by saying the value of y is equal to two times the value of x, plus one. We can show this relationship on a graph by plotting given points such as the ones shown in the table above.

Another way to describe a function is as a process in which one or more numbers are input into an imaginary machine that produces another number as the output. If 5 is input, x, into a machine with a process of x + 1, the output, y, will equal 6.

In real situations, we can describe relationships mathematically. The function y = x + 1 can be used to describe the idea that people age one year on their birthday. To describe the relationship in which a person's monthly medical costs are six times a person's age, we could write y = 6x. We can use this function to predict the monthly cost of medical care. A 20-year-old person would spend $120 per month (120 = 20 * 6). An 80 year-old person would spend $480 per month (480=80*6). Therefore, one could analyze the relationship to say, "As you get older, medical costs increase $6.00 each year."

Example: What is the equation that expresses the relationship between x and y in the table below?

x	y
0	3
1	5
2	7
3	9
4	11
5	13

A. $y = x + 2$

B. $y = \frac{1}{3}x + 3$

C. $y = 2x + 3$

D. $y = 2x - 3$

Solve by plugging in the values of x and y into the equations to see if they work. The answer is C because it is the only equation for which the values of x and y are correct.

Skill 9.5 Choose a graph appropriate to represent a given set of data.

Bar graphs are used to compare various quantities.

Example: For the following set of test scores, what kind of graph would be most appropriate?

	Test 1	Test 2	Test 3	Test 4	Test 5
Evans, Tim	75	66	80	85	97
Miller, Julie	94	93	88	97	98
Thomas, Randy	81	86	88	87	90

A bar graph would be most appropriate because the data is quantitative—each student has taken five tests. A bar graph will show the comparison of each student's own test scores, as well as the comparison among the students' test scores.

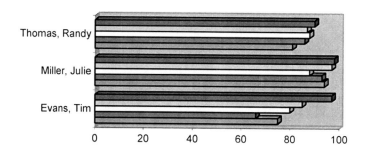

Circle graphs show the relationship of various parts to each other and the whole. Percents are used to create circle graphs.

Example: Julie spends 8 hours each day in school, 2 hours doing homework, 1 hour eating dinner, 2 hours watching television, 10 hours sleeping, and the rest of the time doing other things.

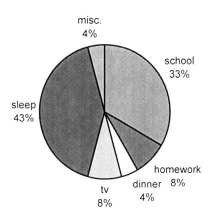

Line graphs show trends in two variables, often over a period.

Example: For the following information about average temperature, what is the most appropriate type of graph?

Month	Jan	Feb	Mar	Apr	May	Jun	Jul	Aug	Sep	Oct	Nov	Dec
Temp (°F)	29	30	39	48	58	68	74	72	65	55	45	34

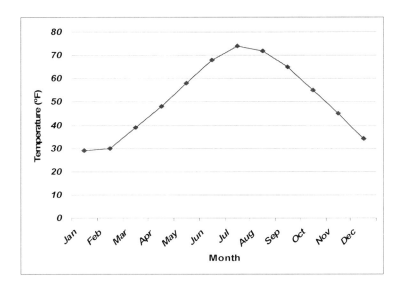

Pictographs can be misleading, especially if drawn to represent 3-dimensional objects. If two or more dimensions are changed in reflecting ratio, the overall visual effect can be misinterpreted. Bar and line graphs can be misleading if the scales are changed. For example, using relatively small scale increments for large numbers will make the comparison differences seem much greater than if larger scale increments are used. Circle graphs, or pie charts, are excellent for comparing relative amounts; however, they cannot be used to represent absolute amounts, and if interpreted as such, they are misleading.

COMPETENCY 10.0   MEASUREMENT AND INFORMAL GEOMETRY

Skill 10.1   Demonstrate basic literacy in the U.S. customary and metric systems of measurement.

Measurements of length (English system)

12 inches (in)	=	1 foot (ft)
3 feet (ft)	=	1 yard (yd)
1760 yards (yd)	=	1 mile (mi)

Measurements of length (Metric system)

kilometer (km)	=	1000 meters (m)
hectometer (hm)	=	100 meters (m)
decameter (dam)	=	10 meters (m)
meter (m)	=	1 meter (m)
decimeter (dm)	=	1/10 meter (m)
centimeter (cm)	=	1/100 meter (m)
millimeter (mm)	=	1/1000 meter (m)

Conversion of length from English to Metric

1 inch	=	2.54 centimeters
1 foot	≈	30 centimeters
1 yard	≈	0.9 meters
1 mile	≈	1.6 kilometers

Measurements of weight (English system)

28 grams (g)	=	1 ounce (oz)
16 ounces (oz)	=	1 pound (lb)
2000 pounds (lb)	=	1 ton (t)(short ton)
1.1 ton (t)	=	1 ton (t)

Measurements of weight (Metric system)

kilogram (kg)	=	1000 grams (g)
gram (g)	=	1 gram (g)
milligram (mg)	=	1/1000 gram (g)

Conversion of weight from English to metric

1 ounce	≈	28 grams
1 pound	≈	0.45 kilogram
	≈	454 grams

Measurement of volume (English system)

8 fluid ounces (oz)	=	1 cup (c)
2 cups (c)	=	1 pint (pt)
2 pints (pt)	=	1 quart (qt)
4 quarts (qt)	=	1 gallon (gal)

Measurement of volume (Metric system)

kiloliter (kl)	=	1000 liters (l)
liter (l)	=	1 liter (l)
milliliter (ml)	=	1/1000 liters (ml)

Conversion of volume from English to metric

1 teaspoon (tsp)	≈	5 milliliters
1 fluid ounce	≈	15 milliliters
1 cup	≈	0.24 liters
1 pint	≈	0.47 liters
1 quart	≈	0.95 liters
1 gallon	≈	3.8 liters

Measurement of time

1 second	=	
1 minute	=	60 seconds
1 hour	=	60 minutes
1 day	=	24 hours
1 week	=	7 days
1 year	=	365 days
1 century	=	100 years

Note: (') represents feet and (") represents inches.

Skill 10.2 **Convert from one unit to another within the same system and between different systems.**

Length

Example: A car skidded 170 yards on an icy road before coming to a stop. How long is the skid distance in kilometers?

Since 1 yard $\approx$ 0.9 meters, multiply 170 yards by 0.9.

$$170 \times 0.9 = 153 \text{ meters}$$

Since 1000 meters = 1 kilometer, divide 153 by 1000.

$$\frac{153}{1000} = 0.153 \text{ kilometers}$$

Example: The distance around a race course is exactly 1 mile, 17 feet, and $9\frac{1}{4}$ inches. Approximate this distance to the nearest tenth of a foot. Convert the distance to feet.

$$1 \text{ mile} = 1760 \text{ yards} = 1760 \times 3 \text{ feet} = 5280 \text{ feet.}$$
$$9\frac{1}{4} \text{ inches} = \frac{37}{4} \times \frac{1}{12} = \frac{37}{48} \approx 0.77083 \text{ feet}$$

So 1 mile, 17 feet and $9\frac{1}{4}$ inches = $5280 + 17 + 0.77083$ feet

$$= 5297.\underline{7}7083 \text{ feet.}$$

Now, we need to round to the nearest tenth digit. The underlined 7 is in the tenths place. The digit in the hundredths place, also a 7, is greater than 5, so the 7 in the tenths place needs to be rounded up to 8 to get a final answer of 5297.8 feet.

Weight

Example: Zachary weighs 150 pounds. Tom weighs 153 pounds. What is the difference in their weights in grams?

153 pounds – 150 pounds = 3 pounds
1 pound = 454 grams
3(454 grams) = 1362 grams

Capacity

Example: Students in a fourth grade class want to fill a 3-gallon jug using cups of water. How many cups of water are needed?

1 gallon = 16 cups of water
3 gallons x 16 cups = 48 cups of water are needed.

Time

Example: It takes Cynthia 45 minutes to get ready each morning. How many hours does she spend getting ready each week?

45 minutes X 7 days = 315 minutes

$$\frac{315 \text{ minutes}}{60 \text{ minutes in an hour}} \quad = \quad 5.25 \text{ hours}$$

Skill 10.3   Recognize and use appropriate units for making measurements and to read a calibrated scale.

Students need to understand that ratios and proportions are used to create scale models of real-life objects, understand the principles of ratio and proportion, and understand how to calculate scale using ratio and proportion.

Scaled drawings (maps, blueprints, and models) are used in many real-world situations. Architects make blueprints and models of buildings. The contractors then use these drawings and models to build the buildings. Engineers make scaled drawings of bridges, machine parts, roads, airplanes, and many other things. Maps of the world, countries, states, roads, etc. are scaled drawings. Landscape designers use scale drawings and models of plants, decks, and other structures to show how they should be placed around a house or other building. Models of cars, boats, and planes made from kits are scaled. Automobile engineers construct models of cars before the actual assembly is done. Many museum exhibits are actually scaled models because the real size of the items displayed would be too large.

Examples of real-world problems that students might solve using scaled drawings include:

- reading road maps and determining the distance between locations by using the map scale
- creating a scaled drawing (floor plan) of their classroom to determine the best use of space
- creating an 8 ½" x 11" representation of a quilt to be pieced together
- drawing a blueprint of their rooms and creating a model from it

Skill 10.4 **Determine the measurements needed to solve a problem.**

Example: Bob wants to put a childproof fence around his pool. What measurements will he need to know in order to purchase the fence?

Bob will need to know the **perimeter** of his pool, that is, the **length** of all of the sides combined, as well as the **price** of the fencing per foot.

Example: Jillian wants to wrap a square gift box. What measurements will she need to know in order to cover the entire box with wrapping paper?

Jillian will need to know the **surface area** of the box and the **area** of the wrapping paper that she has. If the area of the wrapping paper is greater than the surface area of the box, she has enough to wrap the box fully.

Skill 10.5   Recognize and use geometric concepts in making linear, area, and volume measurements.

We name **polygons**, simple closed **two-dimensional figures** composed of line segments, according to the number of sides they have.

A **quadrilateral** is a polygon with four sides.
The sum of the measures of the angles of a quadrilateral is 360°.

A **trapezoid** is a quadrilateral with exactly <u>one</u> pair of parallel sides.

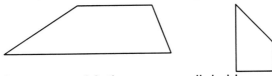

In an **isosceles trapezoid**, the non-parallel sides are congruent.

A **parallelogram** is a quadrilateral with <u>two</u> pairs of parallel sides.

In a parallelogram:
The diagonals bisect each other.
Each diagonal divides the parallelogram into two congruent triangles.
Both pairs of opposite sides are congruent.
Both pairs of opposite angles are congruent.
Two adjacent angles are supplementary.

A **rectangle** is a parallelogram with a right angle.

A **rhombus** is a parallelogram with all sides equal in length.

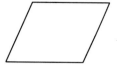

A **square** is a rectangle with all sides equal in length.

Example: True or false?
All squares are rhombuses.   True
All parallelograms are rectangles.   False—<u>some</u>
                                                                        parallelograms are
                                                                        rectangles

All rectangles are parallelograms.   True
Some rhombuses are squares.   True
Some rectangles are trapezoids.   False—only <u>one</u> pair of
                                                                        parallel sides

All quadrilaterals are parallelograms.   False—some
                                                                        quadrilaterals are
                                                                        parallelograms

Some squares are rectangles.   False—all squares are
                                                                        rectangles

Some parallelograms are rhombuses.   True

A **triangle** is a polygon with three sides.

We can classify triangles by the types of angles or the lengths of their sides.

An **acute** triangle has exactly three *acute* angles.
A **right** triangle has one *right* angle.
An **obtuse** triangle has one *obtuse* angle.

        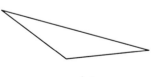

acute   right   obtuse

All *three* sides of an **equilateral** triangle are the same length.
Two sides of an **isosceles** triangle are the same length.

None of the sides of a **scalene** triangle is the same length.

 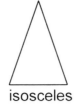 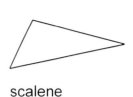

equilateral   isosceles   scalene

Example: Can a triangle have two right angles?
No. A right angle measures 90°; therefore, the sum of two right angles would be 180° and there could not be a third angle.

Example: Can a triangle have two obtuse angles?
No. Since an obtuse angle measures more than 90°, the sum of two obtuse angles would be greater than 180°.

A **cylinder** has two congruent circular bases that are parallel.

A **sphere** is a space figure having all its points the same distance from the center.

A **cone** is a space figure having a circular base and a single vertex.

A **pyramid** is a space figure with a square base and four triangle-shaped sides.

A **tetrahedron** is a 4-sided space triangle. Each face is a triangle.

A **prism** is a space figure with two congruent, parallel bases that are polygons.

The **perimeter** of any polygon is the sum of the lengths of the sides.

The **area** of a polygon is the number of square units covered by the figure.

FIGURE	AREA FORMULA	PERIMETER FORMULA
Rectangle	LW	$2(L+W)$
Triangle	$\frac{1}{2}bh$	$a+b+c$
Parallelogram	bh	sum of lengths of sides
Trapezoid	$\frac{1}{2}h(a+b)$	sum of lengths of sides

Example: A farmer has a piece of land shaped as shown below. He wishes to fence this land at an estimated cost of $25 per linear foot. What is the total cost of fencing this property to the nearest foot?

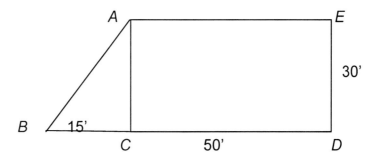

From the right triangle ABC, AC = 30 and BC = 15.

Since (AB) = (AC)^2 + (BC)^2
    (AB) = (30)^2 + (15)^2

So $\sqrt{(AB)^2} = AB = \sqrt{1125} = 33.5410$ feet

To the nearest foot, AB = 34 feet.

Perimeter of the piece of land = $AB + BC + CD + DE + EA$

= 34 + 15 + 50 + 30 + 50 = 179 feet

Cost of fencing = $25 x 179 = $4,475.00

Area
Area is the space that a figure occupies.

Example: What will be the cost of carpeting a rectangular office that measures 12 feet by 15 feet if the carpet costs $12.50 per square yard?

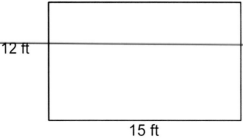

12 ft

15 ft

The problem is asking you to determine the area of the office. The area of a rectangle is *length x width = A*
Substitute the given values in the equation $A = lw$

$A = (12$ ft.$)(15$ ft.$)$

$A = 180$ ft.

The problem asked you to determine the cost of carpet at $12.50 per square yard.

First, you need to convert 180 ft.^{2} into yards^2.

1 yd. = 3 ft.
(1 yard)(1 yard) = (3 feet)(3 feet)
1 yd$^2 = 9$ ft ^{2}

Hence, $\dfrac{180 \text{ ft}^2}{1} = \dfrac{1 \text{ yd}^2}{9 \text{ ft}^2} = \dfrac{20}{1} = 20 \text{ yd}^2$

The carpet costs $12.50 per square yard; thus, the cost of carpeting the office described is $12.50 x 20 = $250.00.

Example: Find the area of a parallelogram whose base is 6.5 cm and the height of the altitude to that base is 3.7 cm.

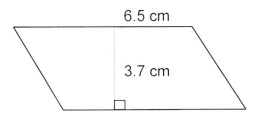

$$A_{parallelogram} = bh$$

$$= (3.7)(6.5)$$
$$= 24.05 \text{ cm}^2$$

Example: Find the area of this triangle.

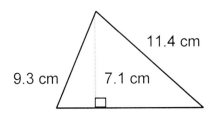

$$A_{triangle} = \frac{1}{2}bh$$
$$= 0.5\,(16.8)\,(7.1)$$
$$= 59.64 \text{ cm}^2$$

Example: Find the area of this trapezoid.

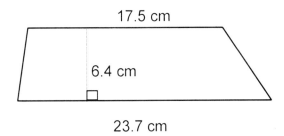

The area of a trapezoid equals one-half the sum of the bases times the altitude.

$$A_{trapezoid} = \frac{1}{2}h(b_1 + b_2)$$
$$= 0.5\,(6.4)\,(17.5 + 23.7)$$
$$= 131.84 \text{ cm}^2$$

The distance around a circle is the **circumference**. The Greek letter pi represents the ratio of the circumference to the diameter.

$$\Pi \sim 3.14 \sim \frac{22}{7}.$$

The circumference of a circle is found by the formula $C = 2\Pi r$ or $C = \Pi d$ where r is the radius of the circle and d is the diameter.

The **area** of a circle is found by the formula $A = \Pi r^2$.

Example: Find the circumference and area of a circle whose radius is 7 meters.

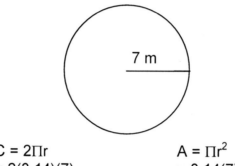

$C = 2\Pi r$	$A = \Pi r^2$
$= 2(3.14)(7)$	$= 3.14(7)(7)$
$= 43.96$ m	$= 153.86$ m^2

We use the following formulas to compute **volume** and **surface area:**

FIGURE	VOLUME	TOTAL SURFACE AREA
Right Cylinder	$\pi r^2 h$	$2\pi rh + 2\pi r^2$
Right Cone	$\dfrac{\pi r^2 h}{3}$	$\pi r \sqrt{r^2 + h^2} + \pi r^2$
Sphere	$\dfrac{4}{3}\pi r^3$	$4\pi r^2$
Rectangular Solid	LWH	$2LW + 2WH + 2LH$

FIGURE	LATERAL AREA	TOTAL AREA	VOLUME
Regular Pyramid	1/2Pl	1/2Pl+B	1/3Bh

P = Perimeter
h = height
B = Area of Base
l = slant height

Example: What is the volume of a shoebox with a length of 35 cm, a width of 20 cm, and a height of 15 cm?

Volume of a rectangular solid
= Length x Width x Height
= 35 x 20 x 15
= 10500 cm^3

Example: A water company is trying to decide whether to use traditional cylindrical paper cups or to offer conical paper cups since both cost the same. The traditional cups are 8 cm wide and 14 cm high. The conical cups are 12 cm wide and 19 cm high. The company will use the cup that holds the most water.

Draw and label a sketch of each.

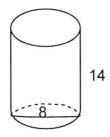

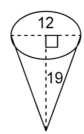

$V = \pi r^2 h$ $V = \dfrac{\pi r^2 h}{3}$ 1. write formula

$V = \pi (4)^2 (14)$ $V = \dfrac{1}{3}\pi (6)^2 (19)$ 2. substitute

$V = 703.717$ cm^3 $V = 716.283$ cm^3 3. solve

The choice should be the conical cup since its volume is more.

Example: How much material do we need to make a basketball that has a diameter of 15 inches? How much air do we need to fill the basketball?

Draw and label a sketch:

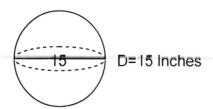

D = 15 Inches

Total surface area	Volume	
$TSA = 4\pi r^2$	$V = \dfrac{4}{3}\pi r^3$	1. write formula
$= 4\pi(7.5)^2$	$= \dfrac{4}{3}\pi(7.5)^3$	2. substitute
$= 706.858 \text{ in}^2$	$= 1767.1459 \text{ in}^3$	3. solve

Skill 10.6   Solve measurement problems by using estimates of measure, rates as measures, making visual comparisons, using scaling/proportional reasoning.

To estimate measurement of familiar objects, it is first necessary to determine the units to be used.

Examples:

Length
1. The coastline of Florida
2. The width of a ribbon
3. The thickness of a book
4. The depth of water in a pool

Weight or mass
1. A bag of sugar
2. A school bus
3. A dime

Capacity or volume
1. Paint to paint a bedroom
2. Glass of milk

Money
1. Cost of a house
2. Cost of a cup of coffee
3. Exchange rate

Perimeter
1. The edge of a backyard
2. The edge of a football field

Area
1. The size of a carpet
2. The size of a state

Example: Estimate the measurements of the following objects:

Length of a dollar bill	6 inches
Weight of a baseball	1 pound
Distance from New York to Florida	1100 km
Volume of water to fill a medicine dropper	1 milliliter
Length of a desk	2 meters
Temperature of water in a swimming pool	80° F

Depending on the degree of accuracy needed, we can measure an object in different units. For example, a pencil may be 6 inches to the nearest inch, or $6\frac{3}{8}$ inches to the nearest eighth of an inch. Similarly, it might be 15 cm to the nearest centimeter or 154 mm to the nearest millimeter.

Given a set of objects and their measurements, the use of rounding procedures is helpful when attempting to round to the nearest given unit. When rounding to a given place value, it is necessary to look at the number in the next smaller place. If this number is 5 or more, we increase the number in the place we are rounding to by one and change all numbers to the right to zero. If the number is less than 5, the number in the place we are rounding to stays the same and we change all numbers to the right to zero.

One method of rounding measurements can require an additional step. First, we must convert the measurement to a decimal number. Then the rules for rounding apply.

Example: Round the measurements to the given units.

MEASUREMENT	ROUND TO NEAREST	ANSWER
1 foot 7 inches	foot	2 ft
5 pound 6 ounces	pound	5 pounds
5 9/16 inches	inch	6 inches

Convert each measurement to a decimal number. Then apply the rules for rounding.

1 foot 7 inches = $1\frac{7}{12}$ ft = 1.58333 ft, round up to 2 ft

5 pounds 6 ounces = $5\frac{6}{16}$ pounds = 5.375 pound, round to 5 pounds

$5\frac{9}{16}$ inches = 5.5625 inches, round up to 6 inches

Example: Janet goes into a store to purchase a CD on sale for $13.95. While shopping, she sees two pairs of shoes, prices $19.95 and $14.50. She only has $50. Can she purchase everything?

Solve by rounding:

$19.95→$20.00
$14.50→$15.00
$13.95→$14.00
             $49.00   Yes, she can purchase the CD and the shoes.

Rated measurements

Example: A class wants to take a field trip from New York City to Albany to visit the capital. The trip is approximately 160 miles. If they will be traveling at 50 miles per hour, how long will it take for them to get there (assuming they are traveling at a steady rate)?

Set up the equation as a proportion and solve:

$$\frac{160 \text{ miles}}{x \text{ hours}} = \frac{50 \text{ miles}}{1 \text{ hour}}$$

(160 miles)(1 hour) = (50 miles) (x hours)

160 = 50x

x = 3.2 hours

Example: A salesman drove 480 miles from Pittsburgh to Hartford. The next day, he returned the same distance to Pittsburgh in half an hour's less time than his original trip took because he increased his average speed by 4 mph. Find his original speed.

Since distance = rate x time, then time = $\frac{\text{distance}}{\text{rate}}$

original time – 1/2 hour = shorter return time

$$\frac{480}{x} - \frac{1}{2} = \frac{480}{x+4}$$

Multiplying by the LCD of $2x(x+4)$, the equation becomes:

$480\left[2(x+4)\right] - 1\left[x(x+4)\right] = 480(2x)$

$960x + 3840 - x^2 - 4x = 960x$

$x^2 + 4x - 3840 = 0$

$(x+64)(x-60) = 0$

$x = 60$ 60 mph is the original speed

                           64 mph is the faster return speed

Cost per unit

The unit rate for purchasing an item is its price divided by the number of pounds/ ounces, etc. in the item. The item with the lower unit rate is the lower price.

Example: Find the item with the best unit price:

$1.79 for 10 ounces
$1.89 for 12 ounces
$5.49 for 32 ounces

$$\frac{1.79}{10} = 0.179 \text{ per ounce} \qquad \frac{1.89}{12} = 0.1575 \text{ per ounce} \qquad \frac{5.49}{32} = 0.172 \text{ per ounce}$$

$1.89 for 12 ounces is the best price.

Congruent figures have the same size and shape. If one is placed above the other, it will fit exactly. Congruent lines have the same length. Congruent angles have equal measures.

The symbol for congruent is $\cong$.

Polygons (pentagons) *ABCDE* and *VWXYZ* are congruent. They are exactly the same size and shape.

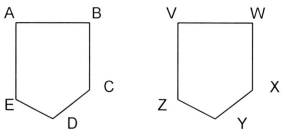

$$ABCDE \cong VWXYZ$$

Corresponding parts are those congruent angles and congruent sides, that is:

corresponding angles	corresponding sides
$\angle A \leftrightarrow \angle V$	$AB \leftrightarrow VW$
$\angle B \leftrightarrow \angle W$	$BC \leftrightarrow WX$
$\angle C \leftrightarrow \angle X$	$CD \leftrightarrow XY$
$\angle D \leftrightarrow \angle Y$	$DE \leftrightarrow YZ$
$\angle E \leftrightarrow \angle Z$	$AE \leftrightarrow VZ$

Example: Given two similar quadrilaterals, find the lengths of sides *x, y,* and z.

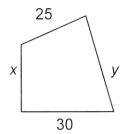
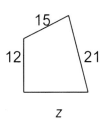

Corresponding sides are proportional,
so the scale is:

$$\frac{12}{x} = \frac{3}{5} \qquad \frac{21}{y} = \frac{3}{5} \qquad \frac{z}{30} = \frac{3}{5}$$

$$3x = 60 \qquad 3y = 105 \qquad 5z = 90$$
$$x = 20 \qquad y = 35 \qquad z = 18$$

Similarity

Two figures that have the same shape are **similar**. Polygons are similar if--and only if—corresponding angles are congruent, and corresponding sides are in proportion. Corresponding parts of similar polygons are proportional.

Example: Given the rectangles below, compare the area and perimeter.

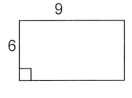
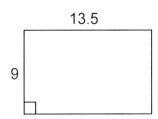

$A = LW$	$A = LW$	1. Write formula.
$A = (6)(9)$	$A = (9)(13.5)$	2. Substitute known values.
$A = 54$ sq. units	$A = 121.5$ sq. units	3. Compute.
$P = 2(L + W)$	$P = 2(L + W)$	1. Write formula.
$P = 2(6 + 9)$	$P = 2(9 + 13.5)$	2. Substitute known Values
$P = 30$ units	$P = 45$ units	3. Compute.

Notice that the areas relate to each other in the following manner:

Ratio of sides: $9/13.5 = 2/3$

Multiply the first area by the square of the reciprocal $(3/2)^2$ to get the second area.

$$54 \times (3/2)^2 = 121.5$$

The perimeters relate to each other in the following manner:

Ratio of sides: $9/13.5 = 2/3$

Multiply the perimeter of the first by the reciprocal of the ratio to get the perimeter of the second.

$$30 \times 3/2 = 45$$

Example: Tommy draws and cuts out 2 triangles for a school project. One of them has sides of 3, 6, and 9 inches. The other triangle has sides of 2, 4, and 6. Is there a relationship between the two triangles?

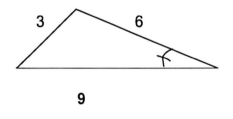

9   6

Take the proportion of the corresponding sides.

$$\frac{2}{3} \qquad \frac{4}{6} = \frac{2}{3} \qquad \frac{6}{9} = \frac{2}{3}$$

The smaller triangle is 2/3 the size of the large triangle.

Skill 10.7   Recognize and use geometric properties and relationships in both pure and real-world situations, using concepts of symmetry and the Pythagorean relationship.

There are four basic **transformational symmetries** that can be used: **translation, rotation, reflection,** and **glide reflection**. The transformation of an object is called its **image**. If the original object was labeled with letters, such as $ABCD$, the image may be labeled with the same letters followed by a prime symbol, $A'B'C'D'$.

A **translation** is a transformation that "slides" an object a fixed distance in a given direction. The original object and its translation have the same shape and size, and they face in the same direction.

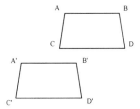

An example of a translation in architecture would be stadium seating. The seats are the same size and the same shape and face the same direction.

A **rotation** is a transformation that turns a figure about a fixed point called the center of rotation. An object and its rotation are the same shape and size, but the figures may be turned in different directions. Rotations can occur in either a clockwise or a counterclockwise direction.

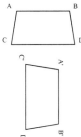

Rotations can be seen in wallpaper and art, and a Ferris wheel is also an example of rotation.

An object and its **reflection** have the same shape and size, but the figures face in opposite directions.

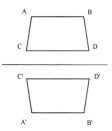

The line (where a mirror may be placed) is called the **line of reflection**. The distance from a point to the line of reflection is the same as the distance from the point's image to the line of reflection.

A **glide reflection** is a combination of a reflection and a translation.

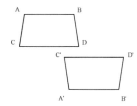

The Pythagorean Theorem

Given any right-angled triangle, $\triangle ABC$, the square of the hypotenuse is equal to the sum of the squares of the other two sides.

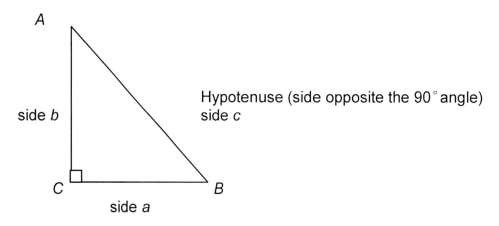

The theorem says that: $c^2 = a^2 + b^2$

Example: Find the area and perimeter of a rectangle if its length is 12 inches and its diagonal is 15 inches.

1. Draw and label sketch.

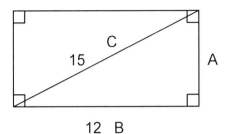

2. Since the height is still needed, use Pythagorean formula to find the missing leg of the triangle.

$$A^2 + B^2 = C^2$$
$$A^2 + 12^2 = 15^2$$
$$A^2 = 15^2 - 12^2$$
$$A^2 = 81$$
$$A = 9$$

Now, use this information to find the area and perimeter.

$$A = LW \qquad\qquad P = 2(L + W)$$
$$A = (12)(9) \qquad P = 2(12 + 9)$$
$$A = 108 \text{ in}^2 \qquad P = 42 \text{ inches}$$

1. Write formula.
2. Substitute.
3. Solve.

COMPETENCY 11.0   FORMAL MATHEMATICAL REASONING

Skill 11.1   Interpret statements that use logical connectives as well as quantifiers.

A simple statement represents a simple idea that can be described either as *true* or *false*, but not both. A small letter of the alphabet represents a simple statement.

Example: "Today is Monday." This is a simple statement since we can determine that this statement is either true or false. We can write p = "Today is Monday."

Example: "John, please be quiet." We do not consider this a simple statement in our study of logic, since we cannot assign a truth value to it.

Simple statements joined by **connectives** (*and, or, not, if then*, and *if and only if*) result in compound statements. Note that we can also form compound statements using *but, however,* or *nevertheless*. We can assign a truth value to a compound statement.

We frequently write conditional statements in *if-then* form. The *if* clause of the conditional is known as the **hypothesis**, and the *then* clause is called the **conclusion**. In a proof, the hypothesis is the information that is assumed true, while the conclusion is what is to be proven true. We consider a conditional to be of the form: **If p, then q,** where p is the hypothesis and q is the conclusion.

$p \rightarrow q$ is read, "If p, then q."
~ (statement) is read, "It is not true that (statement)."

Quantifiers are words describing a quantity under discussion. These include words such as *all, none* (or *no*), and *some*.

Negation of a Statement—If a statement is true, then its negation must be false (and vice versa).

A Summary of Negation Rules:

statement	negation
(1) q	(1) <u>not</u> q
(2) <u>not</u> q	(2) q
(3) π <u>and</u> s	(3) (not π) <u>or</u> (not s)
(4) π <u>or</u> s	(4) (not π) <u>and</u> (not s)
(5) if p, then q	(5) (p) <u>and</u> (not q)

Example: Select the statement that is the negation of "some winter nights are not cold."

A. All winter nights are not cold.
B. Some winter nights are cold.
C. All winter nights are cold.
D. None of the winter nights is cold.

Negation of *some are* is *none is*. Therefore, the negation statement is "None of the winter nights is cold." Therefore, the answer is D.

Example: Select the statement that is the negation of "If it rains, then the beach party will not be held."

A. If it does not rain, then the beach party will be held.
B. If the beach party is held, then it will not rain.
C. It does not rain and the beach party will be held.
D. It rains and the beach party will be held.

Negation of "If *p*, then *q*" is "*p* and (not *q*)." The negation of the given statement is "It rains and the beach party will be held." Select D.

Example: Select the negation of the statement "If they get elected, then all politicians go back on election promises."

A. If they are elected, then many politicians go back on election promises.
B. They are elected and some politicians go back on election promises.
C. If they are not elected, some politicians do not go back on election promises.
D. None of the above statements is the negation of the given statement.

Identify the key words of "if...then" and "all...go back". The negation of the given statement is "They are elected and none of the politicians goes back on election promises." So select response D, since statements A, B, and C are not the negations.

Example: Select the statement that is the negation of "the sun is shining bright <u>and</u> I feel great."

A. If the sun is not shining bright, I do not feel great.
B. The sun is not shining bright and I do not feel great.
C. The sun is not shining bring or I do not feel great.
D. The sun is shining bright and I do not feel great.

The negation of "*r* and *s*" is "(not *r*) or (not *s*)." Therefore, the negation of the given statement is "The sun is <u>not</u> shining bright <u>or</u> I do not feel great." We select response C.

We can diagram conditional statements using a **Venn diagram**. We can draw a diagram with one circle inside another circle. The inner circle represents the hypothesis. The outer circle represents the conclusion. If we take the hypothesis to be true, then you are located inside the inner circle. If you are located in the inner circle then you are also inside the outer circle, so that proves the conclusion is true.

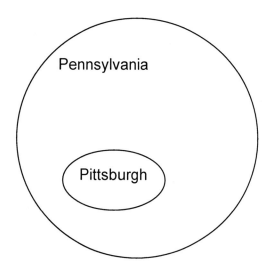

Example: If an angle has a measure of 90 degrees, then it is a right angle.

In this statement, "an angle has a measure of 90 degrees," is the hypothesis. In this statement, "it is a right angle" is the conclusion.

Example: If you are in Pittsburgh, then you are in Pennsylvania.

In this statement, "you are in Pittsburgh" is the hypothesis.
In this statement, "you are in Pennsylvania" is the conclusion.

Skill 11.2   **Use deductive reasoning to determine whether an argument (a series of statements leading to a conclusion) is valid or invalid.**

Deductive reasoning is the process of arriving at a conclusion based on other statements that we know to be true.

A symbolic argument consists of a set of premises and a conclusion in the format of of *if* [premise 1 and premise 2], *then* [conclusion].

An argument is **valid** when the conclusion follows necessarily from the premises. An argument is **invalid** or a fallacy when the conclusion does not follow from the premises.

We need to remember four standard forms of valid arguments:

1. Law of Detachment   If p, then q (premise 1)
                          p (premise 2)
                          Therefore, q

2. Law of Contraposition   If p, then q
                          not q
                          Therefore, not p

3. Law of Syllogism   If p, then q
                          If q, then r
                          Therefore if p, then r

4. Disjunctive Syllogism p or q
                          not p
                          Therefore, q

Example: Can we reach a conclusion from these two statements?

A.   All swimmers are athletes.
        All athletes are scholars.

In *if-then* form, these would be:

If you are a swimmer, then you are an athlete.
If you are an athlete, then you are a scholar.

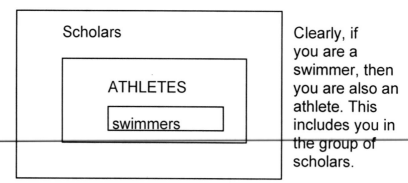

Clearly, if you are a swimmer, then you are also an athlete. This includes you in the group of scholars.

B.   All swimmers are athletes.
      All wrestlers are athletes.

In *if-then* form, these would be:

If you are a swimmer, then you are an athlete.
If you are a wrestler, then you are an athlete.

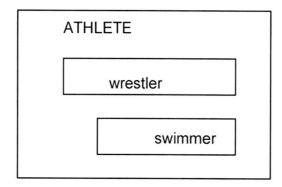

Clearly, if you are a swimmer or a wrestler, then you are also an athlete. This does NOT allow you to come to any other conclusions.

A swimmer may or may NOT also be a wrestler. Therefore, NO CONCLUSION IS POSSIBLE.

Suppose that these statements were given to you, and you were asked to try to reach a conclusion. The statements are:

Example: Determine whether statement A, B, C, or D can be deduced from the following:

(i) If John drives the big truck, then the shipment will be delivered.

(ii) The shipment will not be delivered.

a. John does not drive the big truck.
b. John drives the big truck.
c. The shipment will not be delivered.
d. None of the above conclusion is true.

Let p: John drives the big truck.
q: The shipment is delivered.

Statement (i) gives $p \rightarrow q$, statement (ii) gives $\sim q$. This is the Law of Contraposition.

Therefore, the logical conclusion is $\sim p$ or "John does not drive the big truck." Therefore, the answer is response A.

Example: Given that:

(i) Peter is a jet pilot or Peter is a navigator.
(ii) Peter is not a jet pilot.

Determine which conclusion can be logically deduced.

a. Peter is not a navigator.
b. Peter is a navigator.
c. Peter is neither a jet pilot nor a navigator.
d. None of the above is true.

Let p: Peter is a jet pilot.
q: Peter is a navigator.

So we have $p \vee q$ from statement (i)
$\sim p$ from statement (ii)

So choose response B.

Try These:

What conclusion, if any, can be reached? Assume each statement is true, regardless of any personal beliefs.

1. If the Red Sox win the World Series, I will die.
   I died.

2. If an angle's measure Is between 0° and 90°, then the angle is acute. Angle B is not acute.

3. Students who do well in geometry will succeed in college.
   Annie is doing extremely well in geometry.

4. Left-handed people are witty and charming.
   You are left-handed.

Question #1   The Red Sox won the World Series.
Question #2   Angle B is not between 0 and 90 degrees.
Question #3   Annie will do well in college.
Question #4   You are witty and charming.

Sample Test: Mathematics

1. $-9\dfrac{1}{4}$ ☐ $-8\dfrac{2}{3}$

   (Average Rigor) (Skill 7.2)

   A. =
   B. <
   C. >
   D. ≤

2. 0.74 =
   (Easy) (Skill 7.3)

   A. $\dfrac{74}{100}$

   B. 7.4%

   C. $\dfrac{33}{50}$

   D. $\dfrac{74}{10}$

3. $(3 \times 9)^4 =$
   (Rigorous) (Skill 7.3)

   A. $(3 \times 9)(3 \times 9)(27 \times 27)$
   B. $(3 \times 9) + (3 \times 9)$
   C. (12×36)
   D. $(3 \times 9) + (3 \times 9) + (3 \times 9)$
      $+ (3 \times 9)$

4. $(-2.1 \times 10^4)(4.2 \times 10^{-5}) =$
   (Rigorous) (Skill 7.3)

   A. 8.82
   B. −8.82
   C. −0.882
   D. 0.882

5. $\dfrac{2^{10}}{2^5} =$

   (Rigorous) (Skill 7.3)

   A. 2^2
   B. 2^5
   C. 2^{50}
   D. $2^{\frac{1}{2}}$

6. Choose the expression that is not equivalent to 5x + 3y + 15z.
   (Average Rigor) (Skill 7.5)

   A. 5(x + 3z) + 3y
   B. 3(x + y + 5z)
   C. 3y + 5(x + 3z)
   D. 5x + 3(y + 5z)

7. Choose the statement that is true for all real numbers.
   (Rigorous) (Skill 7.5)

   A. $a = 0, b \neq 0,$ then $\dfrac{b}{a}$ = undefined.
   B. $-(a + (-a)) = 2a$
   C. $2(ab) = -(2a)b$
   D. $-a(b + 1) = ab - a$

8. What is the greatest common factor of 16, 28, and 36?
   (Easy) (Skill 8.1)

   A. 2
   B. 4
   C. 8
   D. 16

9. $\left(\dfrac{-4}{9}\right)+\left(\dfrac{-7}{10}\right)=$

   (Average Rigor) (Skill 8.1)

   A. $\dfrac{23}{90}$

   B. $\dfrac{-23}{90}$

   C. $\dfrac{103}{90}$

   D. $\dfrac{-103}{90}$

10. $(5.6)\times(-0.11)=$

    (Average Rigor) (Skill 8.1)

    A. -0.616
    B. 0.616
    C. -6.110
    D. 6.110

11. $\dfrac{7}{9}+\dfrac{1}{3}\div\dfrac{2}{3}=$

    (Easy) (Skill 8.1)

    A. $\dfrac{5}{3}$

    B. $\dfrac{3}{2}$

    C. 2

    D. $\dfrac{23}{18}$

12. $4\dfrac{2}{9}\ \times\ \dfrac{7}{10}$

    (Rigorous) (Skill 8.1)

    A. $4\dfrac{9}{10}$

    B. $\dfrac{266}{90}$

    C. $2\dfrac{43}{45}$

    D. $2\dfrac{6}{20}$

13. Round $1\dfrac{13}{16}$ of an inch to the nearest quarter of an inch.
    (Easy) (Skill 8.2)

    A. $1\dfrac{1}{4}$ inch

    B. $1\dfrac{5}{8}$ inch

    C. $1\dfrac{3}{4}$ inch

    D. 2 inches

14. It takes 5 equally-skilled people 9 hours to shingle Mr. Joe's roof. Let *t* be the time required for only 3 of these men to do the same job. Select the correct statement of the given condition.
(Rigorous) (Skill 8.3)

A. $\dfrac{3}{5} = \dfrac{9}{t}$

B. $\dfrac{9}{5} = \dfrac{3}{t}$

C. $\dfrac{5}{9} = \dfrac{3}{t}$

D. $\dfrac{14}{9} = \dfrac{t}{5}$

15. 303 is what percent of 600?
(Easy) (Skill 8.3)

A. 0.505%
B. 5.05%
C. 505%
D. 50.5%

16. A restaurant employs 465 people. There are 280 waiters and 185 cooks. If 168 waiters and 85 cooks receive pay raises, what percent of the waiters will receive a pay raise?
(Average Rigor) (Skill 8.3)

A. 36.13%
B. 60%
C. 60.22%
D. 40%

17. In a sample of 40 full-time employees at a particular company, 35 were also holding down a part-time job requiring at least 10 hours/week. If this proportion holds for the entire company of 25,000 employees, how many full-time employees at this company are actually holding down a part-time job of at least 10 hours per week.
(Rigorous) (Skill 8.3)

A. 714
B. 625
C. 21,875
D. 28,571

18. An item that sells for $375 is put on sale for $120. What is the percent of decrease?
(Rigorous) (Skill 8.3)

A. 25%
B. 28%
C. 68%
D. 34%

19. The table below shows the distribution of majors for a group of college students.

Major	Proportion of students
Mathematics	0.32
Photography	0.26
Journalism	0.19
Engineering	0.21
Criminal Law	0.02

If it is known that a student, chosen at random is not majoring in mathematics or engineering, what is the probability that a student is majoring in journalism?
(Rigorous) (Skill 8.5)

A. 0.19
B. 0.36
C. 0.40
D. 0.81

20. If $4x - (3 - x) = 7(x - 3) + 10$, then
(Average Rigor) (Skill 8.6)

A. $x = 8$
B. $x = -8$
C. $x = 4$
D. $x = -4$

21. For each of the statements below, determine whether $x = \dfrac{1}{6}$ is a solution.

i. $6x \le 4x^2 + 2$
ii. $10x + 1 = 3(4x - 3)$
iii. $|x - 1| = x$
(Rigorous) (Skill 8.6)

A. i, ii, and iii
B. i and iii only
C. i only
D. iii only

22. Given $f(x) = (x)^3 - 3(x)^2 + 5$, find $x = (-2)$.
(Rigorous) (Skill 8.6)

A. 15
B. -15
C. 25
D. -25

23. Choose the equation that is equivalent to the following:

$$\frac{3x}{5} - 5 = 5x$$
(Rigorous) (Skill 8.6)

A. $3x - 25 = 25x$

B. $x - \dfrac{25}{3} = 25x$

C. $6x - 50 = 75x$

D. $x + 25 = 25x$

24. Solve for x.

$$3x - \frac{2}{3} = \frac{5x}{2} + 2$$

(Rigorous) (Skill 8.6)

A. $5\frac{1}{3}$

B. $\frac{17}{3}$

C. 2

D. $\frac{16}{2}$

25. Two mathematics classes have a total of 410 students. The 8:00 am class has 40 more than the 10:00 am class. How many students are in the 10:00 am class?
(Average Rigor) (Skill 8.6)

A. 123.3
B. 370
C. 185
D. 330

26. The following chart shows the yearly average number of international tourists visiting Palm Beach for 1990-1994. How many more international tourists visited Palm Beach in 1994 than in 1991?
(Easy) (Skill 9.1)

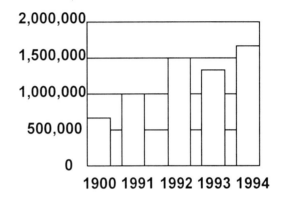

A. 100,000
B. 600,000
C. 1,600,000
D. 8,000,000

27. Consider the graph of the distribution of the length of time it took individuals to complete an employment form.

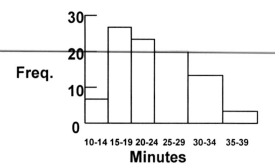

Minutes

Approximately how many individuals took less than 15 minutes to complete the employment form?
(Easy) (Skill 9.1)

A. 35
B. 28
C. 7
D. 4

28. What is the mode of the data in the following sample?
(Average Rigor) (Skill 9.2)

9, 10, 11, 9, 10, 11, 9, 13

A. 9
B. 9.5
C. 10
D. 11

29. Mary did comparison shopping on her favorite brand of coffee. Over half of the stores priced the coffee at $1.70. Most of the remaining stores priced the coffee at $1.80, except for a few who charged $1.90. Which of the following statements is true about the distribution of prices?
(Rigorous) (Skill 9.2)

A. The mean and the mode are the same.
B. The mean is greater than the mode.
C. The mean is less than the mode.
D. The mean is less than the median.

30. What is the equation that expresses the relationship between x and y in the table below?
(Rigorous) (Skill 9.4)

x	y
−2	4
−1	2
0	−2
1	−5
2	−8

A. $y = -x - 2$
B. $y = -3x - 2$
C. $y = 3x - 2$
D. $y = \dfrac{1}{3}x - 1$

31. **What measure could be used to report the distance traveled in walking around a track?**
(Easy) (Skill 10.1)

    A.   degrees
    B.   square meters
    C.   kilometers
    D.   cubic feet

32. **What unit of measurement would describe the spread of a forest fire in a unit time?**
(Average Rigor) (Skill 10.1)

    A.   10 square yards per second
    B.   10 yards per minute
    C.   10 feet per hour
    D.   10 cubic feet per hour

33. **For the following statements:**

    I.   **All parallelograms are rectangles.**
    II.   **Some rhombuses are squares.**
    III.   **All parallelograms are rectangles.**
(Average Rigor) (Skill 10.5)

    A.   All statements are correct
    B.   All statements are incorrect
    C.   Only II and III are correct
    D.   Only II is correct

34. **What type of triangle is △ABC?**
(Average Rigor) (Skill 10.5)

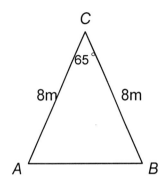

    A.   right
    B.   equilateral
    C.   scalene
    D.   isosceles

35. **What is the area of a square whose side is 13 feet?**
(Easy) (Skill 10.5)

    A.   169 feet
    B.   169 square feet
    C.   52 feet
    D.   52 square feet

36. **The trunk of a tree has a 2.1 meter radius. What is its circumference?**
(Rigorous) (Skill 10.5)

    A. 2.1π square meters
    B. 4.2π meters
    C. 2.1π meters
    D. 4.2π square meters

37. The figure below shows a running track with the shape of a rectangle with semicircles at each end.

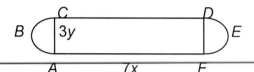

Calculate the distance around the track.
(Rigorous) (Skill 10.5)

A. $6\pi y + 14x$
B. $3\pi y + 7x$
C. $6\pi y + 7x$
D. $3\pi y + 14x$

38. What is the area of this triangle?
(Rigorous) (Skill 10.5)

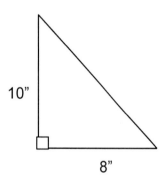

A. 80 square inches
B. 20 square inches
C. 40 square inches
D. 30 square inches

39. Given the formula $d = rt$, (where d = distance, r = rate, and t = time), calculate the time required for a vehicle to travel 585 miles at a rate of 65 miles per hour.
(Average Rigor) (Skill 10.6)

A. 8.5 hours
B. 6.5 hours
C. 9.5 hours
D. 9 hours

40. The price of gas was $3.27 per gallon. Your tank holds 15 gallons of fuel. You are using two tanks a week. How much will you save weekly if the price of gas goes down to $2.30 per gallon?
(Average Rigor) (Skill 10.6)

A. $26.00
B. $29.00
C. $15.00
D. $17.00

41. A car gets 25.36 miles per gallon. The car has been driven 83,310 miles. What is a reasonable estimate for the number of gallons of gas used?
(Average Rigor) (Skill 10.6)

A. 2,087 gallons
B. 3,000 gallons
C. 1,800 gallons
D. 164 gallons

42. Study figures A, B, C, and D. Select the letter in which all triangles are similar.
(Rigorous) (Skill 10.6)

A.

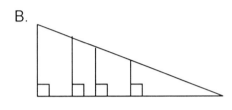

B.

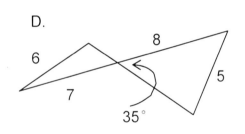

C.

D.

43. The owner of a rectangular piece of land 40 yards in length and 30 yards in width wants to divide it into two parts. She plans to join two opposite corners with a fence, as shown in the diagram below. The cost of the fence will be approximately $25 per linear foot. What is the estimated cost for the fence needed by the owner?
(Rigorous) (Skill 10.7)

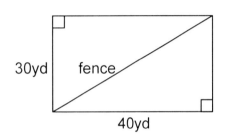

A. $1,250
B. $62,500
C. $5,250
D. $3,750

44. Set A, B, C, and U are related as shown in the diagram.
(Average Rigor) (Skill 11.1)

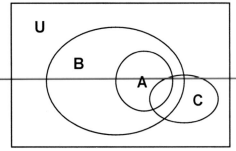

Which of the following is true, assuming not one of the six regions is empty?

A. Any element that is a member of set B is also a member of set A.

B. No element is a member of all three sets A, B, and C.

C. Any element that is a member of set U is also a member of set B.

D. None of the above statements is true.

45. Select the statement that is the negation of the statement, "If the weather is cold, then the soccer game will be played."
(Average Rigor) (Skill 11.1)

A. If the weather is not cold, then the soccer game will be played.

B. The weather is cold and the soccer game was not played.

C. If the soccer game is played, then the weather is not cold.

D. The weather is cold and the soccer game will be played.

46. Select the statement below that is NOT logically equivalent to, "If Mary works late, then Bill will prepare lunch."
(Average Rigor) (Skill 11.1)

A. Bill prepares lunch or Mary does not work late.

B. If Bill does not prepare lunch, then Mary did not work late.

C. If Bill prepares lunch, then Mary works late.

D. Mary does not work late or Bill prepares lunch.

47. Given that:
    i. No athletes are weak.
    ii. All football players are athletes.

    Determine which conclusion can be logically deduced.
    (Average Rigor) (Skill 11.1)

    A. Some football players are weak.
    B. All football players are weak.
    C. No football player is weak.
    D. None of the above is true.

48. Study the information given below. If a logical conclusion is given, select that conclusion.

    Bob eats donuts, or he eats yogurt. If Bob eats yogurt, then he is healthy. If Bob is healthy, then he can run the marathon. Bob does not eat yogurt.
    (Average Rigor) (Skill 11.1)

    A. Bob does not eat donuts.
    B. Bob is healthy.
    C. If Bob runs the Marathon, then he eats yogurt.
    D. None of the above is warranted.

49. Select the rule of logical equivalence that directly (in one step) transforms the statement (i) into statement (ii).

    i. Not all the students have books.
    ii. Some students do not have books.
    (Average Rigor) (Skill 11.2)

    A. "If p, then q" is equivalent to "if not q, then p."
    B. "Not all are p" is equivalent to "some are not p."
    C. "Not q" is equivalent to "p."
    D. "All are not p" is equivalent to "none is p."

50. All of the following arguments have true conclusions, but one of the arguments is not valid. Select the argument that is not valid.
(Average Rigor) (Skill 11.2)

A. All sea stars are echinoderms and all echinoderms are marine; therefore, all sea stars are marine.

B. All spiders are dangerous. The black widow is dangerous. Therefore, the black widow is a spider.

C. All crocodiles are amphibians and all amphibians breathe by lungs, gill, or skin; therefore, all crocodiles breathe by lungs, gill, or skin.

D. All kids have hats and all boys are kids; therefore, all boys have hats.

Answer Key: Mathematics

1.	B		27.	C
2.	A		28.	A
3.	A		29.	B
4.	C		30.	B
5.	B		31.	C
6.	B		32.	A
7.	A		33.	D
8.	B		34.	D
9.	D		35.	B
10.	A		36.	B
11.	D		37.	D
12.	C		38.	C
13.	C		39.	D
14.	B		40.	B
15.	D		41.	B
16.	B		42.	B
17.	C		43.	D
18.	C		44.	D
19.	C		45.	A
20.	C		46.	C
21.	C		47.	C
22.	B		48.	D
23.	A		49.	B
24.	A		50.	B
25.	C			
26.	B			

Rigor Table: Mathematics

	Easy 20%	Average 40%	Rigorous 40%
Questions (53)	3, 4, 5, 8, 14, 15, 28, 29, 33, 37	1, 6, 7, 16, 21, 22, 30, 34, 35, 36, 41, 42, 43, 44, 47, 48, 49, 50, 51, 52, 53	2, 9, 10, 11, 12, 13, 17, 18, 19, 20, 23, 24, 25, 26, 27, 31, 32, 38, 39, 40, 45, 46
TOTALS	10 (18.9%)	21 (39.6%)	22 (41.5%)

Rationales with Sample Questions: Mathematics

1. $-9\dfrac{1}{4}$ ☐ $-8\dfrac{2}{3}$

   (Average Rigor) (Skill 7.2)

   A. $=$
   B. $<$
   C. $>$
   D. $\leq$

Answer: B. $<$

The larger the absolute value of a negative number, the smaller the negative number is. The absolute value of $-9\dfrac{1}{4}$ is $9\dfrac{1}{4}$ which is larger than the absolute value of $-8\dfrac{2}{3}$, which is $8\dfrac{2}{3}$. Therefore, the sign should be $-9\dfrac{1}{4} < -8\dfrac{2}{3}$.

2. $0.74 =$
   (Easy) (Skill 7.3)

   A. $\dfrac{74}{100}$

   B. 7.4%

   C. $\dfrac{33}{50}$

   D. $\dfrac{74}{10}$

Answer: A. $\dfrac{74}{100}$

This is basic conversion of decimals to fractions. $0.74 \rightarrow$ the 4 is in the hundredths place, so the answer is $\dfrac{74}{100}$.

3. $(3 \times 9)^4 =$

    (Rigorous) (Skill 7.3)

    A. $(3 \times 9)(3 \times 9)(27 \times 27)$
    B. $(3 \times 9) + (3 \times 9)$
    C. (12×36)
    D. $(3 \times 9) + (3 \times 9) + (3 \times 9)$
        $+ (3 \times 9)$

Answer: A. (3 x 9) (3 x 9) (27 x 27)

$(3 \times 9)^4 = (3 \times 9)(3 \times 9)(3 \times 9)(3 \times 9)$, which, when solving two of the parentheses, is $(3 \times 9)(3 \times 9)(27 \times 27)$.

4. $(-2.1 \times 10^4)(4.2 \times 10^{-5}) =$

    (Rigorous) (Skill 7.3)

    A. 8.82
    B. −8.82
    C. −0.882
    D. 0.882

Answer: C. −0.882

First, multiply −2.1 and 4.2 to get −8.82. Then, multiply 10^4 by 10^{-5} to get 10^{-1}. $-8.82 \times 10^{-1} = -0.882$.

5. $\dfrac{2^{10}}{2^5} =$

    (Rigorous) (Skill 7.3)

    A. 2^2
    B. 2^5
    C. 2^{50}
    D. $2^{\frac{1}{2}}$

Answer: B. 2^5

The quotient rule of exponents says $\dfrac{a^m}{a^n} = a^{(m-n)}$ so $\dfrac{2^{10}}{2^5} = 2^{(10-5)} = 2^5$.

6. Choose the expression that is not equivalent to 5x + 3y + 15z.
   (Average Rigor) (Skill 7.5)

   A. 5(x + 3z) + 3y
   B. 3(x + y + 5z)
   C. 3y + 5(x + 3z)
   D. 5x + 3(y + 5z)

Answer: B. 3(x + y + 5z)

5x + 3y + 15z = (5x + 15z) + 3y = 5(x + 3z) + 3y   A. is true
                = 5x + (3y + 15z) = 5x + 3(y + 5z)   D. is true
                = 37 + (5x + 15z) = 37 + 5(x + 3z)   C. is true

We can solve all of these using the associative property and then factoring. However, in B, 3(x + y + 5z) by distributive property = 3x + 3y + 15z does not equal 5x + 37 + 15z.

7. Choose the statement that is true for all real numbers.
   (Rigorous) (Skill 7.5)

   A. $a = 0, b \neq 0$, then
      $\dfrac{b}{a}$ = undefined.
   B. $-(a + (-a)) = 2a$
   C. $2(ab) = -(2a)b$
   D. $-a(b + 1) = ab - a$

Answer: A. $a = 0, b \neq 0$, **then** $\dfrac{b}{a}$ = **undefined.**

Any number divided by 0 is undefined.

8. What is the greatest common factor of 16, 28, and 36?
   (Easy) (Skill 8.1)

   A. 2
   B. 4
   C. 8
   D. 16

Answer: B. 4

The smallest number in this set is 16; its factors are 1, 2, 4, 8, and 16. Sixteen is the largest factor, but it does not divide into 28 or 36. Neither does 8. Four does factor into both 28 and 36.

9. $\left(\dfrac{-4}{9}\right)+\left(\dfrac{-7}{10}\right)=$

(Average Rigor) (Skill 8.1)

A. $\dfrac{23}{90}$

B. $\dfrac{-23}{90}$

C. $\dfrac{103}{90}$

D. $\dfrac{-103}{90}$

Answer: D. $\dfrac{-103}{90}$

Find the LCD of $\dfrac{-4}{9}$ and $\dfrac{-7}{10}$. The LCD is 90, so you get $\dfrac{-40}{90}+\dfrac{-63}{90}=\dfrac{-103}{90}$.

10. $(5.6)\times(-0.11)=$

(Average Rigor) (Skill 8.1)

A. -0.616
B. 0.616
C. -6.110
D. 6.110

Answer: A. −0.616

Simple multiplication. The answer will be negative because a positive number multiplied by a negative number is a negative number. $5.6\times-0.11=-0.616$.

11. $\dfrac{7}{9} + \dfrac{1}{3} \div \dfrac{2}{3} =$

(Easy) (Skill 8.1)

   A. $\dfrac{5}{3}$

   B. $\dfrac{3}{2}$

   C. 2

   D. $\dfrac{23}{18}$

Answer: D. $\dfrac{23}{18}$

First, do the division.

$$\dfrac{1}{3} \div \dfrac{2}{3} = \dfrac{1}{3} \times \dfrac{3}{2} = \dfrac{1}{2}$$

Next, add the fractions.

$$\dfrac{7}{9} + \dfrac{1}{2} = \dfrac{14}{18} + \dfrac{9}{18} = \dfrac{23}{18}, \text{ which is answer D.}$$

12. $4\dfrac{2}{9}$ x $\dfrac{7}{10}$

(Rigorous) (Skill 8.1)

A. $4\dfrac{9}{10}$

B. $\dfrac{266}{90}$

C. $2\dfrac{43}{45}$

D. $2\dfrac{6}{20}$

Answer: C. $2\dfrac{43}{45}$

Convert any mixed number to an improper fraction: $\dfrac{38}{9}$ x $\dfrac{7}{10}$. Since no common factors of numerators or denominators exist, multiply the numerators and the denominators by each other = $\dfrac{266}{90}$. Convert back to a mixed number and reduce $2\dfrac{86}{90} = 2\dfrac{43}{45}$.

13. Round $1\frac{13}{16}$ of an inch to the nearest quarter of an inch.
    (Easy) (Skill 8.2)

   A. $1\frac{1}{4}$ inch

   B. $1\frac{5}{8}$ inch

   C. $1\frac{3}{4}$ inch

   D.   2 inches

Answer: C. $1\frac{3}{4}$ inch

$1\frac{13}{16}$ inches is approximately $1\frac{12}{16}$, which is also $1\frac{3}{4}$, which is the nearest $\frac{1}{4}$ of an inch, so the answer is C.

14. It takes 5 equally-skilled people 9 hours to shingle Mr. Joe's roof. Let *t* be the time required for only 3 of these men to do the same job. Select the correct statement of the given condition.
(Rigorous) (Skill 8.3)

A. $\dfrac{3}{5} = \dfrac{9}{t}$

B. $\dfrac{9}{5} = \dfrac{3}{t}$

C. $\dfrac{5}{9} = \dfrac{3}{t}$

D. $\dfrac{14}{9} = \dfrac{t}{5}$

Answer: B. $\dfrac{9}{5} = \dfrac{3}{t}$

$$\dfrac{9 \text{ hours}}{5 \text{ people}} = \dfrac{3 \text{ people}}{t \text{ hours}}$$

15. 303 is what percent of 600?
(Easy) (Skill 8.3)

A. 0.505%
B. 5.05%
C. 505%
D. 50.5%

Answer: D. 50.5%

Use *x* for the percent. $600x = 303$. $\dfrac{600x}{600} = \dfrac{303}{600} \rightarrow x = 0.505 = 50.5\%$.

16. A restaurant employs 465 people. There are 280 waiters and 185 cooks. If 168 waiters and 85 cooks receive pay raises, what percent of the waiters will receive a pay raise?
(Average Rigor) (Skill 8.3)

  A. 36.13%
  B. 60%
  C. 60.22%
  D. 40%

Answer: B. 60%

The total number of waiters is 280 and only 168 of them get a pay raise. Divide the number getting a raise by the total number of waiters to get the percent.

$$\frac{168}{280} = 0.6 = 60\%.$$

17. In a sample of 40 full-time employees at a particular company, 35 were also holding down a part-time job requiring at least 10 hours/week. If this proportion holds for the entire company of 25,000 employees, how many full-time employees at this company are actually holding down a part-time job of at least 10 hours per week. (Rigorous) (Skill 8.3)

  A. 714
  B. 625
  C. 21,875
  D. 28,571

Answer: C. 21,875

$\frac{35}{40}$ full-time employees also have a part-time job. Out of 25,000 full-time employees, the number that also have a part-time job is

$\frac{35}{40} = \frac{x}{25000} \to 40x = 875000 \to x = 21875$, so 21,875 full-time employees also have a part time job.

18.   An item that sells for $375 is put on sale for $120. What is the percent of decrease?
       (Rigorous) (Skill 8.3)

       A.   25%
       B.   28%
       C.   68%
       D.   34%

Answer: C. 68%

Use $(1 - x)$ as the discount. $375x = 120$.
$375(1-x) = 120 \rightarrow 375 - 375x = 120 \rightarrow 375x = 255 \rightarrow x = 0.68 = 68\%$.

19.   The table below shows the distribution of majors for a group of college students.

Major	Proportion of students
Mathematics	0.32
Photography	0.26
Journalism	0.19
Engineering	0.21
Criminal Law	0.02

       If it is known that a student, chosen at random is not majoring in mathematics or engineering, what is the probability that a student is majoring in journalism?
       (Rigorous) (Skill 8.5)

       A.   0.19
       B.   0.36
       C.   0.40
       D.   0.81

The proportion of students majoring in math or engineering is 0.32 + 0.21 = 0.53. This means that the proportion of students NOT majoring in math or engineering is 1.00 – 0.53 = 0.47. The proportion of students majoring in journalism out of those not majoring in math or engineering is $\dfrac{0.19}{0.47} = 0.404$.

21. For each of the statements below, determine whether $x = \dfrac{1}{6}$ is a solution.

    i. $6x \le 4x^2 + 2$
    ii. $10x + 1 = 3(4x - 3)$
    iii. $|x - 1| = x$
    (Rigorous) (Skill 8.6)

    A.   i, ii, and iii
    B.   i and iii only
    C.   i only
    D.   iii only

Answer: C. i only

Substitute $x = \dfrac{1}{6}$ into each equation and solve.

i. $6\left(\dfrac{1}{6}\right) \le 4\left(\dfrac{1}{6}\right)^2 + 2 = 1 \le 4\left(\dfrac{1}{36}\right) + 2 \rightarrow 1 \le \dfrac{1}{9} + 2 \rightarrow 1 \le 2\dfrac{1}{9}$ True.

ii. $10\left(\dfrac{1}{6}\right) + 1 = 3\left(4\left(\dfrac{1}{6}\right) - 3\right) = 2\dfrac{2}{3} = 3\left(\dfrac{2}{3} - 3\right) \rightarrow 2\dfrac{2}{3} = \dfrac{6}{3} - 9 \rightarrow 2\dfrac{2}{3} = -7$ False.

iii. $\left|\dfrac{1}{6} - 1\right| = \dfrac{1}{6} \rightarrow \left|\dfrac{1}{6} - \dfrac{6}{6}\right| = \dfrac{1}{6} \rightarrow \left|\dfrac{-5}{6}\right| = \dfrac{1}{6} \rightarrow \dfrac{5}{6} = \dfrac{1}{6}$ False.

So, only (i) is true, which is answer **C.**

22. Given $f(x) = (x)^3 - 3(x)^2 + 5$, find $x = (-2)$.
    (Rigorous) (Skill 8.6)

    A.   15
    B.   −15
    C.   25
    D.   −25

Answer: B. −15

Substitute $x = -2$.

$f(-2) = (-2)^3 - 3 \times (-2)^2 + 5$

$f(-2) = -8 - 3(4) + 5$

$f(-2) = -8 - 12 + 5$

$f(-2) = -15$

23. Choose the equation that is equivalent to the following:

$$\frac{3x}{5} - 5 = 5x$$

(Rigorous) (Skill 8.6)

A. $3x - 25 = 25x$

B. $x - \dfrac{25}{3} = 25x$

C. $6x - 50 = 75x$

D. $x + 25 = 25x$

Answer: A. 3x − 25 = 25x

A is the correct answer because it is the original equation multiplied by 5. The other choices alter the answer to the original equation.

24. Solve for x.

$$3x - \frac{2}{3} = \frac{5x}{2} + 2$$

(Rigorous) (Skill 8.6)

A. $5\frac{1}{3}$

B. $\frac{17}{3}$

C. 2

D. $\frac{16}{2}$

Answer: A. $5\frac{1}{3}$

$$3x(6) - \frac{2}{3}(6) = \frac{5x}{2}(6) + 2(6)$$ 6 is the LCD of 2 and 3

$$18x - 4 = 15x + 12$$

$$18x = 15x + 16$$

$$3x = 16$$

$$x = \frac{16}{3} = 5\frac{1}{3}$$

25. **Two mathematics classes have a total of 410 students. The 8:00 am class has 40 more than the 10:00 am class. How many students are in the 10:00 am class?**
   (Average Rigor) (Skill 8.6)

   A. 123.3
   B. 370
   C. 185
   D. 330

Answer: C. 185

Let x = # of students in the 8 am class and $x - 40$ = # of students in the 10 am class. $x + (x - 40) = 410 \rightarrow 2x - 40 = 410 \rightarrow 2x = 450 \rightarrow x = 225$. Therefore, there are 225 students in the 8 am class, and $225 - 40 = 185$ in the 10 am class.

26. The following chart shows the yearly average number of international tourists visiting Palm Beach for 1990–1994. How many more international tourists visited Palm Beach in 1994 than in 1991? *(Easy) (Skill 9.1)*

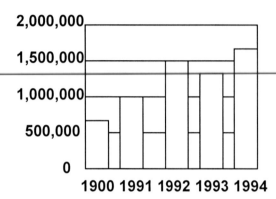

A.   100,000
B.   600,000
C.   1,600,000
D.   8,000,000

Answer: B. 600,000

The number of tourists in 1991 was 1,000,000 and the number in 1994 was 1,600,000. Subtract to get a difference of 600,000.

27. Consider the graph of the distribution of the length of time it took individuals to complete an employment form.

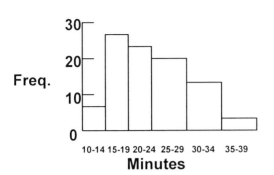

Freq.

Minutes

Approximately how many individuals took less than 15 minutes to complete the employment form?
(Easy) (Skill 9.1)

A. 35
B. 28
C. 7
D. 4

Answer: C. 7

According to the chart, the number of people who took under 15 minutes is seven.

28. What is the mode of the data in the following sample?
(Average Rigor) (Skill 9.2)

9, 10, 11, 9, 10, 11, 9, 13

A. 9
B. 9.5
C. 10
D. 11

Answer: A. 9

The mode is the number that appears most frequently. Nine appears three times, which is more than the other numbers.

29. Mary did comparison shopping on her favorite brand of coffee. Over half of the stores priced the coffee at $1.70. Most of the remaining stores priced the coffee at $1.80, except for a few who charged $1.90. Which of the following statements is true about the distribution of prices?
(Rigorous) (Skill 9.2)

A. The mean and the mode are the same.
B. The mean is greater than the mode.
C. The mean is less than the mode.
D. The mean is less than the median.

Answer: B. The mean is greater than the mode.

Over half the stores priced the coffee at $1.70, so this means that this is the mode. The mean would be slightly over $1.70 because other stores priced the coffee at over $1.70.

30. What is the equation that expresses the relationship between x and y in the table below?
(Rigorous) (Skill 9.4)

x	y
−2	4
−1	2
0	−2
1	−5
2	−8

A. $y = -x - 2$
B. $y = -3x - 2$
C. $y = 3x - 2$
D. $y = \dfrac{1}{3}x - 1$

Answer: B. $y = -3x - 2$

Solve by plugging in the values of x and y into the equations to see if they work. The answer is B because it is the only equation for which the values of x and y are correct.

31. **What measure could be used to report the distance traveled in walking around a track?**
(Easy) (Skill 10.1)

   A.   degrees
   B.   square meters
   C.   kilometers
   D.   cubic feet

Answer: C. kilometers

Degrees measure angles, square meters measure area, cubic feet measure volume, and kilometers measure length. Kilometers is the only reasonable answer.

32. **What unit of measurement would describe the spread of a forest fire in a unit time?**
(Average Rigor) (Skill 10.1)

   A.   10 square yards per second
   B.   10 yards per minute
   C.   10 feet per hour
   D.   10 cubic feet per hour

Answer: A. 10 square yards per second

The only appropriate answer is one that describes "an area" of forest consumed per unit time. Not all answers are units of area measurement, only answer A.

33. **For the following statements:**

   I.   **All parallelograms are rectangles.**
   II.   **Some rhombuses are squares.**
   III. **All parallelograms are rectangles.**
   (Average Rigor) (Skill 10.5)

   A.   All statements are correct
   B.   All statements are incorrect
   C.   Only II and III are correct
   D.   Only II is correct

Answer: D. Only II is correct.

I is false because only some parallelograms are rectangles. II is true. III is false because only some parallelograms are rhombuses. Only II is correct.

34. **What type of triangle is $\triangle ABC$?**
   (Average Rigor) (Skill 10.5)

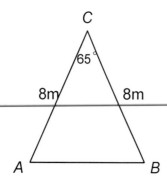

   A.   right
   B.   equilateral
   C.   scalene
   D.   isosceles

Answer: D. isosceles

Two of the sides are the same length, so we know the triangle is either equilateral or isosceles. $\square$ *CAB* and $\square$ *CBA* are equal, because their sides are.

Therefore, $180° = 65° - 2x = \dfrac{115°}{2} = 57.5°$. Because not all three angles are

equal, the triangle is isosceles.

35. **What is the area of a square whose side is 13 feet?**
   (Easy) (Skill 10.5)

   A.   169 feet
   B.   169 square feet
   C.   52 feet
   D.   52 square feet

Answer: B. 169 square feet

Area = length times width (*lw*)
Length = 13 feet
Width = 13 feet (square, so length and width are the same).
Area = $13 \times 13 = 169$ square feet
We measure area in square feet, so the answer is B.

36.   The trunk of a tree has a 2.1 meter radius. What is its circumference?
       (Rigorous) (Skill 10.5)

       A. 2.1π square meters
       B. 4.2π meters
       C. 2.1π meters
       D. 4.2π square meters

Answer: B. 4.2π meters

Circumference is $2\pi r$, where r is the radius. The circumference is $2\pi 2.1 = 4.2\pi$ meters (not square meters because we are not measuring area).

37.   **The figure below shows a running track with the shape of a rectangle with semicircles at each end.**

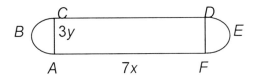

       Calculate the distance around the track.
       (Rigorous) (Skill 10.5)

       A. $6\pi y + 14x$
       B. $3\pi y + 7x$
       C. $6\pi y + 7x$
       D. $3\pi y + 14x$

Answer: D. $3\pi y + 14x$

The two semicircles of the track create one circle with a diameter 3y. The circumference of a circle is $C = \pi d$ so $C = 3\pi y$. The length of both sides of the track is 7x on each side, so the total circumference around the track is $3\pi y + 7x + 7x = 3\pi y + 14x$.

38.   **What is the area of this triangle?**
      (Rigorous) (Skill 10.5)

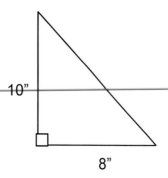

      A.   80 square inches
      B.   20 square inches
      C.   40 square inches
      D.   30 square inches

Answer: C. 40 square inches

The area of a triangle is $\frac{1}{2}bh$. $\frac{1}{2}x8x10 = 40$ square inches.

39.   **Given the formula *d = rt*, (where *d* = distance, *r* = rate, and *t* = time), calculate the time required for a vehicle to travel 585 miles at a rate of 65 miles per hour.**
      (Average Rigor) (Skill 10.6)

      A.   8.5 hours
      B.   6.5 hours
      C.   9.5 hours
      D.   9 hours

Answer: D. 9 hours

We are given d = 585 miles and r = 65 miles per hour and $d = rt$. Solve for t.
$585 = 65t \rightarrow t = 9$ hours.

40.	The price of gas was $3.27 per gallon. Your tank holds 15 gallons of fuel. You are using two tanks a week. How much will you save weekly if the price of gas goes down to $2.30 per gallon?
(Average Rigor) (Skill 10.6)

A.	$26.00
B.	$29.00
C.	$15.00
D.	$17.00

Answer: B. $29.00

15 gallons x 2 tanks = 30 gallons a week
30 gallons x $3.27 = $98.10
30 gallons x $2.30 = $69.00
$98.10 – $69.00 = $29.10 is approximately $29.00.

41.	A car gets 25.36 miles per gallon. The car has been driven 83,310 miles. What is a reasonable estimate for the number of gallons of gas used?
(Average Rigor) (Skill 10.6)

A.	2,087 gallons
B.	3,000 gallons
C.	1,800 gallons
D.	164 gallons

Answer: B. 3,000 gallons

Divide the number of miles by the miles per gallon to determine the approximate number of gallons of gas used. $\dfrac{83310 \text{ miles}}{25.36 \text{ miles per gallon}} = 3285$ gallons. This is approximately 3000 gallons.

42.	Study figures A, B, C, and D. Select the letter in which all triangles are similar.
	(Rigorous) (Skill 10.6)

A.

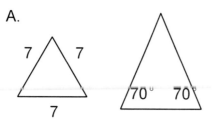

B.

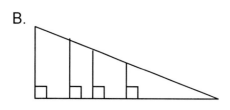

C.

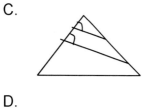

D.

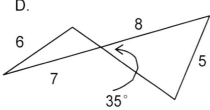

Answer: B.

Choice A is not correct because one triangle is equilateral and the other is isosceles. Choice C is not correct because the two smaller triangles are similar, but the large triangle is not. Choice D is not correct because the lengths and angles are not proportional to each other. Therefore, the correct answer is B because all the triangles have the same angles.

43. The owner of a rectangular piece of land 40 yards in length and 30 yards in width wants to divide it into two parts. She plans to join two opposite corners with a fence, as shown in the diagram below. The cost of the fence will be approximately $25 per linear foot. What is the estimated cost for the fence needed by the owner?
(Rigorous) (Skill 10.7)

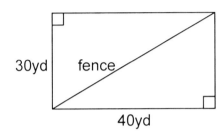

A. $1,250
B. $62,500
C. $5,250
D. $3,750

Answer: D. $3,750

Find the length of the diagonal by using the Pythagorean Theorem. Let x be the length of the diagonal.

$$30^2 + 40^2 = x^2 \rightarrow 900 + 1600 = x^2$$
$$2500 = x^2 \rightarrow \sqrt{2500} = \sqrt{x^2}$$
$$x = 50 \text{ yards}$$

Convert to feet. $\dfrac{50 \text{ yards}}{x \text{ feet}} = \dfrac{1 \text{ yard}}{3 \text{ feet}} \rightarrow 150 \text{ feet}$

It cost $25.00 per linear foot, so the cost is (150 ft)($25) = $3750.

44.   Set A, B, C, and U are related as shown in the diagram.
       (Average Rigor) (Skill 11.1)

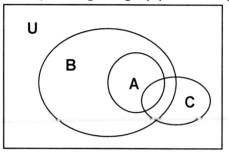

       Which of the following is true, assuming not one of the six regions is empty?

       A.   Any element that is a member of set B is also a member of set A.
       B.   No element is a member of all three sets A, B, and C.
       C.   Any element that is a member of set U is also a member of set B.
       D.   None of the above statements is true.

Answer: D. None of the above statements is true.

Answer A is incorrect because not all members of set B are also in set A. Answer B is incorrect because there are elements that are members of all three sets A, B, and C. Answer C is incorrect because not all members of set U are members of set B. This leaves answer D.

45.   **Select the statement that is the negation of the statement, "If the weather is cold, then the soccer game will be played."**
       (Average Rigor) (Skill 11.1)

       A.   If the weather is not cold, then the soccer game will be played.
       B.   The weather is cold and the soccer game was not played.
       C.   If the soccer game is played, then the weather is not cold.
       D.   The weather is cold and the soccer game will be played.

Answer: A. If the weather is not cold, then the soccer game will be played.

Negation of "if p, then q" is "(not p) and q". The words *not cold* negate *is cold*. Option A negates the circumstances under which the game will be played.

46. **Select the statement below that is NOT logically equivalent to, "If Mary works late, then Bill will prepare lunch."**
    (Average Rigor) (Skill 11.1)

    A.   Bill prepares lunch or Mary does not work late.
    B.   If Bill does not prepare lunch, then Mary did not work late.
    C.   If Bill prepares lunch, then Mary works late.
    D.   Mary does not work late or Bill prepares lunch.

Answer: C. If Bill prepares lunch, then Mary works late.

The second statement must also be an *if-then* statement to be logically equivalent to the first. Use the Law of Contraposition: If *p*, then *q*—not *q*, so, therefore, not *p*.

47. **Given that:**
    i. No athletes are weak.
    ii. All football players are athletes.

    Determine which conclusion can be logically deduced.
    (Average Rigor) (Skill 11.1)

    A.   Some football players are weak.
    B.   All football players are weak.
    C.   No football player is weak.
    D.   None of the above is true.

Answer: C. No football player is weak.

Use the Law of Syllogism: If *p*, then *q*.
                            If *q*, then *r*.
                            Therefore if *p*, then *r*.

In *if-then* form, this would be, "If you are an athlete, then you are not weak. If you are a football player, then you are an athlete." Clearly, if you are a football player, you are an athlete, which means you are also not weak.

48. Study the information given below. If a logical conclusion is given, select that conclusion.

    Bob eats donuts, or he eats yogurt. If Bob eats yogurt, then he is healthy. If Bob is healthy, then he can run the marathon. Bob does not eat yogurt.
    (Average Rigor) (Skill 11.1)

    A. Bob does not eat donuts.
    B. Bob is healthy.
    C. If Bob runs the Marathon, then he eats yogurt.
    D. None of the above is warranted.

Answer: D. None of the above is warranted.

Use Disjunctive Syllogism: *p* or *q*
                              not *p*
                              Therefore, *q*

The fact that Bob does not eat yogurt means that he eats donuts. Because he eats donuts, Option A is incorrect. In addition, Bob is not healthy or running a marathon because he would have to eat yogurt for these things to happen.

49. Select the rule of logical equivalence that directly (in one step) transforms the statement (i) into statement (ii).

    i. Not all the students have books.
    ii. Some students do not have books.
    (Average Rigor) (Skill 11.2)

    A. "If p, then q" is equivalent to "if not q, then p."
    B. "Not all are p" is equivalent to "some are not p."
    C. "Not q" is equivalent to "p."
    D. "All are not p" is equivalent to "none is p."

Answer: B. "Not all are *p*" is equivalent to "some are not *p*."

Identify the quantifiers, *all* and *some*. The negation of "not all have" is "some do not have." *Not all* students *have* books; therefore, *some* students *do not* have books.

50. **All of the following arguments have true conclusions, but one of the arguments is not valid. Select the argument that is not valid.** *(Average Rigor) (Skill 11.2)*

   A.   All sea stars are echinoderms and all echinoderms are marine; therefore, all sea stars are marine.
   B.   All spiders are dangerous. The black widow is dangerous. Therefore, the black widow is a spider.
   C.   All crocodiles are amphibians and all amphibians breathe by lungs, gill, or skin; therefore, all crocodiles breathe by lungs, gill, or skin.
   D.   All kids have hats and all boys are kids; therefore, all boys have hats.

Answer: B. All spiders are dangerous. The black widow is dangerous. Therefore, the black widow is a spider.

Options A and C follow the Law of Syllogism (If p, then q—If q, then r—Therefore, if p, then r.). Option D follows the Law of Detachment. (If p, then q [premise 1] p, [premise 2]—Therefore, q.). Option B is invalid because its conclusion does not follow from the premises.

XAMonline, INC. 21 Orient Ave. Melrose, MA 02176

Toll Free number 800-509-4128

TO ORDER Fax 781-662-9268 OR www.XAMonline.com

WEST SERIES

PO#   Store/School:

Address 1:

Address 2 (Ship to other):

City, State Zip

Credit card number_____-_____-_____-_____   expiration_____

EMAIL _____

PHONE   **FAX**

ISBN	TITLE	Qty	Retail	Total
978-1-58197-638-0	WEST-B Basic Skills			
978-1-58197-609-0	WEST-E Biology 0235			
978-1-58197-693-9	WEST-E Chemistry 0245			
978-1-58197-566-6	WEST-E Designated World Language: French Sample Test 0173			
978-1-58197-557-4	WEST-E Designated World Language: Spanish 0191			
978-1-58197-614-4	WEST-E Elementary Education 0014			
978-1-58197-636-6	WEST-E English Language Arts 0041			
978-1-58197-634-2	WEST-E General Science 0435			
978-1-58197-637-3	WEST-E Health & Fitness 0856			
978-1-58197-635-9	WEST-E Library Media 0310			
978-1-58197-674-8	WEST-E Mathematics 0061			
978-1-58197-556-7	WEST-E Middle Level Humanities 0049, 0089			
978-1-58197-043-2	WEST-E Physics 0265			
978-1-58197-563-5	WEST-E Reading/Literacy 0300			
978-1-58197-552-9	WEST-E Social Studies 0081			
978-1-58197-639-7	WEST-E Special Education 0353			
978-1-58197-633-5	WEST-E Visual Arts Sample Test 0133			
	SUBTOTAL		Ship	$8.25
	FOR PRODUCT PRICES VISIT WWW.XAMONLINE.COM		**TOTAL**	

CPSIA information can be obtained at www.ICGtesting.com
Printed in the USA
BVOW050401190312

285505BV00001B/5/P

9 781581 976380